Describing language

Second edition

David Graddol
Jenny Cheshire
and
Joan Swann

Open University Press
Buckingham · Philadelphia

Open University Press
Celtic Court
22 Ballmoor
Buckingham
MK18 1XW

and
1900 Frost Road, Suite 101
Bristol, PA 19007, USA

First Published 1994
Reprinted 1995

A catalogue record of this book is available from the British Library

ISBN 0 335 19315 3 (pb)

Library of Congress Cataloging-in-Publication Data
Graddol, David.
    Describing language / David Graddol, Jenny Cheshire, and Joan
Swann. — 2nd ed.
        p.   cm.
    Includes bibliographical references and index.
    ISBN 0–335–19315–3 (pbk.)
    1. Language and languages.   2. Linguistics.   I. Cheshire, Jenny,
1946– .   II. Swann, Joan.   III. Title.
P121.G69   1994
410—dc20   94–16918
                                                                              CIP

Typeset by Graphicraft Typesetters Ltd, Hong Kong
Printed and bound in Great Britain by
Biddles Ltd, Guildford and King's Lynn

Contents

Preface

When this book first appeared in 1987, we expected that it would be used mainly by Open University students enrolled on a broadly based course in language study. We have been surprised, but gratified, by the number of other users which the book has acquired over the years, and it is this fact which persuaded the authors to provide an updated version. This new edition contains substantial changes – in particular, to Chapter 1 and Chapter 3. The latter chapter now makes a broader survey of approaches to grammatical description, more in keeping with the introductory nature of the book.

A book such as this shows the work of several hands. It draws on materials which have been written by various authors for undergraduate language courses at the Open University, and it contains much new material which has been improved by comments and ideas from many colleagues and students. Various chapters have benefited greatly from the comments – at some time or another – of James Britton, Penelope Brown, John Green, James Hurford, Angus McIntosh, Harold Rosen, Gordon Wells, colleagues at the Open University and many students throughout the UK.

We are grateful to Janet Maybin for permission to reproduce the field notes on page 176 and to NATE Language and Gender Committee for permission to reproduce the figure on page 177.

David Graddol
Jenny Cheshire
Joan Swann

Introduction

This book is designed as a practical and accessible introduction to various areas of linguistic description. It should be useful to anyone who wishes to refer to technical literature involving linguistic description, who requires a basic conceptual framework and technical vocabulary with which to talk about language, or who has a requirement to make elementary but principled descriptions and analyses of real data, such as classroom interaction or counselling sessions.

The selection and treatment of material is eclectic and practical in orientation, both in the sense that the content is more concerned with methods of usefully describing real linguistic data than with making theoretical points, and in the sense that the selection is designed to be helpful, in a practical manner, to an inexperienced student approaching the literature for the first time.

Different sections of the book have rather different aims which attempt to balance the reasonable ambitions of students against the complexity of the subject matter or special training required. Some sections give an introduction to a general area of linguistic description and others give more detailed instructions and exercises which should allow students to make an analysis of data they have collected themselves.

1 The nature of language

1.1 Introduction

It has been suggested (Harris 1980: 1–3) that anyone who asks 'What is a language?'

> must expect to be treated with the same suspicion as the traveller who inquires of the other passengers waiting on platform 1 whether they can tell him the way to the railway station . . . The language user already has the only concept of a language worth having.

Harris raises several important points with this engaging metaphor. In an important sense, anyone who can speak a language knows something about what a language is. But it cannot be assumed that those who know how to use language can readily tell us what language is. They can *show* us instances of language; we can *observe* them using language; but if they are able to explain articulately and usefully what the nature of language is, then they are demonstrating a special **metalinguistic** skill – usually brought about by an extensive consideration of language as an object of knowledge.

This leads us to the central problem in describing language. Although we all have competence in some language or other, although language plays a central role in our mental and social life, we have no privileged or easy access to its inner workings. It requires methodical effort to discover, describe and analyse the underlying principles which govern its functioning. The result of such effort is a **theory** or **model** of language. That is, an understanding of how language 'works' which can, like other kinds of theory, be tested against the facts which it attempts to explain. Theories and models of language – like those of any other phenomenon such as the weather, the economy, or the nature of the galaxy – will constantly need to be revised whenever more data come to light which prove existing theories inadequate.

This chapter discusses some of the basic issues facing any serious student of language – that is, anyone who wishes to enquire further into the nature of language and learn what others have already discovered. It begins by noting some of the motives for studying language, and then discusses how we can define the object of study more precisely.

Why study language?

Scholars are interested in how language works for a very wide range of reasons. First and foremost, the study of language represents a part of the more general human endeavour to discover more about themselves and the world around them. A great deal of the descriptive and theoretical progress in linguistics has been directed by a simple concern to understand better what is by any criterion a remarkable phenomenon.

But linguistics also has a wide variety of practical applications. Theories of language reflect the motives and interests of the scholars who produce them. For example, **language teaching** requires an explicit knowledge about language, and grammatical models developed for this purpose reflect the needs of learners, teachers, and the institutions within which language teaching usually takes place. To give another example, much of linguistic theory is concerned with understanding the linguistic abilities which are shared by all language users, but **forensic linguistics** (which provides evidence in criminal investigations) is more concerned with the idiosyncrasies of language behaviour which help identify individual people. Other applications make their own special requirements of linguistic theory: **speech therapy**, **natural language processing** by computers, and translation are but a few of the other areas of **applied linguistics** within which specialized models of language have arisen.

Some people want to learn more about how language works in order to have better control over it themselves. This does not necessarily just mean speaking or writing more effectively. A flourishing tradition of **critical language study** (see, for example, Fairclough 1992) suggests that an understanding of how texts embody particular assumptions and views of the world will help make us all more aware of how powerful groups (such as advertisers, politicians and employers) try to persuade us to do things which are against our interests.

Because there are so many different motives for studying language, there are also many different approaches and analytical frameworks. In this sense, there can be no single correct and complete model of language, but rather different approaches, each of which attempts to be internally consistent, tested against the known data, and useful for a particular purpose. This book contains a broad guide to the kind of descriptive and analytical apparatus which has emerged in recent years, largely in connection with the analysis of English (though usually with claims of wider applicability), and within the academic discipline which has become known as linguistics. It focuses on the basic issues which any kind of language description has to deal with, and indicates some key differences between major theoretical approaches.

1.2 What is 'language'?

The object of study in linguistics is surprisingly poorly defined. 'Language', like many terms used by linguists, is one which is taken from everyday language, where it describes a complex and shifting human experience. It carries with it many of the ambiguities and unclarities which make it a usable word in the everyday world. The word 'language', for example, is used to signify many aspects of human and animal communication (the 'language of the bees'; 'body language', and so on). One of the distinctive features of linguistics is its focus on **verbal communication**. It traditionally conceptualizes language as a mechanism for conveying meaning which operates independently of other means of human communication (such as gesture), and which is distinctively different from animal communication.

One problem with an exclusive focus on verbal communication arises from the way words are usually only one part of the complex activity in which humans exchange and understand meanings. There exists a continuing debate between language scholars as to the place of **non-verbal communication** in their models. Should linguistics take account of non-verbal phenomena, such as body movement and facial expression, when providing accounts of how spoken language works? And, in the case of printed texts, should typography, page layout, even the use of illustrations be integrated with accounts of verbal language? Would a failure to examine such non-verbal systems of communication lead to an inadequate account of how verbal language itself works? Or would it merely represent a sensible focusing of research effort? In recent years, there has been a trend among many scholars working in applied fields to take a broader view of how language works, one which draws on descriptions of the wider context in which utterances and texts are produced and understood. We return to this idea later in this chapter.

Some scholars take a yet wider view of what is to be included in language description. **Semiotic theory**, for example, treats a very wide variety of cultural and social behaviour (such as choice of clothes, or architectural design) as **signifying practices**. Within semiotics, such modes of communication are analysed in similar ways to verbal language, and no very distinct boundary between verbal and non-verbal phenomena is recognized. A review of some applications of linguistic theory to visual media (such as TV and film) can be found in Graddol and Boyd-Barrett (1994).

The discipline of linguistics is frequently described as 'the science of language', which reflects the way in which many linguists have sought to emulate the objective investigative techniques of the natural sciences, and to treat language as a natural (rather than human-made) phenomenon. The techniques for investigating language have, over the centuries, reflected ideas as to what constitutes proper research methods in the natural sciences.

For example, if we look at the historical development of language study, the kinds of metaphor which scholars have used to describe language, and the kinds of structure they have proposed to account for its workings have always reflected those areas of science in which rapid advances were currently being made. Language has, at various times, been regarded as a system of logic which can be explained in terms of mathematical principles; as a set of chemical elements which combine with each other in systematic ways; as an organism like a plant or animal which has evolved in a particular habitat and which demonstrates relationships with other species; as a mechanical system with structural properties; or as a computer program which requires certain kinds of input and which, after due processing, yields output. (A fuller discussion of such metaphors can be found in Graddol 1994.)

1.3 What is 'a language'?

There is a systematic ambiguity in the way the word 'language' is used. It can refer to the general human capacity for verbal communication (as we have discussed it above) or it can refer to specific forms of language. We can examine what is meant by 'a language' by looking briefly at the language in which this book is written – the English language.

English has a special place in the world. It has become an international language, both in the sense that it is now the first language of people from several continents and in the sense that many others use it as a subsidiary language. The English language began its life in Britain, but British speakers of English today constitute very much a minority of the world's English speakers. Many people who speak English as a first language speak no other, and imagine that such **monolingualism** is the normal state of affairs in the world. The majority of the world's English speakers, however, are **bi-** or **multilingual**. Different speakers of English can thus have very different experiences of the language, and very different perceptions of the number and status of other languages. Activity 1.1 is intended to encourage you to reflect on this point.

Activity 1.1

Make a list of the languages which you know of. Do not attempt to look anything up – just jot down names as they come to mind.

Mark those six languages which you think are the most widely spoken in the world. Hazard a *very rough* guess at how many million people speak each of them.

If you managed to get more than 20 or so languages on your list, then you did well. But you would have had to spend a very long time writing to make much impression on the stock of world languages. It has been estimated that there are about 4000 languages spoken in the world today. If we take into account identifiable **dialects**, the number is quite staggering. In the index of the world's languages prepared by Voegelin and Voegelin (1977) there are over 20 000 entries. In fact, as we shall see, the distinction between a dialect and a language is a problematical one. For this reason the term **language variety** is often used by linguists where such questions of status can be avoided.

Approaches to language classification

The existence of so many language varieties means that, for practical descriptive purposes, some method of classification is needed. Two approaches are common. The first is **typological** – this groups languages according to their similarities and differences in linguistic structure. The second is **genealogical** (or **genetic**) – this groups languages according to supposed historical relationships.

TYPOLOGICAL CLASSIFICATIONS

One way of classifying languages is in terms of their characteristic patterns of **word order**. For example, the English language uses a word order in which the **subject** (S) usually appears in the sentence before the **verb** (V), which in turn is followed by the **object** (O):

S	V	O
Jill	caught	the mouse

English is sometimes referred to as an **SVO** language, for this reason. Other languages, such as Welsh, are known as **VSO** languages, since they place the verb first. This, then, provides a rough and ready method of classifying languages, and it leads to interesting insights. It turns out, for example, that some word orders, such as **OVS**, are extremely uncommon. However, languages differ in how rigid word order must be, as we shall see shortly.

Another typological classification divides the world's languages into four groups:

Analytic (or **isolating**) – languages like Chinese in which words are simple units without any word endings or affixes. Syntactic relationships are signalled entirely by word order. In Mandarin Chinese (Putonghua) *ta chin fan le* can be translated, literally, as 'he eat meal past' or 'he ate the meal'.

Synthetic (or **inflectional**) – languages like Latin which have elaborate systems of suffixes indicating things like the **tense** of verbs or whether a noun is the subject or object. In the sentence *Octavia amat canem* ('Octavia loves the dog') *canem* consists of *can-* + *-em* where *-em* indicates that the dog is the object of the verb (if it were the subject it would be *canis*), and also that the dog is singular (the plural form is *canes*). Word order tends to be more flexible in synthetic languages, since syntactic relationships can be shown by word endings. In the sentence *Canem Octavia amat*, 'dog' is still the object of the verb.

Agglutinative (or **affixing**) – languages like Turkish, Japanese or Swahili in which words contain a series of 'slots' into which are placed small verbal elements corresponding to **pronouns**, tense and so on. In Turkish, for example, *ev* means 'house', *evler* means 'the houses' (consisting of *ev* 'house' and-*ler*, plural) and *evlerden* means 'from the houses' (where -*den* means 'from').

Polysynthetic (or **incorporating**) – languages like Australian Aboriginal languages in which there exist complex word forms which may function as entire sentences. For instance, Inuktitut, a North American Indian language, has words such as *Qasuiirsarvigssarsingitluinarnarpuq*, which can be translated literally as *qasu-iir-sar* 'tired not cause-to-be', -*vig* 'place-for', -*ssar* 'suitable', -*si* 'find', -*ngit* 'not', -*luinar* 'completely', -*nar* 'someone', -*puq* 'third person singular' – or 'someone did not find a completely suitable resting place'. (This example comes from O'Grady and Dobrovolsky 1992: 333).

Typological approaches have been subject to a number of refinements over the years and for some purposes have proved very useful. One problem, however, is that many languages do not fit neatly into the categories listed. The English language, for example, can be regarded as a mix of analytic, synthetic and agglutinative. It has analytic tendencies, as can be seen in the use of *will* to express future time reference (as in *he will grow cabbage this year*) or in the use of *more* to indicate comparison (*her cabbage is more delicious than his*). It has some inflectional tendencies, as illustrated by the word *loves* in *Jeremy loves eating cabbage*, where the -*s* in *loves* expresses the fact that there is a third person singular subject and that the verb refers to the present tense. And it also has agglutinative tendencies in word formation, as in *unfortunately*, where the *un*- expresses 'not', and -*ly* marks the word as an adverb. The English language used to be more synthetic but its inflectional system has been largely lost over the centuries.

In some ways, the four language types represent points on a continuum (from *analytic* at one end to *polysynthetic* at the other). For this reason, the number of separate types which linguists identify tends to vary.

GENEALOGICAL CLASSIFICATIONS

A genealogical classification attempts to show the historical relationships between languages. All languages tend to change through time, and if a language changes in form faster in one community than another, or if some changes occur in one place and not another, then different language varieties will emerge. How close such varieties are related will depend on how long ago they began to diverge from each other.

All languages which have evolved from a single **parent language** are regarded as belonging to the same **language family**. Many of the European and Indian languages are thought to be derived from a single prehistoric language, which has been called **Proto-Indo-European**. This means that modern English and, say, Gujarati are linguistic relatives; whereas English and Turkish are not. Linguists have tried to represent the relationships between the Indo-European languages by means of a **family tree**. One version of this tree is shown in Figure 1.1.

There are two important limitations with family trees. The first is that the model seems to work particularly well for the Indo-European languages which were most intensively studied during the nineteenth century when genealogical theory was developed. Genealogical models are much less able to give a satisfactory account of the relationships within other language families such as Bantu. This may be in part because of the lack of documentary historical evidence from such languages, but it is also likely that different patterns of population movement, of contact between communities, and of size of community have led to a less clearly structured family tree.

The second limitation is that the genealogical model fails to take into account any contact between languages after the supposed historical divergence. Just as ideas, customs and objects tend to spread from one culture to another, so also are words introduced into one language from another. English has many such **loan words**, and has, in turn, been the source of many in other languages. This borrowing from language to language may give rise to similarities between languages which do not share a common ancestor. Borrowings may occasionally extend beyond vocabulary to include pronunciation or grammatical features. For these reasons the actual historical and present-day relationships between languages are far more complex than the family tree suggests, but it is nevertheless a useful way of drawing attention to certain similarities and differences between modern languages.

Social and political criteria

We have discussed the question of classification as if it were merely a linguistic issue in which different languages, at least, were easy to identify and name. This is far from being the case. Languages have a social and political identity as much as a linguistic one.

This may become clearer if you return to the list of languages which you made in Activity 1.1. What may be more interesting than the number of languages which you managed to think of is the mental strategy you used to get them. Did you, for instance, write down the names of languages as they came to you, or did you go through a mental list of countries and mark down the language spoken in each? Either way, you probably ended

Figure 1.1 The Indo-European family of languages

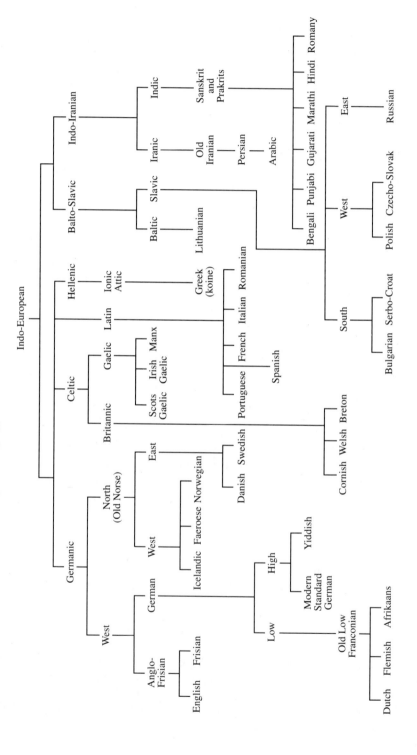

Table 1.1 The major languages of the world

Language	Number of speakers (in millions)		
	A	B	C
Chinese	700(1)	1035(1)	541(1)
English	320(2)	350(2)	300(2)
Hindi	220(3)	225(4)	90(7)
Spanish	200(4)	275(3)	150(3)
Russian	150(5)	220(5)	150(3)
Bengali	140(6)	160(6)	76(8)
Portuguese	130(7)	135(8)	76(8)
Japanese	115(8)	120(9)	100(5)
Arabic	110(9)	150(7)	50–80(10)
German	100(10)	100(10)	95(6)
French	70(11)	75(11)	64(11)
Italian	60(12)	60(12)	56(12)

Source: A, *Sunday Times Magazine* (1993); B, Katzner (1986); C, Voegelin and Voegelin (1977)

up with about one language for each country. In Britain, the USA and Australia, the experience of most English speakers is largely a mono-lingual one – if this is your own background then you may have come to think it natural that one language should serve a whole population. If your list contains such spurious languages as 'Swiss' or 'Belgian', then you have been misled by this experience, since there are four officially recognized languages of Switzerland (German, French, Italian and Romansch) and three in Belgium (Flemish, French and German). The existence of more than one language in a country is by no means unusual. The most extreme example is probably New Guinea, where there are estimated to be around 800 different languages spoken.

Let us now return to your list of the major languages, and the number of speakers. Table 1.1 shows which are the top 12 according to one source (column A), and it also shows how other reference books rate these languages (columns B and C). Column A is ordered by rank, according to the number of speakers. Rank orders of all three columns are shown in parentheses.

Activity 1.2

Table 1.1 shows significant variation among estimates of a language's status. Why should there be this kind of disagreement between authorities? On which languages is there the most agreement and on which the most disagreement? How is it that the first source can claim 130 million speakers of Portuguese when the population of Portugal is only about 10 million people?

The answers to these questions tell us something about the nature of languages and their use in the world. For instance, Portuguese is used extensively in South America and in former Portuguese colonies in Africa. The largest community of Portuguese speakers is in Brazil (over 100 million). One of the smallest is in Goa, on the West Coast of India, where a rapidly dwindling number of older people still speak Portuguese. However, the number of Portuguese speakers in the world as a whole is steadily increasing. One estimate, made by Cristavao in 1987, suggests that there will be over 210 million Portuguese speakers by the end of the 1990s, making the language fifth in rank order (cited in Santarita and Martin-Jones 1991).

A rather different but very practical problem arises with a language like Chinese: how does one arrive at any specific figure for a language which is spoken in areas where census information is hard to come by? Problems of data collection affect many languages: how can one find out, in some isolated part of the world or one experiencing political unrest, what language or languages each and every person speaks? Such difficulties may explain why there is greater agreement over the numbers for European languages – the relevant information may be easier to find and more reliable.

Lastly, there are differences in date among the sources. The relative importance of languages and the absolute numbers of speakers change over time, as we have seen. The figures for Hindi and Chinese, in particular, have notably increased since 1977.

These are straightforward answers, but they leave aside some of the more interesting and problematic issues in constructing such tables. For example, there is disagreement over how languages are to be classified and what 'counts' as a given language. Such titles as 'Chinese' may be little better than our spurious languages 'Swiss' and 'Belgian' – there are at least eight Chinese languages (according to Voegelin and Voegelin 1977) and hundreds of dialects. So although there may be doubt about the size of the Chinese population, this may not be the major problem. There may be disagreement over what should be included in the blanket term 'Chinese'. In fact, the figure given in column A refers specifically to Putonghua, which is estimated to represent roughly two-thirds of Chinese speakers as a whole, whereas the figure in column B includes all Chinese speakers.

Problems of classification arise out of the nature of languages themselves and the way that different language varieties are often closely related. The decision to call certain varieties distinct languages depends as much on political and cultural factors as on linguistic criteria or criteria of mutual intelligibility. The Scandinavian languages are an example. Although Danes, Swedes and Norwegians often find they can understand one another, they each speak a language which has its own agreed standard form, and which is symbolic of the political and cultural integrity of their respective countries.

Classifying speakers

Another problem in constructing 'league tables' like Table 1.1 arises from the way most people in the world speak more than one language. This raises a further issue: what does it mean to be a 'speaker' of a language? The table attempts to show numbers of 'native speakers', but it is not always easy to distinguish between those who speak a given language as a **first language** and those who speak it as a **second language**. The implication for numbers is tremendous. The *Sunday Times* league table (for which David Crystal acted as consultant), for example, estimates that there are 450 million speakers of English as a second language, leading to an aggregate figure of 770 million. Elsewhere, Crystal has argued for the recognition of a category of 'English users' based on readership of English-medium magazines and newspapers. On this basis, he estimates the total number of English speakers as 1000–2000 million people world-wide (Crystal 1985).

Multilingual speakers will use a variety of languages, but they may not have equal fluency in them all. Even monolingual speakers will usually command a range of **language styles**, reserving some for more formal occasions or just for writing, for instance, or they may be able to speak in more than one dialect. For these reasons it is better to think of all speakers as commanding a **language repertoire** rather than a single monolithic language. We can then explore how different language varieties are used in different combinations in different communities.

Let us take two examples of English speakers. In the south Indian state of Tamil Nadu, an educated person is likely to speak the state language of Tamil, English, and (possibly) Hindi, all with fluency in different **communicative domains**. A less well-educated person in this part of India is less likely to speak English or Hindi very well, but is likely to speak a local language and/or one of the neighbouring languages (such as Kannada, Malayalam, or Telugu). Both Tamil and English are also used in Singapore, but in different combinations with other languages and with different social and political statuses. The Tamil community is one of three major ethnic groups in Singapore. The largest of these is Chinese, and the other is Malay. This multi-ethnic situation gives rise to a number of political and cultural issues connected with language use. However, education in Singapore is primarily now conducted in English, with an expectation that students become bilingual in one of the other national languages. (For further details of the languages of education in Singapore see, for example, Kwan-Terry and Kwan-Terry 1993.)

In both India and Singapore (and many other countries) there exist local varieties of the English language. For example, Indian English uses a great many words which do not occur elsewhere. The numeral system, for instance, includes the words *lakh* (100 000) and *crore* (10 million). Words are often used in Indian English with distinctive meanings. In the phrase *wines bar*, the word *wines* includes all alcoholic beverages, including beer and whisky. (In fact 'wine', in the sense in which the word is used in other varieties of English, may not be available from a 'wines bar' at all.) The term *wines bar* also demonstrates a grammatical feature of Indian English. In most varieties of English, singular (uninflected) noun forms are used when they modify another noun: *passenger train; three foot pole.* In Indian English plural forms are common: *guests book; prawns curry.* (This example is taken from Nihalani *et al.* 1979).

Differences of this kind raise the question of where the boundary between different varieties of English is to be drawn. If we recognize that Chinese is a group of distinct languages, then should we not also recognize that the English language is now best regarded as a group of distinct but related languages? The appropriate answer to this lies not just in the linguistic facts, but also in political and cultural sensibilities. In both India and Singapore, for example, local varieties of English have low prestige and are given little official recognition. Linguists, however, do not just take account of governmental policies, but look also at the social and cultural facts of language use. On this basis, linguists are increasingly recognizing that distinct varieties of English have emerged in various parts of the world – these include Indian English, Nigerian English, and Singaporean English.

Minority languages

Even in those countries where most English speakers are monolingual – principally the USA, the United Kingdom, Australia and New Zealand, in which English is the sole official language in the country as a whole – many more languages are also in daily use than most people appreciate. All these countries, for example, have communities who speak indigenous languages – that is, languages which were spoken in the area before the arrival of English. In Britain, there are Celtic languages (Welsh and Gaelic); in the USA, many Indian languages; in Australia, the Aboriginal languages; in New Zealand, Maori. In each of these countries there are also many more languages used in multilingual urban communities. Estimates of the languages spoken by schoolchildren in London for example (Alladina and Edwards 1991), put the number at over 150, and such a number is probably typical for many large Western cities.

It will be clear that languages have very different kinds of status within a community and what makes a language a minority language has nothing to do with how many speakers it has. Faeroese is the native language of only around 40 000 people – about equal to the population of the British towns of Hereford or Scarborough – but has official status within the islands. On the other hand, Chinese is a minority language in a country like Britain, and despite the fact that there exist more than 100 000 speakers of Chinese in Britain (Wong 1991), the language is poorly recognized for the purposes of education and governmental administration.

1.4 Language structure and language use

The components of language

Language is a complex system of communication, and an important task of linguistics is to describe this system, analysing the relationships that exist between different components. To make this task somewhat easier it has become conventional to regard language as if it were composed of a series of 'boxes', each containing a distinct kind of machinery. While the number and nature of the boxes identified vary in different linguistic theories, the most commonly recognized ones are:

SOUND	GRAMMAR	MEANING

Further subdivisions are often made. For example, in the box marked 'sound' it is common to distinguish **phonetics**, the study of the sounds produced by speakers, and **phonology**, the more abstract study of the sound system of a language. In the 'grammar' box a distinction between **morphology** (word structure) and **syntax** (sentence structure) is also usual.

We have followed the convention of distinguishing different components of analysis in the organization of this book: the sounds of language are discussed in Chapter 2, grammar in Chapter 3 and meaning in Chapter 4.

'Duality' or 'double articulation'

However many components one recognizes for the purposes of analysis, it is clear that some of them, at least, are arranged on a series of levels. Furthermore, these levels do not operate independently but only in relation to other levels: the 'units on the "lower" level of phonology (the sounds of a language) have no function other than that of combining with one another to form the "higher" units of grammar (words)' (Lyons 1968: 54).

According to this view, language is seen as having a **dual structure** (sometimes also referred to as **double articulation**). Units of sound, meaningless in themselves, combine to form larger units (words) which have meaning. This leads to considerable economy in the system: it is possible to construct a very large number of words, or meaningful parts of words, from a relatively small number of sound units. This property of human language has been seen as a defining characteristic, distinguishing it from other systems of communication.

The autonomy of language

This way of describing language, as an autonomous system that can be analysed in terms of internal relationships and contrasts, represents a highly abstract view. It is conventional, in linguistics, to make a distinction between such an abstract **system**, and **language in use** (what people actually say or write on any occasion). This distinction is differently expressed in different theories. The Swiss linguist, Ferdinand de Saussure, working early in the twentieth century, distinguished *langue* (often translated as 'language') from *parole* (translated as 'speech' or 'speaking'). *Langue* is a social product (Saussure 1974: 13–14):

> It is a storehouse filled by the members of a given speech community through their active use of speaking, a grammatical system that has a potential existence in each brain, or, more specifically, in the brains of a group of individuals. For language is not complete in any speaker; it exists perfectly only within a collectivity.

Parole is the individual act of speaking or writing. It consists of actual utterances and texts, rather than the abstract system which was used to create them.

The American linguist, Noam Chomsky, made a similar distinction between **competence** and **performance** in the 1960s. 'Competence' here refers to a speaker's knowledge of what constitutes a well-formed sentence in his or her own language; 'performance' is language use, complete with 'numerous false starts, deviations from rules, changes of plan in mid-course, and so on' (Chomsky 1965: 4). Chomsky regarded competence as the proper, or at least prior, object of study for linguistics – recognizing that language in this sense is an idealization (Chomsky 1965: 3):

> Linguistic theory is concerned primarily with an ideal speaker-listener, in a completely homogeneous speech-community, who knows its language perfectly and is unaffected by such grammatically irrelevant conditions as memory limitations, distractions, shifts of attention and interest, and errors (random or characteristic) in applying his knowledge of the language in actual performance.

The study of language in social context

An alternative approach to language description is to give full recognition to 'performance' – to recognize actual utterances and texts produced by real speakers and writers in specific contexts as legitimate objects of study. Rather than disregarding such data as simply imperfect realizations of competence (subject to errors, memory limitations, etc.), some researchers have been able to discern interesting patterns and regularities in use. There has been a rapid growth of interest in this area in recent years, but earlier scholars also saw the dangers of regarding language as an autonomous system.

One such person was an anthropologist, Bronislaw Malinowski, who studied the culture of Trobriand Islanders in the Pacific and, in particular, the role of language in their work and social practices. Malinowski criticized two aspects of the Saussurean tradition of linguistics: first, the way it viewed language as primarily a vehicle for 'information communication' rather than as a means of negotiating and maintaining social relationships; second, its insistence that language study is essentially about the study of linguistic form, rather than meaning.

> The false conception of language as a means of transfusing ideas from the head of the speaker to that of the listener has, in my opinion, largely vitiated the philological approach to language. The view here set forth [in *The Language of Magic and Gardening*] is not merely academic: it compels us, as we shall see, to correlate the study of language with that of other activities, to interpret the meaning of each utterance within its actual context.
>
> (Malinowski 1935: 9)

To Malinowski (1923) we owe the concept of **context of situation**. For Malinowski and many anthropologists, utterances become comprehensible only in the context of the whole way of life of which they form part. The focus of analysis is thus not the sentence but the 'speech event in a context of situation'. These ideas were the foundation of what became known as the **London School** of linguistics.

Working within this tradition, Michael Halliday has taken up Malinowski's ideas and built a formal model which shows how language and context are interlinked in the production of meaning. He claims:

> After a period of intensive study of language as an idealized philosophical construct, linguists have come round to taking account of the fact that people talk to each other. In order to solve purely internal problems of its own history and structure, language has had to be taken out of its glass case, dusted, and put back in a living environment – into a 'context of situation', in Malinowski's term.
>
> (Halliday 1978: 192).

We examine Halliday's model of language more closely in Chapter 3.

It was not just in Britain that an interest in language in use developed. At about the same time as Malinowski was working, the American anthropological linguist, Edward Sapir, wrote:

> In linguistics, abstracted speech sounds, words, and the arrangement of words have come to have so authentic a vitality that one can speak of 'regular sound change' and 'loss of genders' without knowing or caring who opened their mouths, at what time, to communicate to whom.
>
> (Sapir 1949: 578–9)

It was these aspects of language that interested the linguist, Dell Hymes, who established the notion of the **ethnography of speaking**, the study of who spoke to whom, when, why, and so on. Hymes coined the term **communicative competence** by analogy with Chomsky's 'competence'. 'Communicative competence' is, however, far more extensive, encompassing the knowledge a speaker needs to know in order to use language appropriately – depending on the person being spoken to, the context in which an utterance is produced, the communicative goals of the speaker, and so on. Interest in this area has also come from a branch of linguistics known as **sociolinguistics**, which studies the relationship between language and society (for an introduction to this discipline, see Trudgill 1983; or Holmes 1992).

The study of language in context is thus a flourishing one, and one which has engendered a proliferation of descriptive terms. In addition to those mentioned above, the term **pragmatics** will be found in the literature to refer to certain aspects of the study of language in its communicative context. We examine some aspects of pragmatics in Chapter 4.

1.5 Investigating language

In Section 1.4 we discussed two rather conflicting views of language. On the one hand, it could be regarded as an autonomous system; on the other, as inextricably bound up with social and contextual factors. Which view is taken by linguists will clearly affect the methods they select as appropriate to its study. This section briefly discusses two major methods for investigating language: one which draws upon the tacit knowledge which we all have (more particularly, which investigators themselves have); and a more empirical approach which examines language as it is used in real communicative contexts.

The use of intuition

There are some sentences and phrases that we say over and over again in our everyday lives. Many of us will repeat the following examples, or others like them, at fairly regular intervals:

> How's your mother?
> It's a nice day
> We're late again
> Oh no, where are my keys?

On the other hand, a large number of the sentences which we produce and interpret will be ones that we have never heard and never spoken before. It seems, in fact, that we are able to produce and understand an infinite number of new sentences. Consider:

> This weeping walrus does not usually enjoy a meal of fish and chips

It is unlikely that you will have come across this sentence before, but you will probably be able to understand it, even if you think it's a rather silly sentence. This understanding is due, at least in part, to your ability to draw on your intuitive knowledge of the syntactic structure of English.

Chomsky has placed great emphasis on this aspect of 'creativity'. He argued that because the potential number of grammatical sentences is infinite, empirical methods of investigating language were flawed: 'the set of grammatical sentences cannot be identified with any particular corpus of utterances obtained by the linguist in his fieldwork' (Chomsky 1957: 15). Chomsky took as his object of study not just the body of observed utterances (as earlier linguists had done) but the whole potential stock of sentences which were, in principle, allowed by the grammatical rules of a language and which would be recognized as well-formed by any native speaker.

The only means of gaining access to such a store of unused, unspoken sentences was through introspection, and the use of the speaker's intuitive judgements concerning the acceptability of grammatical structures. Such judgements gained something of a special status in Chomsky's theory of **generative grammar** (which we describe in Chapter 3).

The intuitions which linguists make use of in their linguistic investigations are often their own, since they are themselves members of the speech community and should share everyone else's judgements of grammaticality. Some concern has been expressed, however, about the validity of linguists' intuitions. Labov (1975b), for example, suggested that 'experimenter' effects might cause a researcher to perceive linguistic facts that accord with his or her theoretical expectations, and to see points of doubt as clear-cut.

Spencer (1973) demonstrated that a consensus judgement made by non-linguists did not always match those made by linguists. One hundred and fifty illustrative sentences were culled from half a dozen influential linguistics articles and presented to both 'naive' and 'non-naive' native speakers. Although some 80 per cent of these people agreed among themselves on acceptability judgements, little more than half of their judgements agreed with those of the linguists. The conclusion to be drawn is that a linguist who has a particular theoretical motivation in judging an example may not reach the same judgement as a disinterested party. Spencer suggests that, merely by virtue of getting too close to the data, a linguist's perceptions may become distorted. Although linguistically untrained speakers are described in the linguistic literature (rather patronizingly) as 'naive', it may turn out that their judgements are more reliable.

There are, however, problems associated with collecting judgements from non-linguists.

Activity 1.3

How well do you know your own use of English?
  Answer the following questions. Consider, in each case, how sure you are about your answer, and what kind of justification you might give another person.
  Do you say:

1 (a) Put out the light
    or
  (b) Put the light out

2 Do you pronounce the *t* in the word *postman*?

3 At school, you were probably taught that sentences in English can be passive or active. According to this distinction, sentence (a) is active; sentence (b) is passive. What are the others?
   (a) This bus carries forty people.
   (b) This elephant is frightened by helter-skelters.
   (c) This banana will feed the whole family.
   (d) This cottage sleeps the whole family.
   (e) This angel cake eats well with Madeira.

4 Are any of the following sentences ungrammatical?
   (a) A person may need to blow their nose.
   (b) Brian set out to boldly go where no snail had been before.
   (c) Walking down the garden path, the flowers were very striking.

5 Is the following sentence grammatical?
   It has been being tested.

6 If a friend told you that she 'had a bare $100' in her bank account would you understand her as having:
   (a) Exactly $100.
   (b) A little more than $100.
   (c) A little less than $100.

You are probably familiar with both versions of the sentence in Question 1, so much so that you may find it difficult to decide which expression you yourself use. The placement of the object varies to some extent regionally, but also seems to depend on the particular phrasing used. This makes it very difficult for individual speakers to decide exactly what they would say, even though it is highly likely that in each context only one of the two orderings would be used. For example, one might say *At midnight, I put the cat out,* but not *At midnight I put six milk bottles, a note for the newspaper boy, and the cat out.*

Question 2 again requires an accurate knowledge of your own speech habits. You may have convinced yourself that you pronounce the *t*, since the spelling makes this seem like the 'proper' pronunciation. In fact, the usual and accepted pronunciation of this word by native speakers is *posman.*

Question 3 is much more complex. It should illustrate, though, that our ability to describe and analyse sentences depends a great deal on formal training. The traditional categories and classifications which have been used for many years in the English classroom cannot cope with the syntactic relationships which hold between the nouns in some of these sentences. Sentences (d) and (e) look 'active', but is *the family* usefully described as the 'object' of a transitive verb *sleep*, and is *angel cake* really the 'subject' of *eat*? The examples illustrate the extent to which the English language has a more complex structure than is easily captured by traditional grammatical categories. This is a point we return to later (in Chapter 3) when we examine alternative grammatical frameworks which have emerged in recent years.

Question 4 contains a number of traditional solecisms, which are mostly frowned upon by etiquette books, such as Fowler's (1926) *A Dictionary of Modern English Usage*. Had they appeared in the text of this book or in a school essay, they would probably have been corrected by the editor or teacher. If you thought they were ungrammatical, then you are prepared to accept criteria which have more to do with social acceptability than with the linguistic fact that these kinds of expression are governed by grammatical rules and are regularly used.

Question 5 raises a rather different issue about grammaticality. Few people are sure whether expressions like this are grammatical or not (and those who are sure tend to deny that they are grammatical). Nevertheless, expressions like these regularly occur in real data.

Question 6 demonstrates the way some expressions can be ambiguous without this necessarily being appreciated. Different people seem to understand this sentence in different ways, and each of the interpretations given is possible.

A final point in this discussion of our intuitions about language is that the form in which a question is asked of a speaker is likely to affect their response. If you give a native speaker an example of a sentence and ask whether they would say it, if they find it acceptable, or if it is grammatical in their language you may well get three different answers.

These examples show, in different ways, the precariousness of native speaker intuitions about their own usage. A dramatic example of this was discovered by the American sociolinguist William Labov. Labov (1975b) asked members of the Philadelphia speech community about their use of the word *anymore* in a positive sense which was peculiar to the district – that is, said of something which 'was not true at some previous time and is true at this time':

> We now have ample evidence that introspective reports about positive *anymore* have a very weak relation to what speakers actually say. Since 1972 we have collected twelve cases of speakers who used positive *anymore* quite freely though their introspective judgements were entirely negative . . . Faced with a sentence like *John is smoking a lot anymore* they said they had never heard it before, did not recognise it as English, thought it might mean 'not smoking' and showed the same signs of bewilderment that we get from Northern speakers outside the dialect area.
>
> (Labov 1975b: 34)

The embarrassing fact is that native speaker intuitions about 'acceptability' or 'grammaticality' aren't infallible, as Chomsky (1965: 38) concedes:

> Obviously, every speaker of a language has mastered and internalized a generative grammar that expresses his knowledge of his language. This is not to say that he is aware of the rules of the grammar or even that he can become aware of them, or that his statements

about intuitive knowledge of the language are necessarily accurate. Any interesting generative grammar will be dealing, for the most part, with mental processes that are far beyond the level of actual or even potential consciousness; furthermore, it is quite apparent that a speaker's self-reports and viewpoints about his behaviour and his competence may be in error.

Linguists are thus faced with a methodological problem. If competence is the object of study then one needs to access speakers' tacit understanding of the 'rules' of their language. But neither linguists themselves nor native speakers can produce reliable reports of what they understand, presumably at a subconscious level. Competence cannot be tapped by simply reflecting on sentences, or potential sentences, out of their communicative context. Paradoxically, at least as a check on intuition, we need some means of eliciting, or observing, situated utterances – in other words, performance – from which we may make inferences about competence. Halliday, for example, argues that when linguists construct examples to test their linguistic theories, they tend to produce simple grammatical structures which reflect written rather than spoken language structure. As a result, grammatical models which are based on intuition methodology cannot cope with what he calls the 'grammatical intricacy' of spoken language: 'we look at spoken language through the lens of a grammar designed for writing' (Halliday 1987: 67). The complexity of spoken language, according to Halliday, becomes apparent only when you start collecting real data. The example in Question 5 in Activity 1.3 is one which Halliday (1987: 58) recorded:

> About 30 years ago, as a result of being asked to teach English intonation to foreign students, I began observing natural spontaneous discourse in English; and from the start I was struck by a curious fact. Not only were people unconscious of what they themselves were saying; they would often deny, not just that they HAD said something I had observed them to say, but also that they ever COULD say it. For example, I noticed the utterance *it'll've been going to've being tested every day for the past fortnight soon* where the verbal group *will have been going to have been being tested* makes five serial tense choices, present in past in future in past in future, and is also passive. This passed quite unnoticed by both the speaker and the person it was addressed to; yet at the time it was being seriously questioned whether a simple verb form like *has been being tested*, which one can hear about once a week, could ever occur in English.

Corpus linguistics

These are some of the reasons why there has been a great growth in recent years in what has become known as **corpus linguistics** – studies of language based on real usage. Computers have become sufficiently powerful and data storage sufficiently cheap to allow huge collections of utterances and texts from a wide variety of sources to be collected and scrutinized carefully. The size and comprehensiveness of these corpora can partially overcome some of the drawbacks which concerned Chomsky.

For example, the new corpora of English usage being collected in computer databases for commercial and academic exploitation are vast, some approaching 100 million words. An early limitation of such computerized texts was their restricted range of sources – mainly easily obtainable printed texts and little spoken data. This limitation is also now being overcome with the systematic creation of spoken language corpora. The *Longman corpus*, for instance, commissioned a market research organization to equip a cross-section of the British population with portable cassette recorders, with which they were to record their own speech and conversational encounters continuously through a whole week. These tapes were submitted anonymously to the project for transcription and addition to the database.

A corpus of naturally-occurring language data will contain a number of structures and usages which are acceptable to native speakers, but which a theoretical linguist would have missed. One corpus linguist, Jan Aarts remarks: 'Only linguists who use corpus data themselves will know that a corpus always yields a much greater variety of constructions than one can either find in the literature or think up oneself' (cited in Aarts 1991: 46). Aarts (1991) calls a grammar which deals with such instances an **observational grammar**. A methodological problem arises from the fact that the corpus will also contain examples of the performance errors which Chomsky was concerned about. Aarts suggests that intuition can again be used to distinguish between acceptable and unacceptable utterances. Aarts (1991: 55) calls these 'intuitions about the currency of certain structures'. Figure 1.2 shows schematically the relationship between the three sets of sentences implied by this: those contained in a specific corpus; the total set of sentences identified as grammatical by an intuition-based model; and the total set of sentences regarded as acceptable by a native speaker.

Corpus linguistics raises as many methodological questions as it answers (for example, Halliday's comments above make it clear that distinguishing between acceptable and unacceptable sentences is by no means straightforward). Nevertheless, corpus linguistics has already made significant contributions to the study of grammar. Corpus linguistics has also had a major influence in other areas of linguistic inquiry. Later in this book we describe its contributions to dictionary-making, the analysis of cultural and ideological biases in texts, and literary stylistics.

1.6 The ideological basis of linguistic theory

We began this chapter by noting that some of the basic concepts of linguistic study evade easy definition. For example, we have seen how the notion of 'language', or 'a language', gives rise to theoretical and practical difficulties of definition. It will not be surprising that some of the other concepts

Figure 1.2 Testing a grammar on a corpus

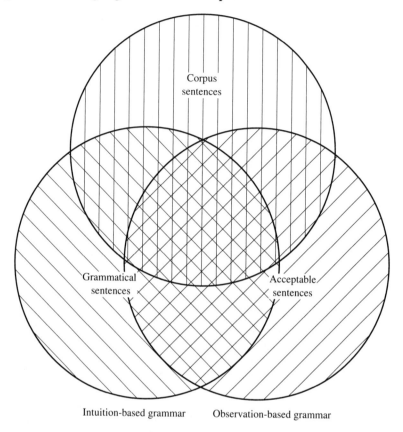

Source: Aarts (1991: 50)

which we have discussed cause similar difficulty. We finish this chapter by discussing two of them – the **speech community** and the **native speaker** – and we point out some of the ways in which the idealizations which linguists regularly make are as much ideological as scientific. That is, they represent a particular way of looking at the world rather than an inevitable consequence of an attempt to make systematic sense of empirical data.

The reason for discussing such issues here is to place traditions of linguistic analysis into a wider context of scientific study. Many of the questions which we ask here are similar to ones being asked within the natural sciences: in what ways does the methodology of linguistic enquiry and the way its objects of study are defined embody fundamental assumptions about the nature of the world which are essentially culturally based? Such assumptions may be so deeply embedded in our ways of thinking that their status is rarely questioned.

What is a speech community?

We mentioned above that the traditional Chomskyan notion of *competence* relies on the idea of an (idealized) homogeneous speech community. Indeed, the use of intuition in any investigation implies homogeneity among a group of speakers – for an intuition to represent valid data, others must share it. This is what Saussure meant when he referred to *langue* as being a 'social fact' and existing only within 'collectivities' rather than individual speakers. In real life, however, speech communities are likely to be far from homogeneous.

Activity 1.3 has already drawn attention to the way different speakers may use and understand linguistic structures and words differently, and that such differences need not necessarily be obvious. Diversity in language use, however, goes well beyond such relatively minor differences. Sociolinguistics, for example, is based on the idea that people who interact and communicate with each other may nevertheless use language differently, and in ways which can be explained in social terms.

The notion of a 'speech community' has always been a central one in linguistic investigation, but a satisfactory definition has never been agreed. Consider the following definitions:

All the people who use a given language (or dialect).
(Lyons 1970: 326)

A regionally or socially definable human group, identified by the use of a shared spoken language or language variety.
(Crystal 1992: 363)

A group of people who interact by means of speech.
(Bloomfield 1935: 42)

A speech community cannot be conceived as a group of speakers who use all the same forms; it is best defined as a group of speakers who share the same norms in regard to language.
(Labov 1972a: 158)

To the extent that speakers share knowledge of the communicative constraints and options governing a significant number of social situations, they can be said to be members of the same *speech community* ... since such shared knowledge depends on intensity of contact and on communicative networks, speech boundaries tend to coincide with wider social units, such as countries, tribes, religions or ethnic groupings.
(Gumperz 1972: 16)

Lyons' definition is inadequate as it stands: it makes no allowance for bilingual – or bidialectal – communities. Nor does 'community' here suggest geographical or cultural proximity: English speakers in Delhi, in New York and in Devon, England, could, according to this definition, be in the same speech community by virtue of speaking English. Crystal adds this requirement, though in a rather vague way. Bloomfield's definition emphasizes communication between speakers, but allows that this need not involve use of the same language. Labov allows for linguistic variation but stresses shared linguistic norms (for instance, that speakers would agree on which variety of the language was most prestigious). This would be inadequate for Gumperz, who argues that speakers would also need to agree on a variety of communicative 'rules' (including when to speak and when to be silent, for instance) – or to share *communicative competence* (see Section 1.4). Hudson (1980) discusses several definitions of 'speech community' (including some of those cited above). See also Romaine (1982) for a detailed consideration of variation in speech communities.

In considering where one draws the boundaries of a speech community, it is likely that the more culturally diverse one allows the community to be the more linguistically heterogeneous it will also be. By definition, members of the same speech community will have some linguistic and communicative features in common, but absolute linguistic homogeneity may well not be found even within an **idiolect** (the variety of language spoken by one individual). This makes more problematical the notion of native speaker intuitions: while many of these may be shared with a larger group of speakers (the majority of speakers in New York, for instance) some will be more restricted (children from a particular housing estate) and some will be idiosyncratic.

What is a native speaker?

Just as there are difficulties with the idea of 'speech community', so there are problems with the concept of 'native speaker'. Originally, the notion of the native speaker arose as a theoretical idealization, similar to that of 'homogeneous speech community' and of a 'competence' which was not marred by performance considerations such as slips of the tongue. Appeal to this notion simply ruled out grammatical constructions which might be produced by someone who did not 'really know' the language properly, and thus helped construct a simplified, coherent object of study.

Davies (1991), in a discussion of the 'native speaker in applied linguistics', examines a range of psychological and theoretical issues, such as the claim by Felix (1987: 114) that 'after puberty a second language speaker cannot become a native speaker'. More interesting, from our point of view, is an experiment by Coppieters (1987). He took a group of non-native speakers of French, who spoke French so well that it was not possible to tell easily from their language use that they were non-native speakers. Nevertheless, he found that they diverged greatly from native speakers when it came to making acceptability judgements of a list of sentences. Davies argues that one important difference between the acceptability judgements of native and non-native speakers lies in the limited experience of communicative contexts which the latter typically possess and which makes it difficult for them to imagine likely contexts in which certain utterances would be acceptable.

There is thus a range of arguments which suggest that the exclusion of non-native speakers from serious linguistic investigation is a sensible one: their judgements are unreliable and the result of imperfect knowledge of the way the target language is used. The concept of the native speaker, however, has in recent years acquired a more problematic status in linguistic theory and professional life. It can be criticized for reflecting a peculiarly monolingual view of language competence, which privileges the experience of powerful countries (particularly English- French- and German-speaking ones) and suggests that monolingualism is the expected 'normal' linguistic situation. As we have already seen, most people in the world (even most English speakers) are bi- or multilingual. What exactly does 'native speaker' mean in multilingual situations, where different languages are typically used for different communicative domains? In such contexts, a speaker may switch between languages according to culturally appropriate norms but may not be equally fluent in all languages in a given domain. The importance of this point becomes clear when it is realized that many languages in the world have no, or extremely few, monolingual speakers. For example, monolingual speakers of the Welsh language are now rare, and these are mostly below the age of 4.

The monolingual viewpoint becomes dangerously close to ideological notions of 'purity' in language and speech communities. Since language is closely linked with ethnicity, one might even suggest that the theoretical insistence on 'native speaker' intuitions is a form of institutionalized racism. 'Non-native speaker', in many Western contexts, suggests 'foreigner'. If heterogeneity among so-called native speakers is recognized, then the distinct category of 'non-native' seems less important – or, at least, a different criterion of language competence needs to be established.

There are commercial considerations also at stake in the 'cult of native speakerdom', certainly in relation to the major world languages which, unsurprisingly, are also the ones on which most modern linguistic theory has been based. The English language teaching business, for example, is a huge international one, and one in which US, British and Australian producers of materials, franchise language schools and so on, are keen to protect their market position. They might be expected to argue that the best teachers of a language will be native speakers.

The modernist nature of linguistic theory

The preceding discussion reflects a trend in linguistic theory over the past decade or so, which recognizes that descriptive linguistics has tended to make assumptions about language and society which have become more and more controversial as theories about society, and the role of language in creating and sustaining particular views of the world, have themselves become more developed. This book focuses on the description and analysis of the linguistic system rather than on sociolinguistic or political processes, and it is not appropriate to discuss these issues in detail here. It is, however, important to note the ways in which linguistic theories incorporate certain assumptions and views of the world which may not be testable – certainly not against the kinds of data usually appealed to in linguistic research. Here we will note some of the traditional assumptions made by linguistic theories which have begun to be challenged by recent approaches to the analysis of language in use.

1 *That the proper objects of linguistic study are 'ideal types'.*
   Idealizations are justified as necessary abstractions from reality needed to model the underlying processes which direct actual behaviour. However, the way such idealizations are made usually makes assumptions of a cultural or ideological nature invisible.

2 *That the structure of language can be regarded as internally coherent and hierarchical in form.*
   Notions of structure in language have tended to mirror changing ideas about structure in the natural world. The hierarchical structures proposed by linguists to describe language in many ways reflect classical ideas about the order of the universe. In an era when such views of the universe and the nature of physical matter have themselves been challenged, it is not surprising that alternative views of language have emerged, which see it as more fluid, less predictable, and with greater complexity in its internal structure.

3 *That linguistic form is the sole, or major, mechanism for the communication of meaning.*
   This assumption takes two forms. The first is by way of a maxim to be followed by linguists: 'interpret language phenomena in such a way as gives maximum importance to linguistic form even where an alternative (perhaps simpler) explanation might be given by appealing to features of context, or mundane reasoning on the part of a speaker'. The second is seen in the model of communication which seems to underlie much linguistic theory: that language 'encodes' ideas which can thus be transmitted and 'decoded' by another person provided the latter knows the language. Some recent theories, which focus on language in use, argue that communication is much more precarious than this model suggests, and that different members of the same 'speech community' may arrive at rather different interpretations of the same text.

4 *That society is homogeneous and there exists a consensus about linguistic norms.*
   We have already seen the status of this assumption in our discussions above. Alternative ideas suggest that the 'normal' state of societies is one of internal conflict and struggle between social groups, that different people have different experiences of language, and that such

heterogeneity needs to be recognized as the primary 'social fact' by linguistic theory. See, for example, Fairclough (1989) for an account of language in use which takes the latter approach.

5 *That speakers are rational and autonomous beings.*
Just as language is theorized as an autonomous system, so speakers are typically regarded as autonomous individual beings who each possess a comprehensive language competence, who have readily identifiable social identities (such as 'working class', 'ethnic Chinese' or 'female'), and who are in control of the meanings they communicate to others. In Chapter 7 we will discuss ideas which challenge this view and suggest that human identities are more complex – people often make contradictory statements about their identity, for instance. Furthermore, utterances and texts are often produced by several people in ways which make it very difficult to sustain the notion of the individual, autonomous speaker or writer.

Linguistics is not peculiar in making the kinds of assumption listed above. They belong to a view of the natural and social world which has been called modernist, and reflect liberal, humanist ideas which have been prominent in Western thought for many centuries. They have, however, been vigorously contested by more recent theories in the natural and social sciences. These postmodern ideas about the structure of the universe, the nature of individual identity, and the kinds of social institution within which people live and work, are touched upon again in Chapters 6 and 7.

Here it is sufficient to note that any kind of language description embodies wider assumptions and values of a social and political nature. Furthermore, it is becoming less possible to avoid recognizing this, as the social world itself becomes more complex (with consequent implications for the nature of language use) and as linguistic theory itself matures and develops ways of dealing with complex ideas and data. Recognition of this aspect of language study does not absolve us from responsibility to make our investigations as methical and careful as possible, and to ensure that the theories of language which we produce are both internally consistent and consistent with agreed empirical facts of language. This book describes the ways in which linguists attempt to do this.

2 The sounds of language

2.1 Introduction

Phonetics is one of the oldest traditions of linguistic analysis, being well developed in ancient India. In Europe it was regarded throughout the nineteenth century, and well into the twentieth, as the prime basis for any scientific study of language. The principles of description, therefore, which are laid out in Sections 2.2 and 2.3 are very well-established ones, and have served as a practical framework of description for scholars over many decades.

Section 2.4 ventures on to less well-trodden ground. The linguistically important characteristics of speech delivery – particularly stress and intonation – have been studied for a somewhat shorter time than have consonant and vowel sounds, and with less clear results. The section attempts to pick out some basic features of stress and intonation on which there seems to be some agreement among scholars.

This chapter contains some rather technical and complex material, and it may seem that our decision to give it so much space in an introductory book is a mere hangover of the Victorian tradition. A solid grasp of phonetics is, however, still very important when attempting to understand a wide variety of research in language. In historical linguistics, for example, it helps explain why some changes in pronunciation occur and not others; in sociolinguistics it is necessary in order to understand the principles of social variation in pronunciation. There is still a sound argument for insisting that basic phonetic and phonological description should be one of the first areas to be studied.

Nevertheless, this chapter is no more than an introduction to the subject and makes no attempt to give training in **phonetic transcription**. The ability to transcribe accurately requires much ear-training and practice and cannot be successfully acquired from a textbook.

2.2 Phonetic description of sounds

Phonetics is the name given to the scientific study of the sounds of language. Phoneticians set about the task of describing and analysing sounds in a variety of ways. One approach, known as **articulatory phonetics**, has been particularly important, and it is this which is introduced here.

The organs of speech

When we make the sounds of our language we modify the flow of breath through the mouth and nose by moving the tongue and other organs in and around the mouth. This modification gives each sound its characteristic quality. For thousands of years it has been realized that a study of what we do with these organs of speech affords a useful way of classifying and describing sounds.

Let us start by looking at which muscles and organs are particularly important in producing sounds. Figure 2.1 shows a cross-section of what is known as the **vocal tract**. What is interesting about the organs used in

Figure 2.1 The vocal tract

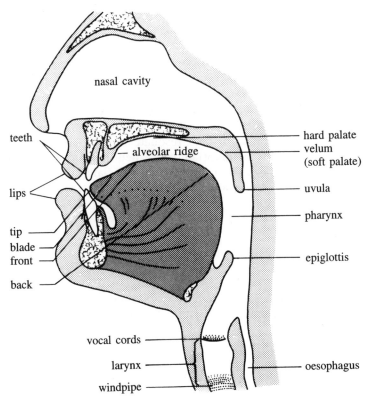

speech production is that none of them are used exclusively for this purpose. In fact, they all seem to have more basic functions. The tongue and teeth, for example, are used for eating, and the **vocal cords** are folds of muscle (they are sometimes referred to as the **vocal folds** for this reason), rather like a pair of lips, which form a valve at the top of the windpipe. These lips are what enable us to close off the windpipe, which we do when we cough or hold our breath under pressure. Although none of the speech organs are used exclusively for language, they seem to have evolved in humans in ways which aid their dual function.

VOICING

To make any sounds we first need to set air in motion. We normally do this naturally by letting air escape from the lungs. If we follow this airstream from the lungs up the windpipe, we can see that the first point at which we can do anything to interfere with it is where it passes through the gap between the vocal cords. Of course, if the cords are fully open, then the air simply passes through. Breathe out forcefully – as if you were breathing on a pair of spectacles to clean them. The only sound you should hear is a sort of rushing sound caused by general turbulence in the airstream. If you had breathed out less forcefully, there would be less turbulence and scarcely any noise. But what if the vocal cords were firmly closed, so that no air could escape? Take a deep breath and then hold it. Make sure you maintain lung pressure while you do this. Now let go. You should have been able to feel the vocal cords release as you let your breath go. The sensation is similar, but more forceful, when you cough.

In addition to these two states – fully open and firmly closed – the vocal cords can be loosely closed in a way which allows the air to be forced through. When this happens the cords vibrate and allow pulses of air to pass through. This vibration or buzz resonates in the oral cavities and is known as **voice.** Voice is an important constituent in many speech sounds. Try saying the word 'her'. Do not whisper it – declaim it boldly and prolong the vowel sound. You should be able to hear the resonant vibration clearly. Compare the sound with the 'breathing on spectacles' sound you made earlier. That was made without voice; the vowel sound in 'her' is made with voice.

Consonants

By no means all speech sounds require vibration of the vocal cords. Many of the consonants of English form pairs of sounds which are distinguished only by the presence or absence of voice. Activity 2.1 deals with some of them. To do it, you will need to find a quiet corner where you can hum and make noises to yourself. Do not feel foolish when you do this – trying out the sounds for yourself is the only way of learning how they are made.

Activity 2.1

Below is a list containing ten different consonantal sounds. They all share one feature – they are **continuants**, i.e. you can indefinitely lengthen them or continue them until you run out of breath.

1	rum	mmmm . . .	6	bus	sss . . .
2	buzzing	zzzz . . .	7	vision	zhzh . . .
3	rush	shsh . . .	8	buff	ffff . . .
4	love	vvv . . .	9	this	thth . . .
5	run	nnnn . . .	10	thistle	thth . . .

(a) Go through the list, making sure you know which sounds are represented. Pronounce each sound in turn, both in the word given and then on its own, and prolong the sound for a second or two.

(b) Try singing each sound, i.e. try to produce a pitched note (it does not matter what note or whether it is steady) as if you were humming or buzzing. Again, it is important to do this boldly, not hesitantly. You should find that only some sounds can be sung like this. The others cannot be sung without their turning into one of the sounds that can. Draw a line down the middle of a piece of paper. In the first column make a list of the sounds which can be sung; in the second column list the sounds which cannot be sung.

(c) Lastly, mark against each sound in the second column which of the sounds in the first it turns into if you attempt to sing it.

What you have just done is identify some of the voiced and voiceless continuants of English. Since, in order to sing a note, the vocal cords must vibrate, those consonants which could be sung must be voiced ones. You should have the following sounds in your first column: *m, z, v, n, zh, th* (as in *this*). The remaining four sounds belong in the second column. Each of the four voiceless consonants has a voiced counterpart, i.e. there are voiced consonants which are formed in exactly the same way, except for the fact that they are uttered with the vocal cords vibrating. You should have found that the letters *th* can signify either a voiced sound (as in *th*is) or a voiceless one (as in *th*istle). Indeed, if there were no difference between these two sounds, we would not be able to distinguish between the words *thy* (which begins with a voiced consonant) and *thigh* (in which the initial consonant is voiceless) or between the verb *mouth* (voiced) and the noun *mouth* (voiceless). Although these are distinct sounds, the English alphabet does not distinguish between them. These two, then, should be one of the pairs you found. The other pairs are *v* and *f*, *z* and *s* and *zh* and *sh*.

Although every variety of English makes a contrast between voiceless and voiced sounds, not all make the contrasts in the same way. The sounds represented by *th* are especially variable and in some accents of English it is not pronounced as a continuant but as a plosive (see below). So don't worry if, in your own speech, you can't hear all the contrasts as described here.

Figure 2.2 Articulation of [f]

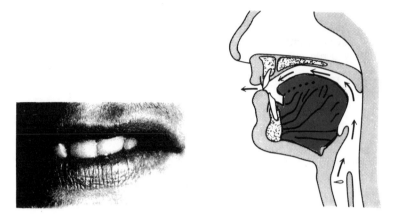

MANNER OF ARTICULATION

What, then, distinguishes each pair of these sounds from other pairs? The answer lies in what you do to the airstream after it has passed through the vocal cords, but before it finally escapes from the mouth. There are a number of ways of interfering with the airstream and thus affecting the quality of the sound, but most involve manipulating the tongue. Of all the organs of speech, the tongue is the most flexible. This, no doubt, is why the word 'tongue' is used figuratively in many languages for language itself. Indeed, our own word 'language' derives from the Latin word for tongue, *lingua*. Besides using the tongue, we can do more limited things by moving the lips, the lower jaw and some of the soft parts at the back of the mouth.

Make the *f* sound again. Notice what happens to your lips as you make this sound. The lower lip touches the upper teeth and air is forced through the constriction, creating friction (Figure 2.2). Exactly the same happens when you utter the voiced counterpart *v*, except that now the vocal cords are vibrating in addition.

Make the *s* sound again. Feel what happens to your tongue. The air is forced between the tongue and the roof of the mouth (Figure 2.3). The action is happening out of sight now, but the principle involved in making the sound is similar. Both these sounds, *f* and *s*, are called **fricatives**, because of the way the airstream is forced through a constriction.

It is also possible to make a sound by blocking the airstream completely and then letting it go. Make a *p* sound. Notice what happens to your lips. Here, both lips start by being firmly pressed together, preventing any escape of air (Figure 2.4). If there is a complete blockage like this, there can be no sound, of course. The sound comes when the lips are opened again and the sudden release of the airstream causes a small explosion of air.

Make a *t* sound. Feel what happens to your tongue. Again, a complete

Figure 2.3 Articulation of [s]

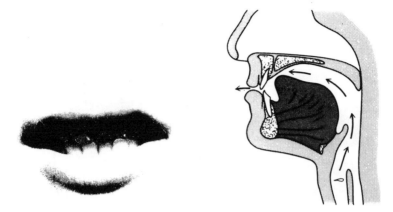

blockage is formed, but out of sight in the mouth (Figure 2.5). When the blockage is released, a characteristic *t* sound is produced. Sounds like *p* and *t* which are made in this way are called **plosives** or, sometimes, **stops**.

   The **manner of articulation**, as it is technically called, is one of the important dimensions along which sounds are classified. Unlike voicing, which is largely a two-way distinction, manner of articulation is more variable. There are half a dozen or so different categories, but the categories of fricative and plosive are two of the most important.

PLACE OF ARTICULATION

We have now identified two of the three major dimensions along which consonants are classified. The third is quite a straightforward one. It

Figure 2.4 Articulation of [p]

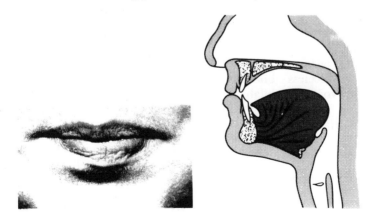

Figure 2.5 Articulation of [t]

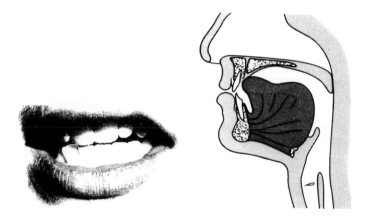

describes where in the mouth the airstream is interfered with, regardless of whether the interference is a complete blockage or a partial constriction. The only difficult thing about describing the place of articulation is that it requires you to know something about the anatomy of the mouth and what the different parts are called.

The *f* sound and *v* sound which you made earlier were created by placing the lower lip on the upper teeth. This, then, is where the place of articulation is for these two sounds. They are called **labio-dental** sounds, after the Latin names for lip and teeth. So, we now have the three elements which provide the minimal phonetic description of these sounds:

sound	voicing	place of articulation	manner of articulation
f	voiceless	labio-dental	fricative
v	voiced	labio-dental	fricative

The *p* sound was made by placing both lips together. This place of articulation is called **bilabial**. Although *p* is a voiceless sound, it too has a voiced counterpart. This is *b*. So we can give this pair of sounds their three-part description:

sound	voicing	place of articulation	manner of articulation
p	voiceless	bilabial	plosive
b	voiced	bilabial	plosive

THE PHONETIC ALBHABET

In an ideal world we would be able to represent each distinct sound with a separate letter of the alphabet. We have already seen, however, that the English alphabet is not ideal in this way. Two separate sounds were represented by *th*, for example, which is in any case two letters put together. We can get around this problem by devising a special alphabet, with special regular rules for its use, in which we reserve one letter for each sound. We can then avoid the confusion which is sometimes caused by the spelling system of English. Many such phonetic alphabets have been devised, but one of the most widely used today is the **International Phonetic Alphabet (IPA)**. As far as possible, familiar letters are used and you will find this is true of many of the consonant symbols. But because there are far more sounds than there are letters, special symbols are also employed. The two sounds which th usually represents in English, for instance, are written as θ (voiceless) and ð (voiced). The first symbol comes from the Greek alphabet and is known as 'theta'; the second was once used in the English alphabet, but originated in Scandinavia, where it was called 'eth' pronounced as in leather. It is still used in modern Icelandic and in Faeroese writing.

The consonant symbols of IPA are usually laid out in a table which lists the place of articulation horizontally and the manner of articulation vertically. In each cell of this table, symbols are given for both voiceless and voiced sounds. Table 2.1 shows some of the IPA consonant symbols. By reference to the table you can work out which is the correct symbol for a particular sound or, conversely, what sound is represented by a particular symbol.

By convention, phonetic symbols are enclosed within square brackets [ ] to indicate that it is the sound of some utterance which is being described and that a phonetic alphabet and not the ordinary one is being used. If you know the value of the symbols, then you will be able to read off not just the word or words used in the original utterance, but also how the utterance was pronounced.

The next activity is intended to help you try out what you have learned so far. You will need to refer to the labelled diagram of the vocal tract (Figure 2.1) and to the table of IPA consonant symbols (Table 2.1).

Activity 2.2

Figure 2.6 shows a cross-section of the vocal tract. It differs from Figure 2.1 in that the **soft palate** (or **velum**) is raised so that the nasal cavity is sealed off. This position is the usual position for sounds which are not **nasal**. (Nasal sounds are those in which the air in the nasal cavities is allowed to resonate with air in the oral cavities.) Work through the following questions.

(a) State whether the sound is voiced or voiceless. (Note: The vocal cords are not shown as vibrating.)
(b) Where does the tongue make contact with the roof of the mouth? Refer back to Figure 2.1 if you are not sure what the part is called and look across the top of the IPA chart for the place of articulation term which seems appropriate. (This term will be the adjectival form of the noun shown on Figure 2.1.)
(c) If the tongue created a complete blockage in the airstream at this point and then released it, what manner of articulation would this be? Look down the left-hand side of the IPA chart and select the appropriate term.

Table 2.1 Some IPA consonant symbols

	Bilabial		Labio-dental		Dental or interdental		Alveolar		Retroflex		Palato-alveolar		Palatal		Velar		Uvular		Labio-velar		Glottal
Manner of articulation	voiceless	voiced	voiceless	voiced	voiceless	voiced	voiceless	voiced	voiceless	voiced	voiceless	voiced	voiceless	voiced	voiceless	voiced	voiceless	voiced	voiceless	voiced	voiceless
Nasal		m						n						ɲ		ŋ					
Plosive	p	b			t̪	d̪	t	d	ʈ	ɖ					k	g					ʔ
Fricative	ɸ	β	f	v	θ	ð	s	z	ʂ	ʐ	ʃ	ʒ			x	ɣ	χ	ʁ	ʍ		h
Approximant								ɹ		ɻ				j						w	
Lateral fricative							ɬ														
Lateral approximant								l													
Trill								r									ʀ	ʀ			
Tap or flap								ɾ		ɽ											

Note: affricates contain both a plosive and a fricative element and can be written as digraphs, e.g. ʤ ʧ.

Figure 2.6 Tongue position for a consonant

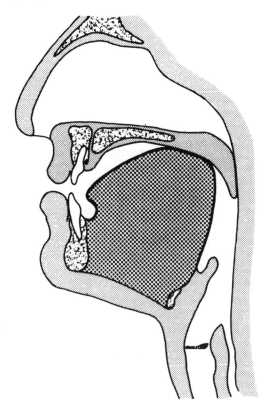

(d) You should now have the necessary three-part description of the sound. Look at the IPA chart and decide which symbol is appropriate for this sound.

(e) In (a) you recorded whether or not the sound was voiced. What sound would result if the opposite had been true? Use the appropriate symbol.

(f) What if the tongue did not create a complete closure at this point, but, instead, air were forced between the tongue and the roof of the mouth? Give the manner of articulation that would result.

(g) Look at the IPA chart again. What symbol would now be used for this sound if it were (i) voiced, (ii) voiceless?

(h) Try making these sounds. Are they normally used in English?

The answers to this activity can be found in the Appendix.

___

Vowels

In this section we consider how vowel sounds are made, how they can be described and classified, and what symbols are used for them in the IPA alphabet. Most of the section consists of activities. Work through these carefully.

Activity 2.3

When doctors or dentists want to examine your mouth, they ask you to say 'aahh'. Why should they choose that vowel sound? Why, for example, do they never ask you to say 'eee' instead?

(a) Figure 2.7 shows the tongue position for four vowels. First find the tongue position marked [ɑ] (this is the IPA symbol for the sound dentists ask for, as in British English Received Pronunication (RP) *part* [pɑːt]); and [i] (this is the IPA symbol for the 'eee' sound, rather like that in RP *peat* [piːt]). Compare the position of the two tongues carefully. Answer the following questions.
   (i) Is the tongue generally higher in the mouth for [ɑ] or [i]? State which is higher.
   (ii) Mark the highest point of the tongue on each of the two diagrams with a cross. Is the highest point of the tongue nearer the front or nearer the back of the mouth? For which sound is the tongue highest nearest the front?
   (iii) Try saying each of these two sounds [ɑ] and [i] to yourself. Does your tongue feel to be in the position shown for these vowels?
(b) Now find the tongue positions marked [a] (as in *pat* – particularly the northern British English pronunciation [pat]) and [u] (as in *boot* [buːt]). Again compare the position of the tongues and answer the following questions:
   (i) Is the tongue generally higher in the mouth for [a] or for [u]? State which is higher.
   (ii) Mark the highest point of each tongue with a cross. Is the highest point of the tongue nearer the front or nearer the back of the mouth? For which sound is the tongue highest near the front?
   (iii) Try saying each of these two sounds [a] and [u] to yourself. Does your tongue feel to be in the position shown for these vowels?
(c) You should now have four crosses marked on the diagrams. Next, copy three crosses so that all four are on one diagram (you may find tracing paper helps you do this accurately). Identify each cross with its appropriate IPA symbol. Draw a line from one point to another, forming a rough rectangle. This shows the outermost limits of the space swept by the highest point of the tongue during the articulation of vowel sounds. At no point is the airstream completely constricted, but the available space is modified and this gives a characteristic resonance to each of the vowels.
(d) The four vowels given do not, of course, exhaust the possible number of distinct vowel sounds. Others are made by putting the tongue in intermediate positions. We can describe these positions by stating where the highest part of the tongue falls on a **high–low** and **front–back** dimension. These positions are commonly plotted on a diagram resembling the shape you arrived at by marking the location of the tongues. Thus, the vowel [e] (heard in northern British English pronunciations of *date* [det]) is a front vowel like [i]

Figure 2.7 Tongue position for four vowels

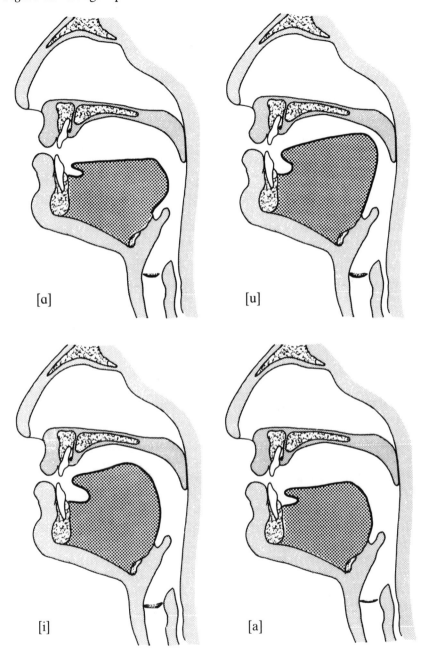

[ɑ]

[u]

[i]

[a]

Figure 2.8 The position of eight vowels on the vowel chart

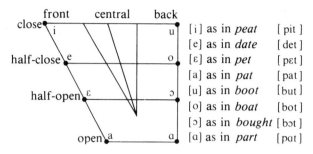

[i] as in *peat*   [pit]
[e] as in *date*   [det]
[ɛ] as in *pet*   [pɛt]
[a] as in *pat*   [pat]
[u] as in *boot*   [but]
[o] as in *boat*   [bot]
[ɔ] as in *bought*   [bɔt]
[ɑ] as in *part*   [pɑt]

but is a little lower. [ɛ] (the sound in *pet* [pɛt], particularly northern British English pronunciations) is likewise a front vowel, but is distinguished from [i] and [e] by being lower still, but not quite as low as [a]. A similar range of tongue heights separates the **back** vowels. Thus many of the vowels of English can be represented on a standard *vowel chart*. The four degrees of tongue height are often described as being on a **close** (or **high**) to **open** (or **low**) dimension, the two mid-way points being **half-close** and **half-open**. For example, [i] is a close vowel and [a] is an open vowel (see Figure 2.8).

(e) The position of the tongue does not tell us everything we need to know about the quality of a vowel, however. Just as we needed at least a three-way description of consonant sounds, so we do for vowels. What could such a third dimension be?

   (i) Say the words *keep* [kip] and *coop* [kup] one after the other. Observe what happens to your lips as you make the two sounds. Use a mirror, if this helps, or place a finger lightly on your lips as you pronounce the sounds. One of these is made with the lips bunched up and rounded; the other made with the lips spread. Which is a **rounded vowel**? Write down the appropriate IPA symbol.

   (ii) Work your way around the vowel chart in Figure 2.8 pronouncing each vowel in turn. Which are the other rounded vowels shown on the chart?

The answers to this activity are given in the Appendix.

CENTRAL AND PERIPHERAL VOWELS

Vowel sounds are classified according to tongue height and where the tongue comes closest to the roof of the mouth. In addition, the degree of lip rounding affects the quality of the vowel. In principle, it is possible to produce an infinite variety of vowel sounds, each subtly differing from one another according to tongue height, where they fall on the front–back dimension, and lip rounding. Vowels which fall somewhere in between front and back vowels are known as **central** vowels. Central vowels often have a less distinct quality than **peripheral** vowels, but one central vowel [ə], sometimes known as **schwa**, is one of the commonest English vowels, occurring frequently in unstressed syllables, as in *about* [əbaut].

Figure 2.9 IPA symbols for unrounded and rounded vowels on the vowel chart

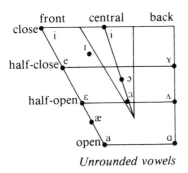

Unrounded vowels

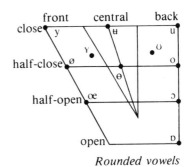

Rounded vowels

CARDINAL VOWELS

Since vowel sounds are infinitely variable, both in principle and practice, it may take a great deal of ear-training before some can be reliably differentiated. One technique used by phoneticians to describe subtle differences in tongue position is to compare the sound they wish to describe with a set of 'reference' vowels which they have been trained to remember. These **cardinal vowels**, as they are called, are situated at well-spaced intervals around the vowel chart. Thus cardinal [i] represents the highest front vowel and [a] the lowest. The continuum from [i] to [a] is then divided into equal auditory intervals by [e] and [ɛ]. Similarly, cardinals [u], [o], [ɔ] and [ɑ] are chosen on the high–low continuum for back vowels. By agreeing on the quality of these eight vowels (more or less the ones used in Activity 2.3), phoneticians can say, for example, when they meet with a particular vowel in someone's speech, that 'it is slightly lower than cardinal [e]' or that 'it is halfway between [ɛ] and [a]'.

DIPHTHONGS

All the vowels so far described are single or 'pure' vowels. You will have noticed though, that in many instances we have had to specify 'northern British English' pronunciation when giving examples. This is because many vowels in English, and especially in southern British English, are not pure, but begin with one quality and move towards another. Such 'double' vowels are known as **diphthongs**. The RP pronunciation of *date*, for instance, begins at a point somewhere between cardinal [e] and [ɛ], but ends with a vowel slightly higher and more central. We can show diphthongs on the same kind of vowel chart as we use to show 'pure' vowels, albeit a little more clumsily, indicating where the starting and finishing points lie in relation to the cardinal vowels. RP *date*, which could be transcribed as [deɪt], is shown in Figure 2.10. All diphthongs can be described in terms of their initial and final vowel qualities, and thus do not require special symbols.

Figure 2.10 The diphthong [eɪ] in RP *date*

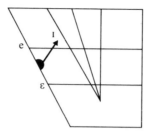

You will be able to work out the values of diphthongs by referring to the same chart as used for 'pure' vowels (see Figure 2.9).

VOWEL LENGTH

In the course of this section and the section on consonants we have discussed all the major dimensions by which the qualities of language sounds are described. Both vowels and consonants can vary in **quantity** as well as **quality**, however. Fortunately, although English consonants do vary in length, it is rarely necessary to describe this. Variation in the length of vowels in English is often more important, as we shall see, but it is rarely necessary to classify vowels more finely than into the two categories of long vowels and short vowels. A number of ways of symbolizing long vowels exist, some of which may be familiar to you: a length-mark may be placed above a symbol, for example $\bar{a}$, or a letter may be doubled, for example *aa*. The method used by the IPA alphabet, however, will be adopted here. A mark ':' after a symbol indicates that the sound is long, for example [ɑː].

2.3 Segmental phonology

We have now looked at the production of both consonants and vowels, but only as isolated sounds. Usually, of course, these sounds are pronounced in words or utterances, where one sound follows closely on the next. In such 'joined-up speech' there are many transitional effects as one sound merges into the next, and we find that many sounds are modified in systematic ways according to what other sounds surround them. This means that there is considerable variation in the articulation of what might have appeared as instances of the same sound – far more so than is apparent when we study sounds in isolation. But, as we shall show, underneath the complex patterns of phonetic variation lie much simpler functional patterns. In this section we shall discuss the respects in which continuous speech displays complex variation and the ways in which the simpler functional patterns can be discerned within this.

Figure 2.11 Transitional sounds in the pronunciation of *cleaned* (adapted from O'Connor 1973: 64)

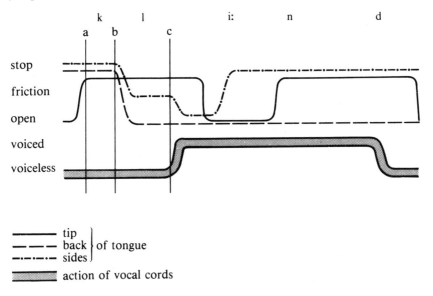

The composite nature of sounds

In connected speech there is a continuous movement of the vocal organs from one position to another, not an abrupt cut-off after one sound followed by a short silence as the muscles move to take up the position required to articulate another pure sound. If we examine the transition from one sound to another, we can find some rather strange sounds which are not normally regarded as occurring in English. For example, the voiced bilabial fricative [ß] does not normally occur in English, but, if we examine continuous speech very carefully, it is possible to find examples of this as a transitional sound. In pronouncing the word *obvious*, for instance, a speaker must make the transition from a voiced bilabial plosive [b] to a voiced labio-dental fricative [v]. As tension on the lips is relaxed, preparatory to making the fricative sound of [v] but before taking up the necessary lip position, a bilabial fricative sound occurs: [ɒbßviəs]. Try pronouncing *obvious* slowly and see if you can detect this happening in your own speech.

Transitional sounds of this kind appear frequently in everyday speech. Figure 2.11 is a profile diagram which shows the movement of the tongue and the action of the vocal cords during the articulation of the word *cleaned*. It shows that, as one would expect, the back of the tongue starts with a complete closure (i.e. a plosive position) but that before this velar plosive is released, the tip of the tongue rises to touch the alveolar ridge – time (a) – in anticipation of the [l] sound. Thus, when the plosive is released, the tongue is already positioned for [l] – the two articulations [k] and [l] overlap to some extent.

In spite of this state of readiness, what we might regard as a proper [l] is a voiced sound, yet there is a delay between releasing the voiceless plosive [k] and beginning the voicing for [l]. Thus, a voiceless variant of [l] occurs between times (b) and (c). But this is not all that is going on at this point. There is more to an isolated [l] than the fact that the tongue tip touches the alveolar ridge and the fact that it is voiced. [l] is said to be a **lateral** sound, which means simply that the sides of the tongue are not sealed against the upper teeth (as they are for the alveolar plosive [d], for instance) but instead allow air to escape. We can see from Figure 2.11, however, that in the pronunciation of *cleaned* the sides of the tongue, in moving from an airtight to an open position, create a brief intermediate 'leaky', or fricative, position between times: [kɬliːnd]. In this way, what we might regard as a proper [l] does not begin until time (c) and it is preceded by a voiceless fricative sound not unlike that found in Welsh in words like *llyn* [ɬin] (lake).

We could go through the profile diagram (Figure 2.11) and find other transitional phenomena (such as the fact that [d] starts voiced, as expected, but finishes voiceless), but the point is probably sufficiently illustrated by looking at one example in detail. We have found that we cannot strictly think of sounds as discrete units joined together like beads on a necklace. They are non-unitary, both in the sense that the articulation of one sound may overlap with that of the next, so that we cannot easily define the boundaries of a sound, and in the sense that what we hear as a single sound may actually consist of several phonetically distinct sounds flowing one into another.

The influence of surrounding sounds

These two phenomena mean that a far greater variety of sounds occurs in ordinary speech than might at first be apparent. In particular, the overlapping of one sound with the next is a source of considerable variation. One of the consequences of the overlap between [k] and [l] in *cleaned*, for example, is that the [k] itself will be given a characteristic quality which is heard only in those [k] sounds which precede an [l]. We can see, in fact, that the [k] in *cleaned* is not exactly the same as the [k] in *keen* or *cow*. If we examined every sound which we heard in someone's speech and identified as a [k], we should find that a surprising variety of sounds was included.

The [k] in *cool* [kuːl] is different from that in *keel* [kiːl] in at least two respects. In [kuːl] the lips are already rounded in anticipation of the rounded vowel [uː] which follows, and the point of articulation of the [k] is further back in the mouth than for [kiːl], anticipating the fact that [uː] is a back vowel. What is happening is that the lips and tongue are preparing to make the vowel sound when the [k] is articulated, and so some of the

features of the vowel are imposed on the preceding consonant. Try saying
cool and *keel* to see if you can feel the difference between the two [k]
sounds.

ASSIMILATION

So far, we have identified at least three phonetically distinct [k] sounds.
The differences are, admittedly, subtle ones – too subtle, in fact, for us to
distinguish them easily with symbols. For many purposes, as we will show,
it is unnecessary to distinguish them. Indeed, it is notable that our problem
has not been to try and persuade you that several easily distinguished
sounds are really the same thing. On the contrary, we have had to take
pains to demonstrate that what appeared to be the same sound was in
reality a very variable phenomenon. For the moment, though, we want to
concentrate on the fact that it is entirely predictable where each kind of
[k] will be used. The predictability arises because of the way the special
qualities of each sound derive from its juxtaposition with certain other
sounds in connected speech. But if we continued studying [k] sounds, we
would soon find that we had by no means discovered all the possible
variants. There would be many more which resulted from [k] sounds overlapping with other sounds and acquiring a characteristic colouration. This
phenomenon of adjacent sounds becoming more like each other is called
assimilation.

A certain degree of assimilation is more or less inevitable in connected
speech, but it is not always possible to draw the line between what is
unavoidable and what is not. An unmodified sequence of sounds might, in
some cases, be physically possible, just a little awkward to produce, or
there may be some alternative modification which might equally ease an
awkward articulation. So, when we say that one [k] sound rather than
another is predictable in a particular position, this is not the same as saying
that it is inevitable. This is demonstrated by the fact that there are some
modifications which occur predictably in one person's speech but do not
occur in another's.

ASPIRATION

When [k] occurs at the beginning of a stressed syllable in RP and precedes
a vowel (as in *kip* but not *skip*), it is usually followed by a puff of air as
the plosive is released. This puff of air, called **aspiration**, does not occur
when [k] appears in other positions in a word (for brevity's sake we will
refer to these as non-initial positions). This is quite an interesting modification. In RP its occurrence is quite predictable – it only occurs when the
[k] is initial – but it is not explained nearly so easily in articulatory terms
as the modifications we have already looked at. Aspiration, then, is predictable but avoidable. Although characteristic of RP, it does not occur in
many varieties of English (so you may have difficulty in detecting it in
your own speech) and it does not apply to [g] in RP, even though this

shares both place and manner of articulation with [k]. For RP speakers, then, this modification, at least, must be regarded as a characteristic part of their language, rather than a simple necessity of speech production.

Phonetic redundancy

This example shows that it would be wrong to think of these systematic modifications merely as lazy articulations. It is probably true that assimilatory phenomena are greater in casual than in precise formal speech, but even very precise speech contains many systematic modifications which are a proper and important part of the sound pattern of the language. They aid communicational efficiency, which may be one reason why they appear everywhere in natural language. By overlapping sounds and inserting additional systematic variation, we distribute the information required to identify sounds. Even if we fail to hear a segment of sound – perhaps because it was masked by noise – it may be possible to reconstruct the missing sound by listening to the clues in adjacent sounds. So, for example, that puff of air in RP gives us an additional clue that the preceding sound was voiceless and, indeed, in some instances this clue may be more important than the lack of vibration of the vocal cords itself. We know from experimental evidence that clues such as this are of great importance to listeners. **Phonetic redundancy** of this kind aids efficiency in communication.

Predictability

All these variants of [k] are, of course, phonetically very similar, and you may be tempted to think that we could classify them more easily as variants of a single sound unit on the basis of their phonetic similarity than on the predictable way in which they alternate with each other. Phonetic similarity is, however, by no means a reliable guide, as we shall see, and it is the predictable way in which these sounds are distributed in speech which is the important criterion in linguistic analysis. A very similar phenomenon occurs in written language, and it may be easier to grasp the argument if we use writing as an analogy.

Activity 2.4

Up to the close of the eighteenth century, many printed books used the 'old-fashioned' letter shapes 'ſ' and 'f' for 's'. If you study texts printed at this time, you will find that not all 's's were printed in this way, though. Sometimes an ordinary 's' appears. In addition, a capital 'S' was used. In these books, then, four distinct letter shapes were employed, but their distribution in text was never random. Study the piece of text below (from Priestley, *The Rudiments of English Grammar*, 1761, pp. vii–ix, published in a facsimile edition by Scolar Press, Menston, 1969) and try to establish what rules the typesetter must have been following when he decided which symbol was appropriate in each case.

As to a publick *Academy*, invefted with authority to afcertain the ufe of words, which is a projeCt that fome perfons are very fanguine in their expeCtations from, I think it not only unfuitable to the genius of a *free nation*, but in itfelf ill calculated to reform and fix a language. We need make no doubt but that the beft forms of fpeech will, in time, eftablifh themfelves by their own fuperior excellence : and, in all controverfies, it is better to wait the decifions of *Time*, which are flow and fure, than to take thofe of *Synods*, which are often hafty and injudicious. A *manufaCture* for which there is a great demand, and a *language* that many perfons have leifure to read and write, are both fure to be brought, in time, to all the perfeCtion of which they are capable. As to the little varieties which the interpofition of an academy might prevent, they appear to me very far from having a difagreeable effeCt in the ftyle of different perfons writing upon different fubjeCts. What would *Academies* have contributed to the perfeCtion of the *Greek* and *Latin* languages? Or who, in thofe free ftates, would have fubmitted to them ?

The propriety of introducing the *Englifh grammar* into *Englifh fchools*, cannot be difputed ; a competent knowledge of our own language being both ufeful and ornamental in every profeffion, and a critical knowledge of it abfolutely neceffary to all perfons of a liberal education. The little difficulty there is apprehended to be in the ftudy of it, is the chief reafon, I believe, why it hath been fo much neglected. The *Latin* tongue was fo complex a language that it made of neceffity (notwithftanding the *Greek* was the learned tongue at Rome) a confiderable branch of Roman fchool education : whereas ours, by being more fimple, is perhaps lefs generally underftood. And though the *Grammar-fchool* be on all accounts the moft proper place for learning it, how many Grammar-fchools have we, and of no fmall reputation, which are deftitute of all provifion for the regular teaching it? All the fkill that our youth at fchool have in it, being acquired in an indirect manner; *viz.* by the mere practice of ufing it in verbal tranflations.

Indeed it is not much above a century ago, that our native tongue feemed to be looked upon as below the notice of a claffical fcholar; and men of learning made very little ufe of it, either in converfation or in writing: and even fince it hath been made the vehicle of knowledge of all kinds, it hath not found its way into the fchools appropriated to language, in proportion to its growing importance; moft of my cotemporaries, I believe, being fenfible, that their knowledge of the grammar of their mother tongue hath been acquired by their own ftudy and obfervation, fince they have paffed the rudiments of the fchools.

You should have found that the large capital 'S' was used in the same way as in present times. In fact, only one example appears in this piece of text, at the beginning of the word *Synods*. Capital 'S' was used at the beginning of sentences, and as the initial letter of proper names and other important words, particularly nouns. This latter use was much more frequent than is the case today. The other three letter shapes are used in a less obvious way. The 'ʃ' is only used in italicized words where it replaces the 'f'. The small 's' is used only at the end of a word. Hence 's' alternates with 'S' and 'f' according to the position of the letter in a word.

Here, then, we have an example of various letter shapes being used in predictable ways, rather as the various [k] sounds were used in speech. Handwriting is a closer analogy to speech than printing, however, in that there is greater variation in the shape of letters and in that handwriting is accomplished by means of a series of flowing muscular movements. It is not surprising, therefore, that we can find regularity in the distribution of handwritten letter shapes and see that the form of a letter is affected by the shape of adjacent letters. In the following example, for instance, four shapes are used for 's':

These different shapes are used in a systematic way, according to the preceding and following letters.

The term **graph** is applied to any written or printed letter shape. We can summarize the analysis of the examples above by saying that certain graphs seem to alternate with other graphs in a predictable way. This means that we can consider a given set of graphs as being variable tokens of a single functional letter. This functional unit is called a **grapheme**. In the example of printed text given in Activity 2.4 the graphs 'S' 's' 'f' 'ʃ' could be regarded as all representing an 's' grapheme. These variants are known as **allographs**. So 'S' 's' 'f' 'ʃ' are allographs of a single grapheme.

Phonemic analysis

Exactly the same is true of speech, except that in speech the tokens are known as **phones** rather than graphs. If we studied continuous speech for long enough, we could identify a vast number of phonetically different phones. But we could also work out how the distribution of these phones could be predicted in any one speaker's speech. This would enable us to identify how many significant sound units, or **phonemes**, were used by that speaker and what tokens, or **allophones**, were used to represent them.

So, we can say that in RP [k] and [kʰ] – the [ʰ] indicates that the [k] is aspirated – are allophones of a single /k/ phoneme. This will not surprise you, so familiar will you be with the fact that these sounds are functionally the same. But this functional equivalence is by no means inevitable. Just as a new printer might decide to use the 'f' symbol as an allographic variant of some other grapheme, for example 'f', so the way sounds are organized and assigned to functional units – phonemes – varies from language to language, or from dialect to dialect. For instance, in some languages the difference between aspirated and non-aspirated 'k' is most important. In Basque, Lappish and Hindi, for example, the two sounds [k] and [kʰ] are not variants of the same unit. If you substituted one sound for the other, you would not be heard to pronounce a word curiously, rather to utter a different word. *Kana* means 'one-eyed' in Hindi, but if you were an RP speaker and assumed you could aspirate the initial *k* with impunity, you would be mistaken. *Khana* means 'to eat'. So we can say not only that in RP [k] and [kʰ] are allophonic variants of a single /k/ phoneme, but that in Hindi they represent different phonemes.

Phonemic analysis is a useful way of reducing the very large number of sounds which actually occur in a language or are used by a speaker to a manageable set of items which are functionally distinct. We can test for the phonemic status of sounds in any language or dialect by looking for **minimal pairs** of words. 'Minimal pair' is the term given to two words that are differentiated – 'kept apart' – solely by one sound, for example *gap* and *cap*, which differ only in the initial sound. Since the difference between [g] and [k] leads to a difference in word meaning, these two sounds must represent different phonemes. A number of minimal pairs can be found to establish the phonemic distinction between [g] and [k] in English, for example: *got* and *cot*; *bag* and *back*; *granny* and *cranny*. But we can find no minimal pair for [k] and [kʰ] in English: [kap] and [kʰap] would be heard as different pronunciations of the same word.

Phonemic transcriptions are distinguished from phonetic ones by the use of oblique strokes rather than square brackets: /kap/. This indicates that a transcription is not intended as a faithful indication of pronunciation, rather as an analysis showing the phonemic structure of an utterance.

Table 2.2 RP phoneme inventory

Consonants

/p/ poppy	/f/ fife	/h/ ha-ha
/b/ bible	/v/ verve	/m/ mimic
/t/ totter	/θ/ thigh	/n/ nine
/d/ dad	/ð/ they	/ŋ/ singing
/k/ kick	/s/ sea-sick	/l/ loyal
/g/ gag	/z/ zoos	/r/ rarer
/tʃ/ church	/ʃ/ shush	/j/ yo-yo
/dʒ/ judge	/ʒ/ azure	/w/ wayward

Vowels

/iː/ peat	/ʊ/ put	/ɪə/ pier
/ɪ/ pit	/uː/ pool	/eə/ pear
/e/ pet	/ɜː/ pearl	/ʊə/ poor
/a/ pat	/eɪ/ pail	/ə/ banana
/ʌ/ putt	/əʊ/ pole	
/ɑː/ part	/aɪ/ pile	
/ɒ/ pot	/aʊ/ foul	
/ɔː/ port	/ɔɪ/ foil	

It will be obvious that the ordinary alphabet in which we write English is partially phonemic. But English dialects contain more phonemes than there are letters in the alphabet. Those letters which we do have are not always used in a consistently phonemic way. Written English has developed a regularity and system of its own (as is discussed in Section 5.3); the alphabet and the phoneme inventory make a different set of distinctions. Table 2.2 is the **phoneme inventory** for the speech of many RP speakers. You will see that it contains 44 phonemes – many more than the 26 letters of the alphabet.

A phonemic account is a structural one, i.e. it allows us to characterize the sound system of a dialect or language in terms of the internal system of contrasts and relationships between sounds without regard to the phonetic quality of the sounds themselves. You may find it easier to grasp this idea if you think of this analogy. The British monetary system consists of units – such as pence and pounds – which are defined in relationship to each other, not in terms of their individual physical properties. Indeed, physical appearance, although not highly variable, is little more than a practical clue which helps us identify instances of the different units. A good example of this is the one pound note, which, at time of writing exists in Scotland whereas in England a coin is used. Both represent the same functional unit, but it is clear that there is nothing in their physical shape which define them as being of the same value. Rather, it is their common transactional value.

Phonology versus phonetics

Just as the value of a unit in a monetary system is defined in terms of its relationships with other units in that system and not by its physical appearance, so a phoneme is defined in terms of its contrast with other phonemes and not by its phonetic properties. The phoneme system is thus an abstract system, but this should not worry you. It is largely at this abstract level, as we have seen, that you are aware of your own language. Furthermore, the description of regularities in language is much simpler at this abstract level than at the superficial level of phonetics. This abstract level of description is called **phonology** and is regarded by most linguists as a branch of grammar. If phonetics is concerned with the physical properties of speech sounds, then phonology is concerned rather with the way these sounds are functionally organized and distributed in a particular language or dialect.

Phonemes are by no means the only units in phonological analysis. Although we have assumed that features such as voicing are entirely phonetic (to do with the fact that the vocal cords are vibrating or not), it appears on closer inspection that such features have a phonological rather than a phonetic status. The profile diagram for *cleaned* (see Figure 2.11), for example, showed that although we would regard /d/ as a voiced phoneme, it was partially unvoiced if pronounced at the end of a word. Might not such devoicing – which is a regular phenomenon – cause confusion between pairs of words such as *bead* and *beat*? Fortunately, other phenomena occur at the phonetic level which keep these words apart. We described above how aspiration in RP of the voiceless plosive /k/ helped to indicate that the sound was voiceless. Likewise we have another clue in words such as *bead* and *beat* which indicates the voicing of the last phoneme. The sound before a voiced phoneme is characteristically longer than that before a voiceless one. So, the length of the /iː/ in *beat* and *bead* may be more important to us in distinguishing the /d/ from the /t/ in these words than any vibration of the vocal cords. In this way we can see that the feature of 'voicing' is an abstract one – in actual speech it is signalled in a number of regular but complex ways.

Phonological rules

Although there are complex and regular patterns at the phonetic level, it is necessary to operate at a more abstract analytical level – that of phonology – before we can see clearly the structural and functional properties of sounds. It makes sense to describe the sounds in terms of straightforward phonological features – such as voiced, plosive, velar, etc. – and leave as a separate exercise the description of how such abstract features, or abstract units, are realized in actual speech.

One succinct way of making the link between phonological and phonetic levels is by devising 'rules'. Such **phonological rules** are no more than a description of the way different sounds are systematically distributed in speech. Another way of looking at rules is to think of them as character-izing the knowledge that speakers must have about how phonemes are to be realized in speech. Take the aspiration of /k/ in RP, for example. We noticed that the /k/ in *skip* is not aspirated, but that the /k/ in *kip* is. After looking at many such words, we can formulate the rule as follows:

> Aspirate /k/ whenever it occurs in an initial position before a stressed vowel.

Since RP speakers must know this rule in the same way as they know the rules of English grammar, let us coin the term *sound-grammar*. We can now say that this rule is contained in the sound-grammar of RP.

The aspiration rule in RP does not just affect /k/ – it applies also to /p/ and /t/. Rather than make three different rules for the sound-grammar, one for each of these consonants, it would be much more succinct to capture this regularity in a single, more general rule. What we need is a means of describing the sounds /k/, /p/ and /t/ as a single but exclusive group. This we can do by using the (phonological) features *plosive* and *voiceless*. We can state that the rule applies to all voiceless plosives in an initial position.

We can also describe in terms of a rule the modification of /k/ which depends on the quality of the following vowel. In fact, wherever there is systematic variation of this kind, we can devise a rule which captures the regularity. Such a rule will contain two parts:

(a) A description of what is to happen, for example:
   (i) voiceless plosives are to be aspirated;
   (ii) velar plosives are to be rounded.
(b) A description of the context or conditions in which the rule is to be applied, for example:
   (i) when the voiceless plosive occurs in an initial position;
   (ii) when the velar plosive precedes a rounded vowel.

Each rule should be as succinct as possible, yet as broad as possible in application. The art – and point – of devising rules is to make occurrences of apparently quite different things appear as instances of a single, more general phenomenon. Employing phonological features in a rule of this kind has allowed us to make a useful generalization. It should, of course, be clear that rules such as these describe what we observe happens; they are far from being instructions from linguists to speakers about the 'cor-rect' way to talk.

2.4 Prosody

The term **prosody** is used to describe a variety of phenomena connected with the pitch, loudness and duration of speech sounds. All three features operate in a domain which is longer than individual phonemic segments. For this reason they are often also called **suprasegmental** features.

The description of prosody, despite the familiarity of the basic ingredi-ents, is extremely complex and difficult. There is probably less agreement among linguists about prosody than about any other area of descriptive linguistics and, as Lieberman (1986: 239) put it: 'Although these aspects of speech [intonation, stress and general "melody" of speech] are among the first that develop in human infants, we still have much to learn concerning the biological bases, the development and the linguistic function of these aspects of human speech.'

On one thing, at least, however, there is some agreement. This is that the three features we have described above are not in themselves of great interest. In order to analyse how utterances are organized at a prosodic level, we have to appeal to a more abstract level of description, and in this respect, prosody is no different from other aspects of phonological de-scription. Two phenomena are usually identified at this abstract level: **rhythm** and **intonation**.

Rhythm

THE DIFFERENCE BETWEEN SYLLABLE STRESS AND SENTENCE FOCUS

A sense of rhythm in speech comes about from a regular pattern of **stressed** and **unstressed** syllables. The term *stress*, like those of pitch and loudness, is a familiar one, but there are various sources of possible confusion in the way the term is used in linguistic description. The word is used to describe two different phenomena. It is used to refer to the way individual syllables are heard to be more prominent than others, as in the phrase

(1) syllabic prominence sɪ'labɪk 'prɒmənəns/

(The IPA marker of stress ['] is placed before the stressed syllable.) Here one syllable of each word is stressed compared with the others.

The term 'stress', however, is also sometimes used to refer to the way one part of an utterance is given emphasis or focus for contextual or semantic reasons:

(2) I bought potatoes

can be said with any one of the three words emphasized, and each version would be appropriate according to what question had been asked or implied:

(3) *I* bought potatoes (as opposed to *you* or *Jane*)
(4) I *bought* potatoes (as opposed to *stole* or *found*)
(5) I bought *potatoes* (as opposed to *carrots* or *asparagus*)

Since it is confusing to use the same term for these rather different phen-omena, we will refer to this kind of sentence emphasis as **sentence focus** and reserve the term 'stress' for syllable prominence. Sentence focus will be discussed below in the section on intonation.

There are two interesting problems attached to stress phenomena. The first is the phonetic problem of what stress consists of, and hence how it might be recognized. The second is what determines which syllables in an utterance are stressed.

THE PHONETIC NATURE OF STRESS

It might be thought that a stressed syllable is simply one which is louder than others, but in fact variation in intensity has been found to be only one, and perhaps a not important, aspect of stress. The intuition that stressed syllables are articulated more forcefully is probably correct, but higher pitch and longer duration seem to be more important indicators of this forcefulness (to listeners) than increased intensity (for reports of the classic experiments on listeners' perceptions of stress, see Fry 1955; 1958).

These features of pitch, duration and intensity combine to mark stressed syllables. In addition, unstressed syllables in English may be marked. Unstressed vowels may be reduced in quality to schwa [ə] or may be centralized in quality. Thus an alternation of vowel qualities may be associated with an alternation in stress and help support the perceived sense of rhythm.

ALLOCATION OF STRESS

Lexical stress   Some languages have a strict system of **fixed stress** on a particular syllable of every word. Polish, for example, stresses the penultimate syllable of every word, while Czech places the stress on the first syllable. English is, by comparison, a language with **free stress**. A speaker of English cannot predict easily which syllable of a word should be stressed – it must be learned and must be given as part of the pronunciation details in dictionaries.

Free stress means that occasionally it is possible for two different words to contrast only in stress (e.g., *billow* /'bɪləʊ/ and *below* /bə'ləʊ/), and such contrasts are quite frequent with noun-verb pairs ('*contrast* and *cont'rast*). Some longer or compound words may have more than one stressed syllable ('*civiliz'ation*, '*co-oper'ation*).

Although the allocation of stress in simple words seems unsystematic, when words are given affixes (see Section 3.3 for a fuller discussion of word division) or are put together to form compound words, certain regular patterns do emerge.

Stress in connected utterances   When words are strung together in connected speech, the resulting stress pattern is not, as might be supposed, a simple stringing together of the stress pattern of individual words. There are at least two phenomena which need to be explained. First, it seems to be the case that some words in an utterance are given more stress than others and in a way which cannot be explained by sentence focus. In the phrase *white elephants*, the word *white* seems more lightly stressed than the stressed syllable in *elephants*. There are, therefore, differences in degree of stress which need explaining. Second, expected stress patterns seem to rearrange themselves on occasion. A well-known example is the word *thirteen*, where the stress migrates to the first syllable from the last in phrases such as *thirteen men*. Phonologists have directed much effort to describing the patterns of such shifting.

It might be thought that all such variation in stress patterns takes place for reasons of ease of articulation. Since word stress may fall on any syllable, it is often the case that two stressed syllables may occur one after the other, and such sequences seem more difficult to articulate fluently. This can be experienced by comparing a sentence with monosyllabic words (excluding words like *of* or *the* which are usually unstressed) with one which contains a mixture of stressed and unstressed syllables.

(6) No cat caught mice
(7) A second animal was caught

There is indeed a difference between the sentences, but it is difficult to say whether or not it is a matter of ease of articulation. There is, however, a sense of impeded progress when one tries to utter the first sentence, as if each syllable refuses to be hurried. In the second sentence, the intervention of unstressed syllables seems to allow a more satisfying rhythm. This, of course, is a highly subjective way of looking at things. The very existence of sentences which consist of stressed monosyllables demonstrates that they can be articulated and hence that 'ease of articulation' is not sufficient explanation for stress patterns.

It is noticeable that English speakers tend to impose a fairly regular rhythm on their speech. English has been called a **stress-timed** language, in that the timing from one stressed syllable to another is roughly equivalent, regardless of how many unstressed syllables may intervene. French, by contrast, is **syllable-timed**, in that roughly equal time is given to each syllable.

(8) No cat caught a mouse
(9) No cat caught any mice

In (8) there is an extra unstressed syllable between *caught* and the next stressed syllable as compared to (6) but the duration of the articulation of *caught* is reduced. The result is that roughly the same amount of time elapses between the two stressed syllables (*caught/mice* and *caught/mouse*) in each case, despite the existence of an extra syllable. In (9) yet another syllable is introduced, and the duration of *caught* seems to reduce again.

Such a principle is known as **isochrony** and demonstrates that there are language-specific rhythmic patterns, but it is still insufficient to explain why some syllables are stressed and others unstressed. Indeed, the distinction between stress-timed and syllable-timed languages is not accepted by all linguists, and there exist varieties of English in some parts of the world which (if the distinction is accepted) are syllable-timed.

Many linguists have observed that stress assignment is closely related to
the syntactic structure of a sentence. Probably the best-developed theory
of this kind is the **metrical theory** proposed by Liberman and Prince (1977).
They note that relative syllable prominence tends to be assigned one way
in compound words and another way in phrases. To see this, we have to
imagine we are in a situation which is not yet confused by the addition of
sentence focus (which might alter the neutral rhythm to give special emphasis or meaning). Take the pair of words 'white house'. This might be
a phrase *white house* (which describes the colour of the house) or it might
be a compound noun *White House* (the building in Washington, USA).
The stress is different in the two cases. In the phrase, it is the right-hand
word which seems to be more prominent, in the compound it is the left-
hand one. This can be represented diagrammatically:

Phrase

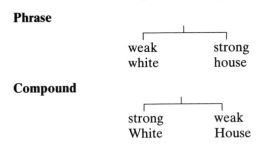

```
        weak        strong
        white       house
```

Compound

```
        strong      weak
        White       House
```

These relationships of relative prominence hold true even when each
pair (a **constituent**) is embedded into a larger structure. A phrase such as
White House official has a syntactic structure which can be represented as
follows:

```
        White       House       official
```

(for a more detailed discussion of syntactic structure and phrase diagrams
see Chapter 3).

We can use exactly the same simple rules to assign relative prominence
between the higher-order constituents:

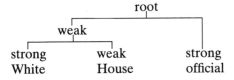

```
                    root
            weak
        strong      weak        strong
        White       House       official
```

This suggests that the constituent 'official' will be relatively stronger than
that of 'White House' while 'White' retains its prominence as compared to
'House'.

Such a process generates a pattern of relative prominences and allows
us to predict which items are stressed and how. It also predicts, however,
that there is a range of stress levels, some items being more highly stressed

than others. The hierarchical range of stress strengths assigned to different items will reflect the way those items are embedded through strong and weak branches in the structure.

Liberman and Prince do not claim that syntactic structure is entirely sufficient to predict where stress will fall. The two rules described above, for example, assume that relative prominences assigned within a constituent will be retained, even if that constituent has been embedded in larger structures. Yet the example we started with of *thirteen men* indicates that this is not always true. Here the relative prominence assigned to the syllables in *thirteen* has changed as a result of embedding the word into the phrase.

Liberman and Prince suggested that the pattern of strong and weak items generated by the above rules may contain clashes of rhythm which require readjustment. Such clashes were not to be seen as an ease-of-articulation requirement since what exactly counts as a clash varies from language to language. Rather, certain kinds of scansion seem to be avoided in English. Liberman and Prince proposed a **metrical grid** as a device for readjusting rhythm so that it fits into an appropriate and permissible pattern. Whether something counts as a clash, however, may depend on the constituent structure of the sentence and not just the final outward rhythmic pattern. In this sense, it would be wrong to think of the grid arrangement as simply being a list of possible metric patterns, like those available to a poet writing in a particular metre.

Metrical theory describes the rhythm of a sentence in terms of a hierarchical pattern of stress levels, but it is important to realize that these levels – and indeed the notions of strong and weak – are abstract categories. The theory provides for an indefinite range of stress levels which are unlikely to be identifiable in an acoustic analysis. Nevertheless, metrical theorists claim that there is a psychological justification for positing so many differential levels of stress. We may perceive a more subtle gradation in stress levels than acoustic cues warrant since we are, they claim, aware of the abstract syntactic structure and hence abstract metrical structure of the utterance.

Intonation

People do not usually talk in a complete monotone. Indeed, monotonous speech is not only difficult to listen to, but also difficult to understand. Speakers give many clues to the syntactic structure of their utterances, as well as to how what they say is to be taken, by altering the pitch of their voice. What is important, though, is not the absolute level of pitch – the natural pitch range of different speakers varies greatly – but rather the relative changes in pitch. Hence, in RP we can pronounce a word such as *sure* with rising intonation and indicate that it is to be taken as a question:

$\overline{\text{sure}}\nearrow$

Or we can give it a falling intonation and imply, perhaps, a reassuring reply to a question:

↘
sure

In longer utterances, intonation patterns work with stress patterns to organize the delivery and meaning of utterances. Rhythm, for example, helps divide utterances into separate **intonational groups**. We can distinguish *I don't know* from *I don't, no* by giving separate intonational groups to *I don't* and *no* and showing the unity of structure by a single intonational group for *I don't know*.

The length of intonational groups is generally restricted by the fact that they are usually said in one breath, so that they rarely exceed seven words or so. Here is a passage divided up into possible intonational groups.

[When I go to London] [I like to make a day of it] [and go to a museum] [John] [on the other hand] [likes to rush there and back as soon as possible]

The boundaries between groups usually come at points where there is a major break in grammatical structure, so that such groups often correspond with a clause (*When I go to London*), sometimes with the subject only (*John*), or the predicate only (*likes to rush there and back as soon as possible*), and sometimes with an adverbial phrase (*on the other hand*). (These syntactic descriptions are more fully explained in Chapter 3.)

The intonational group itself has been analysed in a number of ways. The pattern of pitch movement over the whole intonational group is often referred to as the **pitch contour**. An early British tradition, not entirely superseded in some American analyses, treated the whole contour as carrying a particular meaning. This approach, which may be termed an **intonational lexicon**, suggests that an intonation contour cannot profitably be broken up into smaller units. Instead, the whole prosodic envelope of the intonational group must be regarded as a single entity.

In most current analyses of intonation, however, a number of distinct subdivisions are recognized. An intonational group must consist of at least one syllable (which will necessarily be stressed) which will carry a major pitch movement. In longer utterances the last stressed syllable of the intonational group will carry the main pitch movement. This part of the pitch contour is known as the **nuclear tone** or simply the **nucleus**. Exactly which syllable is given this stress will depend on **sentence focus**, that is, the word which is picked out for special emphasis by the speaker.

The kinds of pitch movement which form the nuclear tone vary slightly from dialect to dialect. Different linguists also come to different conclusions about how many basic pitch movements exist. Ladd (1978) has identified four basic types in RP: a fall, a fall-rise, a high rise, and a low-rise.

All utterances must contain a nucleus, but there may be (and usually is) other material in the intonational group which precedes the nuclear tone. The stretch from the first stressed syllable up to (but not including) the last stressed syllable is known as the **head** and any preceding unstressed syllables form the **pre-head**. If there are any syllables after the nucleus, then these are known as the **tail**. The following utterance, for example, has a tripartite structure:

pre-head	**head**	**nucleus**
I	'wanted to 'go to the	'zoo

This analysis assumes that the sentence focus, and hence the nuclear tone, falls on *zoo*. If the speaker placed the focus on *go* then the organization would be as follows:

pre-head	**head**	**nucleus**	**tail**
I	'wanted to	'go	to the zoo

The pitch patterns in the head are regarded as acting independently of those in the nucleus. Furthermore, unlike the nucleus, the head may vary in length. The actual organization of head and nucleus will depend not just on the syntax of the utterance, but crucially on where the speaker places the sentence focus. This in turn depends on a variety of contextual and semantic factors.

PARAGRAPHING

There are various intonation-like phenomena which occur over longer passages than the intonation group itself. We recognize syllable prominence and pitch movement by identifying deviations from the general pitch level of the utterance. The general pitch level may itself decline gradually over the length of an utterance. Some researchers have suggested that such effects are to be regarded as a part of intonation, in that the speaker plans their execution to help segment the utterance into various clausal groups. In support of this claim they have shown that although the general pattern is a decline in the level which pitch peaks reach throughout the utterance, there appears to be a mild resetting of the level on clause boundaries. The tracing of a pitch contour in Figure 2.12 shows the pattern. Such patterns are referred to as **declination patterns**. There is, however, a certain controversy as to whether such patterns should be regarded as a part of the intonational system, or whether, indeed, they exist at all. Lieberman (1986) has argued that the declinations observed are merely reflections of breath control, and, while listeners must take them into account in some way when picking out local prominences and significant deviations from the baseline, the declination pattern itself does not carry intonational information. Umeda (1982) has queried whether declinations exist outside experiments in which long sentences are read aloud. Short spontaneous and conversational utterances do not seem to show declination behaviour at all.

Figure 2.12 Tracing of a pitch contour

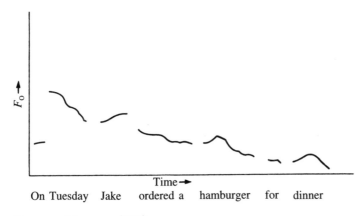

Time →

On Tuesday   Jake   ordered a   hamburger   for   dinner

Source: Cooper and Sorensen (1981)

Even if declination is still a controversial issue, there are other well-attested intonational effects which range over longer stretches of talk. If you listen to newsreaders, for instance, you will hear that the intonation groups at the beginning of a new subject are relatively high, whereas by the end of a subject the overall height of the intonation group will be very much lower. With the introduction of a new topic, the overall pitch goes back to relatively high again. Such pitch movement is rather different from declination, since it regularly occurs over several sentences and breath groups. Furthermore, the ending of such passages is also prosodically marked, not just by a special lowering of pitch, but by a regular lengthening of segments and slower rhythm. It has been shown that listeners can tell whether brief tape-recorded clauses have been taken from the beginning or end of such paragraphs.

Transcription of prosody

There is no single transcription method for prosody which has widespread currency, though this is scarcely surprising in view of the disagreement about the basic phenomena themselves. The International Phonetic Alphabet provides a stress marker ['] and a half stress marker [,], but offers no further help apart from length markers. A variety of notations for intonation are to be found in the literature, representing a variety of solutions to the problem of how to show how pitch movement fits with the segmental structure of the utterance (as shown in a phonemic transcription). Perhaps the simplest, but also most unsatisfactory, method has been adopted by conversation analysts (see Section 7.3). Arrows showing direction of movement can be inserted into the textual transcription, as in the following example from Atkinson and Heritage (1984):

↓ ↑ Thatcher: I am however (0.2) very ↓fortunate (0.4) in having
(0.6) a ↑mar:vlous dep↓uty

This is unsatisfactory from the point of view of an intonational analysis
because it fails to distinguish between a generally high or low level of pitch
and actual pitch movement. It fails also to cope with compound movement, such as fall-rise. It is useful, however, when no sophisticated analysis
of intonation is intended, and only a general impression of pitch behaviour
is needed.

A better method but much disliked by publishers, involves the physical
rearrangement of words on the line, as in this example from Bolinger
(1985):

                    that
      What does
                    have to do with it?

Another, less clumsy, method is to show the direction of pitch movement by means of lines and arrows above the words (as in our own examples above). This has the benefit of being immediately interpretable, but
shares with Bolinger's method the disadvantage that the relationship between pitch movement and stress cannot be easily shown. This problem
has been overcome elegantly by some British linguists (e.g. O'Connor and
Arnold 1961), who use a system of blobs on an imaginary stave below the
orthographic representation. A large blob shows stress:

||I *want* to be *absolutely sure* about it.||

This system is also used in a more refined version by Crystal (1969), who
adds lines which show the precise relationship between pitch movement
and location of stress:

the |ninety NĪNE [|point ĺNĪNE [per |cÈNT]]|

'no refe↑rendum of [↑ÂLL] "↑JÛDGES|

the ap↑PÈAL [ma|chinery in the cōŪRTS]|

These by no means exhaust the variety of notations used, particularly in American writing, but they do demonstrate the range of problems which all methods must face.

It must be admitted that transcription of intonation is a somewhat arcane skill. Newcomers will find it sometimes difficult to decide exactly where the main pitch movement is and where it is heading, and two different listeners are quite likely to disagree. This is partly a reflection of the complexity and speed of the phenomena, and the need for a keen and trained ear. It may also be in part, however, an indication that the analytical frameworks within which the various transcriptions are made do not entirely capture the kinds of thing which are salient to ordinary listeners.

Some researchers, particularly psychologists and some conversation analysts, prefer to work directly with analyses of pitch made by machines (as in Figure 2.12). This certainly lends a more objective appearance to analyses but it is notable that such researchers rarely invoke any well-developed intonational framework. Such tracings are not, in fact, sufficient and are often not helpful in making intonational analyses. Intonational analyses require such tracings to be mapped on to the actual syllables and patterns of stress in the utterance, for example. In addition, the use of instrumental tracings raises various new methodological and analytical questions. Since they contain various incidental perturbations, due to breath control and segmental articulation, and contain gaps due to voiceless segments, they require a theory (as yet even more poorly developed than intonational theories) which relates the abstract categories of nuclear movement to the actual phonetic characteristics of a pitch contour. For these reasons, linguists tend to be rather sceptical about the usefulness of instrumental tracings, as this typical comment by Gussenhoven (1986: 77) shows:

> The analysis was carried out by the author on an auditory basis. This was not out of a cavalier attitude towards instrumental registrations of periodicity, but because the recognition of nuclear tones on the basis of periodicity tracings is still beyond the power of man or machine.

The functions of prosody (see p 53)

The fact that the internal workings of intonation and rhythm have proved difficult to describe does not seem surprising when one considers the different functions they serve.

The first and foremost is a segmenting function. In written language we use punctuation, capital letters, paragraphing and other visual means of dividing language up into smaller units and showing significant structural boundaries. Prosody carries out this function in speech.

Prosody also serves several pragmatic functions. Sentence focus, in particular, is used to mark out the **given** (old) information from the **new**. Such marking depends on speakers' and listeners' knowledge of prior discourse or prior information and it can be used to signal what is to be regarded as mutual knowledge. Since the use of sentence focus implies certain **presuppositions** (these are discussed more fully in Section 4.3), it can be used to communicate information indirectly. If someone says *I didn't do it*, this carries a presupposition that someone else did do it and that there is agreement about the fact that an action was actually carried out. If Fred utters this as Aunt Edith comes into the room, but before she could be expected to have noticed anything wrong, it might be heard as an indirect way of telling her that her favourite vase has been broken.

Prosody, particularly intonation, can be used to establish the **illocutionary force** (see Section 4.3 for a fuller discussion of **speech acts**) of an utterance, where this is not clear from the syntax. *Has John gone to London?* may be said as easily with a falling intonation as with a rising, questioning one. If word order does not show that this is a question, however, the fact can be shown by the use of a questioning intonation: *John's in London?*

Another function of prosody is the signalling of **attitude**. Exactly how this is done is not very clear, but the fact that it is done is familiar to us all. The area is one of greater interest to psychologists, perhaps, than to linguists. One issue has been the question of whether there is a set of intonational categories through which attitude can be conventionally signalled. A second issue is the way in which the intonational system for marking linguistic categories fits in with that of attitude.

Prosody has yet another important function in conversational interaction. It helps speakers indicate that they are coming to the end of a turn, and is used to mark interruptions and other competitive situations. These **management functions** are described in Section 6.3.

3 Sentence and word structure

3.1 Introduction

The great expansion of linguistics as a discipline in the 1960s and 1970s was associated with advances which were then being made in theories of grammar. The work of Noam Chomksy and others not only generated great excitement within linguistics, but also had a considerable impact in other fields as diverse as psychology and architecture. Today, there is a more even balance in the major areas of linguistic research, but theories of grammar are still considered a central part of language study.

The idea of 'grammar' and of doing grammatical analysis, seems to frighten many people. In part, this may have to do with the nature of language itself – a grammar attempts to make generalizations about language structure, but language has the habit of being more complex in its structure than first appears and often evades simple analysis. However, the way grammar has traditionally been taught in schools in many parts of the world – almost as a matter of punishment than for any enjoyment of discovery and learning – has probably alienated generations of students. But it has to be admitted that linguists themselves have not been entirely helpful in this matter: a whole range of theories and terminologies have emerged in recent years and it is sometimes hard to keep up with changing and conflicting ideas about sentence structure. One linguist, in a review of modern theories of sentence structure complains: 'The study of syntax, for reasons that have never been clear (to me, at least) has always been a more acrimonious business than the pursuit of sister-disciplines in formal linguistics. Phonologists, morphologists, semanticists and phoneticians can all survive and cooperate in courteous disagreement, but syntacticians seem to thrive on a more robust diet of anger, polemic and personal abuse.' (McCloskey 1988: 18).

In view of the revolutionary nature of some of the new theories of language, it may seem surprising that they still incorporate many traditional and familiar concepts and categories. **Nouns** and **verbs**, and **subjects** and **objects**, to name just a few, still appear in modern accounts of sentence structure. At the level of rudimentary description, less has changed than might be supposed. In this chapter, we discuss some of the basic characteristics of sentence and word structure that any theory of language has to take into account, and we give an outline of two major theoretical grammars to show how they account for such basic facts of sentence and word structure.

3.2   Grammar and grammars

The scope of grammar

The word 'grammar' is used by linguists in a variety of ways, which can be confusing to a newcomer to the discipline. The first ambiguity has to do with the scope of grammar: what range of language phenomena does it include? In the days when the study of language meant mainly the study of Latin and Greek, grammar was concerned largely with **morphology** (which we described in Chapter 1 as being concerned with the study of word structure). This narrow focus was appropriate for the study of inflected languages, where the relations between words in a sentence is shown primarily by word endings. It was less suitable for the English language, but the focus of grammatical studies remained largely on morphology until well into the twentieth century. The American linguist, Zellig Harris, was able to complain in 1946 that 'many grammars have carried little or no syntactic description' (1946: 161).

As systematic techniques for analysing word order were developed in the second half of the century, so the term 'grammar' came to include both morphology and syntax (syntax was described in Chapter 1 as being the study of how words are combined into longer stretches of language). Such a definition conforms to the traditional use of the word 'grammar' in linguistics, and it coincides, more or less, with popular everyday usage. We used 'grammar' in this way in Chapter 1.

Some linguists, however, particularly those working in the tradition established by Chomsky, use 'grammar' to refer to the entire system of organization of language – including **phonology** and **semantics**, as well as morphology and syntax. For them, all the 'boxes' which we described in Section 1.4 as being components of language are regarded as being a part of grammar.

There is a further ambiguity attached to 'grammar'. Just as the word 'language' is used in two different ways – *language* and *a language* – so the word 'grammar' can be used to describe either the general structural properties of human language, or the characteristics of a specific language. The kind of grammar which Chomsky is associated with has become known as **universal grammar**, which reflects the first of these usages. On the other hand, we can use expressions such as a 'grammar of Sanskrit', to mean a description of the regular patterns of sentence and word structure in Sanskrit.

These different usages of 'grammar' may sound confusing, but in fact the meaning that different linguists intend is usually quite clear. A linguist who provides a general account of language tends to use the word 'grammar' in the wider sense – to include all the components of a linguistic theory. A linguist who provides an account of a particular language tends to use 'grammar' in the narrower sense – to include only morphology and syntax.

Good and bad grammar

In everyday language, people sometimes talk of 'bad grammar', usually referring to features that they do not consider current 'standard' usage. This could mean, for English, sentences with two or more negatives, such as *I haven't got no money on me*, rather than the standard *I haven't got any money on me* or *I have no money on me*. In French, however, it is sentences with a single negative particle that are regarded by some people as 'bad grammar'. Formal French requires both *ne* and *pas* in simple negative sentences (*je n'ai pas d'argent sur moi*) but in colloquial spoken French *pas* often occurs alone (*j'ai pas d'argent sur moi*). Linguists do not think of features such as these in terms of 'good' or 'bad' grammar, though they may be interested in considering what is involved in our everyday concept of 'bad' grammar (see, for discussion, Milroy and Milroy 1985; Andersson and Trudgill 1990). Linguists have to decide whether to base their analysis on the standard variety of the language or on a non-standard variety, or whether to analyse a formal style of the language or informal, colloquial speech; but judgements about 'good' or 'bad' language are irrelevant to the analysis of sentence and word structure.

Types of grammar

These differences in the way the word 'grammar' is defined and used reflect the different motives and purposes for which grammars are designed. At least four kinds of grammar can be usefully identified, each of which employs different methods and frameworks to describe language:

Theoretical grammars: It is these that have revolutionized the study of language during the course of the second half of the twentieth century. Theoretical grammars aim to go beyond describing the morphology and syntax of a particular language, in order to discover what is universal to all languages. Their goal is to describe and to try to explain the general human phenomenon of language. This involves discovering what exactly it is that people 'know' when we say that they 'know' a language, how this knowledge is acquired by children, and how it can best be formulated. Not surprisingly, linguists do not necessarily agree on the precise nature of this human phenomenon, and they have different views about exactly what the grammar should try to explain. This means that theoretical grammars sometimes have very different starting-points, and offer very different kinds of explanation. Theoretical grammars tend to use the term 'grammar' in a wider sense: to include all the components of a linguistic theory.

Descriptive grammars: These aim to make precise, systematic statements about the morphology and syntax of specific languages. They are often written for academics and students of a specific language, such as English, Italian or Pali, or for students, teachers and practitioners in language-related fields such as education or psychology. The best descriptive grammars make use of any relevant insights that have been gained by researchers working on theoretical grammars. An example of a descriptive grammar of this type is Huddleston's (1984) *Introduction to the Grammar of English*. A **reference grammar** is a descriptive grammar that aims to provide a fully comprehensive account of all the major morphological and syntactic structures of a language and that can be consulted on particular points of syntax in much the same way that a dictionary can be consulted about the meaning or spelling of individual words. For English a widely used modern reference grammar is *A Comprehensive Grammar of English* (Quirk *et al.* 1985).

Pedagogic grammars: These are used by students and teachers involved in teaching or learning a foreign language. Typically they contain simplified, explicit accounts of the main morphological and syntactic structures of a language, often with exercises or drills intended to help students to learn these structures. Modern pedagogic grammars are usually informed by work in theoretical and descriptive linguistics, although they rarely discuss points of morphology and syntax in detail, and it would be difficult for them to achieve their objectives if they did. An example of a pedagogic grammar of this kind, again for English, is Murphy and Altman's (1989) *Grammar in Use*.

Prescriptive grammars: Modern linguists make a clear distinction between *descriptive* grammars, which aim to give an objective description of how people actually speak, and *prescriptive* grammars, which lay down rules about how people ought to speak. The notions of 'bad' and 'good' grammar belong to the prescriptivist tradition. Some prescriptive grammars, usually older ones, are idiosyncratic and riddled with inconsistent value judgements. Their prescriptions often try to force speakers of English to conform to rules that were appropriate for Latin but are meaningless when applied to English: some recommend *It is she*, for instance, instead of *It is her*, because the verb *to be* in Latin was followed by a pronoun in the **nominative** (subject) **case**. It is pointless, however, to apply the patterns of sentence structure that exist in one language to those of another language: each language must be described in its own terms and the structure of Latin is very different from the structure of English, as we see in Section 3.3.

Although linguists have generally been at pains to distance themselves from the prescriptivist tradition, prescriptive grammars continue to be bought and consulted regularly by large numbers of people. Native speakers seem to want clear norms for using their own language, and where there is variation between two forms (such as *I'll come provided it isn't raining* or *I'll come providing it isn't raining*) they want to be advised on which one to use. Modern prescriptive grammars now base their advice on the way educated speakers use language rather than on the author's personal whims and preferences. An example of a modern grammar of this type (some would consider 'a guide to good usage' to be a more appropriate term than 'a prescriptive grammar') is Greenbaum and Whitcut's revised edition of *The Complete Plain Words* (Gowers 1986), whose purpose was originally to help civil servants to be clear in their professional writing.

In this chapter we focus on descriptive and theoretical grammars, since it is these that provide suitable frameworks for describing morphology and syntax.

3.3 Descriptive grammars

Any grammatical analysis will show how linguistic elements are ordered and structured within longer stretches of language. In this section we will begin by examining the smallest unit of analysis and show how such units are assembled into larger structures.

Word structure

When it comes to deciding on the smallest unit of analysis common sense suggests that the word will be a suitable unit, but this gives rise to several difficulties. One is that the form which words take is affected by their arrangement into longer stretches of language. The word *love*, for example, has a different form in (1) and (2) below:

(1) We love growing prize cabbages
(2) Jeremy loves eating them

It would be possible to say that *love* and *loves* are completely different words, reflecting the fact that they have different forms, but this would neither take account of a native speaker's intuition that these are, in some sense, variations of the 'same' word, nor recognize that there exists a general pattern of verb forms in English. The verb *love* is by no means the only one that has an -s suffix when it occurs with a singular subject such as *Jeremy*: in fact, most verbs inflect in this way. Consider, for example, *we sing madrigals*, but *Jeremy sings them*; or *I prepare the potatoes, you prepare the beans* but *Jeremy prepares the leeks*.

We can give a better description of English word structure by taking account of the regular patterns of word formation, identifying those elements that occur over and over again in a language, always with the same meaning. This entails describing *loves* in (2), above, as a word that consists of two elements: *love* and -*s*. It is elements such as these – termed **morphemes** – that are considered to be the minimal units of analysis of sentence and word structure.

BOUND AND FREE MORPHEMES

Consider the following words:

jumped	walked	laughed	danced	philosophized
unfair	unhappy	untrue	unfortunate	unimportant

These words can be divided into morphemes as follows:

jump + ed	walk + ed	laugh + ed	dance + ed	philosophize + ed
un + fair	un + happy	un + true	un + fortunate	un + important

The morphemes that we have identified are of two different types: the -*ed* and the *un*- morphemes are recurrent elements of English word structure, but they occur only in combination with other morphemes. They are therefore termed **bound morphemes**, and the way in which they are bound to other morphemes is conventionally shown by the position of their hyphen: -*ed* indicates that the bound morpheme follows another morpheme; *un*- indicates that the bound morpheme precedes another morpheme. **Free morphemes** are then morphemes that can occur alone, such as *jump* or *true* (since they can occur alone, they are written without a hyphen). Agglutinating languages, inflectional languages and polysynthetic languages typically have a large number of bound morphemes. The example given in Section 1.3 from Inuktitut, a polysynthetic language, contains nine bound morphemes: (the example was *Qasuiirsarvigssarsingitluinarnarpuq*, which, as we saw, can be translated literally as *qasu-iir-sar* 'tired not cause-to-be', -*vig* 'place-for', -*ssar* 'suitable', -*si* 'find', -*ngit* 'not', -*luinar* 'completely, -*nar* 'someone', -*puq* 'third person singular' – 'someone did not find a completely suitable resting place'). The example from Turkish, an agglutinative language, *evlerden* ('from the houses'), can now be seen to consist of a free morpheme, *ev*, and two bound morphemes, -*ler* and -*den*.

In English, words can be formed by combining bound and free morphemes, as the following examples show:

free + free:	black-bird, father-in-law
free + bound:	wet-ness, dry-ing
bound + free:	dis-please, be-friend
bound + bound:	con-ceive, re-sist

Allomorphs, or **morpheme variants** of a single morpheme, can be identified in a similar way to the method of establishing allophones and phonemes (see Section 2.3). The morpheme *-ed*, for example, expresses 'past tense' in English, but there are irregular verb forms such as *took* or *saw* that can be considered to contain allomorphs of the past tense morpheme. They are **lexically conditioned** – that is, their form is determined by the particular **lexical item** they represent. ('Lexical item' is the term used to describe the abstract 'word' which underlies all the variant morphological forms which the real word takes. Lexical items are conventionally indicated by means of capitals. Hence here the lexical items are the verbs TAKE and SEE, respectively.) Other allomorphs are **phonologically conditioned**; that is, their form is affected by the sounds that surround them: consider, for example, the pronunciation of the *-ed* morpheme in the following verbs:

lifted	jumped	pulled
descended	walked	died

After /t/ and /d/ (termed **alveolar plosives** – see Section 2.3), as in *lifted* and *descended*, the past tense morpheme is pronounced /ɪd/; after other voiceless consonants, such as in *jumped* and *walked*, it is pronounced /t/; and after all other voiced sounds it is pronounced /d/, as in *pulled* and *died*.

INFLECTIONAL AND DERIVATIONAL MORPHOLOGY

A distinction can also be made between morphemes that express further information about a particular word, and morphemes that are used to construct entirely new words in the vocabulary of a language. The *-ed* morpheme is an example of the first kind, expressing, as we have seen, the past tense forms of English verbs. This process of word formation is typical of inflectional languages, as the name suggests, and is termed **inflectional morphology**. English regular verbs, like JUMP and WALK, can be considered to have a base form *jump* and inflectional forms *jumps, jumped* and *jumping*. Similarly, nouns usually form plurals by the addition of the *-s* morpheme. Thus CAT has the base form *cat* and an inflected form *cats* in the expression *these two cats*. The addition of the extra morpheme does not alter the basic meaning of JUMP or CAT.

Derivational morphology, on the other hand, involves morphemes which are used to form different words such as, for English, *un-*, or *-er*. *Unfortunate* and *unimportant* do not have the same meaning as *fortunate* and *important* (they are **converse** in meaning – see Section 4.2). Similarly, the addition of *-er* to *run* or to *love* not only changes the meaning of the words (from the *process* of running or loving to a *person* who runs or loves) but also changes their **word class**, from verbs to nouns.

Derivational processes are an important way of adding new words to a language, so a morphological analysis can be a useful way of describing the changes that are taking place in the vocabulary of a language. For example, modern English contains many verbs that have been formed by adding the bound morpheme *-ize* to a noun: these include *winterize, immortalize, hospitalize* and *customize*, to name just a few. Many of these verbs were first coined in the USA, and are now spreading to other varieties of English. The bound morpheme *-wise* is similarly responsible for the development of some new words in English, this time for the formation of some new sentence adverbs from nouns: consider *Moneywise, we're not doing too badly* and *Weatherwise, it should be a good day tomorrow*. Another example is the bound morpheme *-ee* which allows nouns to be formed from verbs, as in *employee, divorcee, mortgagee, payee*.

A morphological analysis can also be used to describe new words that are typical of 'Euro-English': in some European countries English morphemes are sometimes used to produce new words that do not exist in native language varieties. The shopping complex at some Swiss railway stations, for example, is called *Shoppyland* (from English *shop + y + land*); and a French commercial chain of garden centres has been given the hybrid name *jardiland* (from French *jardin* and English *land*).

Morphology and word order

How far morphological analysis takes us in analysing larger stretches of language depends on the language that we are analysing. For example, one of the central functions of grammar is to indicate how the words in a sentence are related to each other in meaning. In inflectional languages, this function is largely accomplished by morphology. If you were a writer living in ancient Rome and using classical Latin, you would know that (3) and (4) below have different meanings, with Octavia, as the subject of the verb, loving her dog in (3) and the dog, as the subject of the verb, loving Octavia in (4):

(3) Octavia canem amat (Octavia loves the dog)
(4) Octaviam canis amat (the dog loves Octavia)

The Latin word for 'dog' has the form *canis* when it functions as the subject of the sentence and the form *canem* when it functions as the object; similarly, Octavia is referred to as *Octavia* when she is the subject of the sentence and as *Octaviam* when she is the object. Changing the order of the words in a Latin sentence may create some differences in emphasis, but it does not affect the syntactic relations between the words. Thus, example (5) may stress the fact that it is the dog that is loved, but it does not alter the fact that it is Octavia who loves it:

(5) Canem Octavia amat (Octavia loves the dog)

In English, and other analytic languages, word order is the main mechanism for indicating syntactic relationships between words. Hence (6) and (7) below have different meanings:

(6) The farmer killed the chicken
(7) The chicken killed the farmer

We understand the subject of (6) to be *the farmer* and the subject of (7) to be *the chicken*, since these are the words that occur before the verb. In Welsh, on the other hand, the subject usually occurs after the verb: if you know Welsh, therefore, you will know that the subject of (8) is *y dyn*, 'the man' (a word-for-word translation of (8) is 'saw the man the dog'):

(8) Gwelodd y dyn y ci

Part of the linguistic knowledge that speakers have about their language, then, is the extent to which syntactic relations such as subject and object are expressed by the internal structure of words (the morphology of the language) and the extent to which they are expressed by the order of words (the syntax). As we saw in Chapter 1, languages can be classified according to the relative importance of morphology and word order in indicating such syntactic relations.

Word classes

The ways in which words can be used within sequences depend on their word class (or syntactic category). If you have studied traditional grammar at school, you will probably be familiar with terms like *noun*, *verb*, *adjective* and *adverb*. You may have known them as 'parts of speech'. In traditional grammar these were defined in *notional* terms, such as:

noun: name of a person, place or thing
verb: 'doing' word

or in *functional* terms:

adjective: qualifies a noun
adverb: modifies a noun

One problem with the definition of a verb as 'a doing word', is that it does not apply very well to verbs such as *feel* (as in *I feel hot*). Many children who were taught this definition found it difficult to understand why some nouns describing processes (such as the word 'process' itself) were not verbs. A more objective way of determining word classes is in terms of their distributional properties and syntactic function. One practical way of investigating such distributional properties is to examine the **syntagmatic** and **paradigmatic** relations that words have with each other in sentences. A **syntagm** is a sequential pattern which reflects the restrictions on word order in a language. A **paradigm** is the set of alternative words which could be used equally legitimately in a particular position in the syntagm. Words can be regarded as belonging to the same word class if they can occur as alternatives at the same point in a specific sequence.

As an example, consider the sequence *the grey mare*. We could substitute various different words for *grey*, without upsetting the acceptability of the sequence:

the _____ mare

> old
> gentle
> delightful

Native speakers of English are aware that there are restrictions on what words can be put in this position. They agree that it is ungrammatical, for example, to say *the which mare or *the loves mare (ungrammatical examples are conventionally preceded by an asterisk). Words such as grey, old, gentle, delightful that can occur in this position in the sequence are all considered to be members of the same word class, which in this case is usually labelled **adjective**.

By continuing to investigate the patterns of substitution that are possible in this sequence, two further classes can be identified, termed **determiners** and **nouns**:

determiner	adjective	noun
the	grey	mare
an	old	dog
that	gentle	creature
which	delightful	garden

Such tests show that the, an, that, which can all be used in sequences where they are followed by an adjective and noun.

We can get a pretty good idea of our unconscious knowledge of word classes by analysing nonsense poetry. Lewis Carroll's verse may be nonsense, but it is very much 'English' nonsense, since it conforms to English patterns of syntactic structure.

Activity 3.1

Using the traditional labels 'noun' and 'adjective', identify the words belonging to these two word classes (or 'parts of speech') in the Jabberwocky verse below. Then try to explain how you knew that the word belonged to that class.

'Twas brillig, and the slithy toves
  Did gyre and gimble in the wabe;
All mimsy were the borogoves,
  And the mome raths outgrabe.

We would expect you to identify the nouns and adjectives either like this:

nouns	adjectives
toves	brillig
wabe	slithy

borogoves	mimsy
raths	mome

or like this:

nouns	**adjectives**
toves	brillig
wabe	slithy
borogoves	mimsy
mome	

(In this second analysis *raths* is a verb and *outgrabe* an adverb.)

The -*s* on *toves, borogoves* and *raths* may have helped you to decide that these words were nouns (though the -*s* ending also functions as a present tense marker on third person verbs, which is how the alternative interpretation of the last line of the verse becomes possible). Similarly, you may have taken the -*y* ending on *slithy* and *mimsy* as an indication that these words were adjectives (though by no means all English adjectives end in -*y*). However, these clues would not have been enough on their own. In addition to your knowledge of English word structure, you must have drawn on your knowledge of the syntagmatic patterns of sequence and the paradigmatic relations of choice that are part of the syntactic structure of English – though your explanation may not have been in these terms.

Activity 3.2

The extract below is an example of the problems that occur when distributional criteria are *not* used to set up word classes. The extract is from a traditional grammar book designed for learners of English as a foreign language (Eckersley 1958).

THE ADJECTIVE

An ADJECTIVE is a word that qualifies a noun; it adds to its meaning, but limits its application, e.g. the *new* book; the *black* sheep.

An adjective may be used (i) to qualify a noun, i.e. as an EPITHET as in the examples above, or (2) to form PART OF THE PREDICATE and say what the person or thing denoted by the subject is declared to be, e.g. The book is *new*; the sheep is *black*. It is then said to be used PREDICATIVELY.

Kinds of Adjectives

(1) ADJECTIVES OF QUALITY: which show WHAT KIND, e.g. a *brave* boy; a *German* student.

(2) ADJECTIVES OF QUANTITY: which tell *how many* or *how much*. These may be:

    (i)   *Definite* e.g. one, two, etc.

    (ii)   *Indefinite*, e.g. all, some, several, half, no.

(3) POSSESSIVE ADJECTIVES: which show possession, e.g. *my, her, its, our, their,* etc.

(4) DISTRIBUTIVE ADJECTIVES: which show that the persons or things denoted by the noun are taken singly or in separate lots, e.g. *each, every, either, neither.*

(5) INTERROGATIVE ADJECTIVES: which are used in questions, e.g. *Which* man did you see? *What* time is it?

(6) DEMONSTRATIVE ADJECTIVES: which point out, e.g. *this, that, these, those, a, an, the.*

The definition of an adjective that is given in the first two paragraphs works well for the words *new* and *black*, which are given as the examples, but does it work so well for the six different types of adjective that are listed in the rest of the extract?

Only the first type of adjective (adjectives of quality) can occur both attributively (i.e. before a noun, as an epithet) and predicatively (in the sequence *the + noun + is + ——*). Types 2–6 all occur before a noun (for example, *one book, all books, my book, each book, which book, this book*) but they do not normally occur in the sequence *The book is ——*. We cannot say, for example, *The book is each, or *The book is my, and although it is conceivable that we may say, *The book is this* or *The book is which?* we would only do this if we wanted particularly to emphasise the word *this* or *which*.

Traditional grammar classified these words as adjectives because they were using categories that described the syntax of Latin to try to describe the syntax of English. As we saw earlier, however, English and Latin differ in their morphological and syntactic structure. Latin is an inflectional language, but modern English is not: in Latin the equivalent words to most of the kinds of adjective listed in the extract agree with their noun in gender and case, but this does not apply to English. Modern grammars of English term 'adjectives' of types 2–6 'determiners', as we have seen, to take account of the fact that they have similar patterns of distribution, and belong, therefore, to the same word class.

It is important to identify the word classes of a language or a dialect using patterns of substitution and choice as a guide, rather than to try to impose categories that are suitable for one language or one variety of a language on to the words that occur in another. Consider, as an example, the word *them*. In standard English *them* is a plural pronoun, often substituting for nouns that have just been mentioned, as in the following quotation from Ian McEwan's *The Innocent*: 'until now, it was as though he had never really had any serious feelings. Only now, as he came to name them – shame, desperation, love – could he really claim them for his own' (McEwan 1990: 101). Here *them*, in *he came to name them* substitutes for *any serious feelings* in the previous sentence. We identify *them* as a **pronoun** by virtue of its syntagmatic and paradigmatic relationships: it is in a syntagmatic relationship with the verb phrase *came to name* and in a paradigmatic relationship with other pronouns, such as *these*, that could occur in the same sequence. In some non-standard varieties of English, however, *them* functions not only as a pronoun but also as a determiner, occurring in the same position in the noun phrase as *the, a, which* and other determiners, as in the following quotation from a speaker in Belfast: *Them two fellas was hit* (from Harris 1993). If we are describing a variety of English that is non-standard, it would be very misleading to simply assume that the word *them* enters into the identical relationships that it has in standard English. We describe the notion of a phrase in more detail below.

The need to identify word classes on the basis of distributional criteria can also be seen by comparing different languages, such as French and English. In English, as we saw earlier, one of the criteria used to identify the class of adjectives is that adjectives can occur between a determiner and a noun. This allows us to decide that *white*, in the noun phrase *the white mare*, is a member of the adjective word class. But although this works for English, it would not necessarily allow us to identify adjectives in French, since in French adjectives frequently follow their nouns, as in the equivalent phrase *la jument blanche.* Word classes in French, or in any other language or language variety, must be set up separately for that language or language variety, taking into account the syntagmatic and paradigmatic relations (relationships of distribution and choice) that are characteristic of that language.

FUZZINESS IN LINGUISTIC CATEGORIES

Like all human behaviour, language does not always fit neatly into clear-cut categories. It is very helpful when describing language to set up word classes as part of a syntactic analysis, but it is equally helpful to recognize that these classes have 'fuzzy' edges to them. The adjective *white*, which we have just mentioned, is a prototypical English adjective. Not only does it occur in the adjective position in a noun phrase sequence, preceded by a determiner and followed by a noun (*the white mare*) but it conforms to other criteria that together identify the class of typical English adjectives: it can also occur after the verb BE (*The mare is white*), it can be **graded** (we can say that something is *very white* or *slightly white*), it has a comparative form (a 1960s song has the title *A whiter shade of pale*), a **superlative** form (*the whitest possible shade of pale*), and the noun that it modifies can be replaced by the pronoun *one* (*a white mare and a grey one*). There are other adjectives in English, however, that have some of these characteristics, but not all of them. Some cannot occur after the verb BE (we can say *my former employer* but not **My employer is former*), some can occur only after the verb BE (we can say *The baby is awake* but not **the awake baby*).

Similarly, using distributional criteria we could class the words *rich* and *poor* as adjectives, since they occur in the sequence determiner–adjective–noun (as in *the rich magnate* or *the poor beggar*) as well as after the verb BE (*The magnate is rich, the beggar is poor*). But we can also say *The rich should give to the poor.* Do these words now belong to the class of noun (in the same way that a word like *round* can be both an adjective (as in *the round table*) and a noun (as in *Let's have another round of drinks*)? Or are they still members of the adjective word class? We undoubtedly understand the sentence above as meaning 'the rich people should give to the poor people'.

There is no right or wrong answer to questions like this. We set up word classes to help in our analysis of syntactic structure, but word classes are not necessarily water-tight categories. There is vagueness and indeterminacy in syntax, just as there is vagueness in semantics (see Section 4.2). It is better to acknowledge this vagueness than to try to squeeze languages into hard and fast categories into which they do not fit. The idea that some words are prototypical members of a class while others are more marginal is one way in which we can take account of the indeterminacy that exists in syntax.

OPEN AND CLOSED WORD CLASSES

Word classes can be divided into open and closed sets. The words that belong to a **closed set** are relatively small in number, and if we use one member of the set the rules of syntax usually prevent us from using another in the same sequence. An example of a closed set is the set of determiners: thus we can say, *my book* or *the book* but not **my the book*.

The members of an **open set**, on the other hand, are usually very numerous. The set is open in the sense that new members are continually being added: for example, *ecu* and *firefighter* are fairly recent additions to English nouns, and *le jogging* is a recent addition to French. Nouns, verbs, adjectives and adverbs are examples of open sets; pronouns, prepositions and conjunctions are examples of closed systems.

As with most of the distinctions that we make when analysing language, the distinction is not absolutely clear-cut, but it can be a useful one. It helps explain, for example, why attempts in recent years to invent a new 'non-sexist' pronoun to replace *he* and *she* have not enjoyed the same success as new nouns. The closed sets do change, but only very slowly over centuries.

Halliday (1985) notes that members of closed sets are **grammatical items** rather than **lexical items**. It is the latter which form the 'content' words of a sentence, and the former which provide the linguistic 'glue' to link them together. We discuss one way in which this distinction can be used to describe differences between spoken and written language in Chapter 7.

Hierarchical structure

Sentences do not consist simply of ordered sequences of words. A further fact that we know, as speakers of English, is that sentences have an internal structure, in which sequences of words are grouped together. For example, sentence (9) has two interpretations:

(9) Harry is a cuddly toy seller

Harry could be a pleasant, slightly overweight person who sells many different kinds of toys – train sets, boxed games, dolls or jigsaw puzzles – or he could be a person of any size or shape, who specializes in the sale of teddy bears and other soft toys. In the first case it would be *Harry* who would be cuddly rather than the toys that he sells. We can divide up the words in the sequence *cuddly toy seller* in two different ways to show how this ambiguity in meaning arises from a structural ambiguity:

[cuddly]   [toy seller]
[cuddly toy]   [seller]

Such instances demonstrate that we intuitively know that sequences of words can possess internal structure and grouping. This grouping is hierarchical. For example, the three-word sequence is what is usually called a **noun phrase** – that is, a sequence of words including a noun which can be substituted for a single noun in any sentence.

Harry is a $\begin{cases} \text{cuddly toy seller} \\ \text{toy seller} \\ \text{person of great probity and vision} \\ \text{man} \end{cases}$

Linguists differ in their views about the number of levels of syntactic organization that need to be recognized in the hierarchy of structural relationships. Most recognize at least three levels. Thus, Huddleston (1984: 3–6) identifies the levels of sentence, phrases and word class. In this way sentence (10), below, can be described as a sentence consisting of a noun phrase (*Maud*), a **verb phrase** (*will buy*) and a second noun phrase (*his new teddy bears*); the phrases consist of word classes, with the noun phrase (*his new teddy bears*) containing a determiner, *his*, an adjective, *new*, and a noun, *bears*, and the verb phrase *will buy* containing an **auxiliary**, *will*, and a **lexical verb**, *buy*.

(10) Maud will buy his new teddy bears

At each of these levels of organization, the units (sometimes referred to as **constituents**) are identified by taking account of both word order and hierarchical structure. Sentence (10) is divided into its three constituents of phrase structure (that is, the verb phrase and two noun phrases), by considering the choices that can be made at different points in the sentence. For example, the following noun phrases could all occur instead of *his new teddy bears* after *Maud will buy*:

Maud will buy $\begin{cases} \text{a pound of apples} \\ \text{an anti-wrinkle preparation} \\ \text{the sonnets of Shakespeare} \end{cases}$

A selection of other choices that could be made at different points in our example is given in sentences (11)–(16):

	Noun phrase	Verb phrase	Noun phrase
(11)	Harry	is	a cuddly toy manufacturer
(12)	Maud	will buy	his new teddy bears
(13)	The old grey mare	loves	sugar
(14)	She	may have been going to drive	the fast motorbike
(15)	My mother	has baked	sixty mince pies
(16)	Hermione	would like to soak	her aching feet

There are, of course, restrictions on the choices that can be made. As speakers of English we know that (17) and (18) are not possible:

(17)	*May have been going to drive	is	a cuddly toy manufacturer
(18)	*By the sea	loves	sugar

When analysing phrase structure it is conventional to identify the **head** of a noun phrase or a verb phrase. The head is the word class that has to be present within the phrase: thus a noun phrase has to contain a noun, as we can see by trying to shorten the noun phrase *his new toys*: we can say *his toys*, keeping the determiner and the noun, but not *his new*. The head also determines relationships between the phrase and other elements of the sentence. The head of the verb phrase in sentence (10) is *buy*, and this verb requires an object: we can say, therefore *Maud will buy his teddy bears* or *Maud will buy a present for her granddaughter* but not *Maud will buy*. If the head of the verb phrase had been a different verb, other sentence elements may have been required: the verb *put*, for instance, requires both an object and an adverb element, so that although we can say *Maud will put the teddy bears in the toy cupboard* we cannot simply say *Maud will put* or *Maud will put the teddy bears*. In English the smallest possible sentence normally has at least one noun phrase, as subject, and a verb phrase (provided the verb is one that does not require an object or some other obligatory element): we could say, for instance, *Maud laughed* or *The old grey mare was snoring*.

Activity 3.3

Divide the examples below into their phrase-level constituents of noun phrases and verb phrases and identify, in each case, the head of the noun phrase and the verb phrase:

(a) All the nice girls love a sailor
(b) This bad egg stinks
(c) The ozone layer is shrinking
(d) A change of government can bring about social changes

Using our knowledge of patterns of distribution and choice in English the examples can be divided as follows:

noun phrases	verb phrases	noun phrases
all the nice GIRLS	LOVE	a SAILOR
this bad EGG	STINKS	
the ozone LAYER	is SHRINKing	
a CHANGE of government	can BRING ABOUT	social CHANGES

The heads of the phrases are in small capitals.

The phrase-level constituents of a typical sentence of the types that we have considered here are often represented in an abstract, general way as follows:

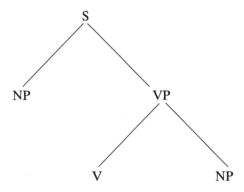

This abstract representation is termed a **tree diagram**, with the branches of the tree showing the relationships between the levels of structure. In such a notation the abbreviation S is used for sentence, NP and VP for noun phrase and verb phrase, and V for verb. The diagram represents the structure of all the sentences (11)–(16), demonstrating that their hierarchical organization is similar.

CLAUSES

You may be wondering why we have not used the term *clause* in the analysis of sentence structure. The reason is that many linguists distinguish just three basic levels of sentence analysis which we have here called *sentence*, *phrase* and *word*. Some linguists prefer to use the term **clause** instead of sentence for the uppermost layer of analysis but theoretical grammars rarely regard them as separate levels. Of the theoretical grammars discussed later in this chapter universal grammar (associated with Chomsky) uses the term *sentence* as we have here, whereas systemic-functional grammar (associated with Halliday) uses the term *clause*.

Traditional grammatical terminology, however, and some descriptive grammars, do use both the terms *sentence* and *clause*. In the simple examples we have been discussing each sentence consists of a single clause, so the distinction is not obvious. But complex sentences can be created by combining simple sentences in various ways – the simplest way is probably to join two sentences with *and* – and in such cases it can sometimes be useful to distinguish the individual clauses from the complex sentence.

Functional categories

We have so far identified the constituents of a sentence by examining possible patterns of substitution. Although this requires the intuitions of a speaker of the language to decide whether a substitution is possible or not, such an analysis does not otherwise depend on interpretation or meaning. The categories which emerge from such an analysis are sometimes referred to as **formal categories**. Word classes and types of phrase (e.g. *noun phrase* or *verb phrase*) are examples of formal categories.

The goal of grammatical analysis is to describe not only the structure of a sentence but also the relationships and functions of its different parts. Establishing the constituents and classifying them is thus only the first stage. In the tree diagram above there are two NPs, for example, and we need some way of describing the different roles they play in the sentence as a whole. This requires us to establish **functional categories**, which show how different elements of a sentence or phrase relate to each other in meaning.

Traditional grammar divides the sentence into two main parts on functional grounds: the **subject** and the **predicate**. Modern grammars also use the term subject, but analyse the predicate into more elements. One influential descriptive grammar (Quirk *et al.* 1985) identifies five sentence elements in all: the **subject** (S), **verb** (V), **object** (O), **complement** (C), and **adverbial** (A). The object can be either a **direct object** or an **indirect object** (O_d, O_i), and the complement can be either a **subject complement** (C_s) or an **object complement** (C_o).

The tree diagram above shows the second noun phrase (*cuddly toy seller* in sentence (9), *his new teddy bears* in sentence (10), and so on) at a lower level of phrase structure than the first. This maintains the traditional distinction between subject (first NP) and predicate (second NP). Functional labels do not normally appear on tree diagrams because they are implicit in the way the branches are drawn. The NP which is immediately dominated by the VP is always the object. The NP which is immediately dominated by the S is the subject.

The internal construction of phrases can also be described in functional terms. We have already referred to the 'head' of a phrase – any remaining words in the phrase form the **modifier**. Hence phrases can be divided into modifier and head. So in the first example in activity 3.3 *all the nice* is the modifier and *girls* the head of the subject noun phrase.

When you study tree diagrams and syntactic descriptions you need to be aware of the two kinds of analysis (formal and functional) and of the possible confusions which labels and abbreviations create. For example, *S* can signify 'sentence' or 'subject', *verb* can refer either to the word class (a formal category) or to the sentence element (a functional element which may consist of a number of words). Because of this possible confusion, some linguists use the term **predicator** to refer to the verb element of a sentence.

Sentence relations

A further aspect of linguistic knowledge the grammars need to take into account is the relationships that exist between different types of sentence. For example, most speakers of English would agree that the following pairs of sentences are related to each other:

(19) The frogs ate the crickets
(20) The crickets were eaten by the frogs

(21) I gave the cat your dinner
(22) I gave your dinner to the cat

(23) The cat had a good meal
(24) The cat did not have a good meal

In order to account for our intuitive knowledge, a syntactic analysis should make explicit the precise relationship that exists between pairs of sentences like these. For example, the relationship between sentences (23) and (24) can be formulated explicitly by saying that (24) can be formed from (23) by adding the auxiliary verb DO and the negative word *not* between the subject and the verb, and then ensuring that DO has the same tense as the verb *had* in (23). We can then describe the structure of the negative sentence (24) by relating it to (23), as follows:

subject + DO + *not* + rest of sentence

This formulation is a useful descriptive generalization that accounts not just for sentence (24) but for all simple negative sentences in English of this type (compare, for instance, *The frogs ate the crickets*, *The frogs did not eat the crickets*; *I gave the cat your dinner*, *I did not give the cat your dinner*). As before, however, it is important to describe sentence relations in terms of the language that we are analysing, rather than in terms of any pre-existing ideas we may have. Consider, as an example, the language of a young English-speaking child. Some of the negative sentences that were used by the child when aged between 18 months and two years are as follows (the examples are adapted from Clark and Clark 1977):

no wipe finger
not a teddy bear!
wear mitten no
no sit there
no the sun shining

These negative utterances are clearly different in structure from those produced by adult speakers of English, but if we are trying to create a grammar to account for this variety of English, then they can be regarded as belonging to the set of well-formed sentences which our grammar has to describe. The negative word can be *no* as well as *not*, and it can be inserted either at the beginning of the sentence or (in one case) at the end, rather than between the subject and the rest of the sentence. The structure of the child's negative sentences can be described as:

$$\left.\begin{array}{c} no \\[1em] not \end{array}\right\} + \text{sentence}$$

or

sentence + *no*

Semantic roles

As competent speakers of English we can recognize that (25) has two interpretations:

(25) The chicken is ready to eat

The first interpretation is that the chicken is alive, hungry and about to eat; the second is that the chicken is dead, has been cooked and is about to be eaten. We can distinguish between the two interpretations of the sentence by considering the **semantic roles** of the sentence elements. In the first interpretation the element *the chicken* can be described as a **senser** (the conscious being that is experiencing the desire to eat) whereas *ready to eat* can be described as a **phenomenon** (something which is 'sensed'); in our second interpretation, on the other hand, *the chicken* is better described as a **carrier** of the **attribute** *ready to eat*.

The pairs of sentences (19) and (20) above can also be analysed from this point of view. Although the grammatical subjects of these sentences differ (the subject of (19) is *the frogs* and the subject of (20) is *the crickets*), the semantic roles of the noun phrases are identical. The noun phrase *the frogs* can be analysed as the **actor** (the initiator of the process represented by the verb *eat*) and *the crickets* can be analysed as the **goal** of the process.

Different linguists sometimes use different terms to represent semantic roles of this type. The term **agent** is sometimes used for what we have referred to as the 'actor', and the terms **affected** or **patient** may be used where we have used 'goal'. Our terms are taken from Halliday's (1985) systemic-functional grammar.

3.4 Theoretical grammars

Introduction

Theoretical grammars have the ambitious aim of explaining the general human phenomenon of language, rather than describing the morphology and syntax of specific languages, and they tend to differ more radically in their approaches than descriptive grammars. Theoretical grammars, like descriptive grammars, must take account of the kinds of basic facts of word and sentence structure which we described in the previous section, but they differ in the relative importance which they attach to analysing them, and in what they regard as the proper limits of theory.

This can be clearly seen by comparing the theoretical approaches of two of the best-known twentieth-century linguists: Noam Chomsky and Michael Halliday. Chomsky and his associates analyse sentence structure by formulating precise rules and statements which exclude any consideration of meaning. Chomsky (1965) has justified this by considering sentences such as:

(26) Colourless green ideas sleep furiously

Despite the fact that this sentence does not seem to convey any obvious meaning (except perhaps as a piece of poetry), most speakers of English would agree that it is well-formed: it conforms to the grammatical structure of English. Chomsky's aim is simply to explain intuitions of this kind, and he leaves the question of meaning to be dealt with by separate theories of semantics and pragmatics (which we discuss in Chapter 4). Halliday, however, considers the construction of meaning to be so fundamental to our use of language that it is inconceivable for him to exclude meaning from the analysis of sentences and word structure. Halliday and others working within the framework of systemic-functional grammar therefore take the expression of meaning as their starting-point. We give outlines of both Chomsky's and Halliday's theories below, and we briefly mention some other, more recent approaches.

Generative grammars

Generative grammars have developed within a research tradition – particularly associated with the work of Noam Chomsky and his associates – which began in the USA during the 1950s. Generative grammars aim to provide a rigorous, explicit framework that can produce (or **generate**), from a small number of elements and general principles, all the sentences of a language that a native speaker would find well-formed, and no others. For example, in English, the grammar should be able to generate *We all feel better when the sun shines* but not **We better when the sun shines*.

Generative linguists use the languages of the world as a source of data from which they can derive and test out the universal principles that may govern the general phenomenon of language. They devise successive models of a language that are powerful enough to generate the same 'output' as a native speaker and hope that, ultimately, they will be able to do this for every known human language. By constructing models of this type it is thought that we will begin to understand the kinds of general constraints within which all human languages operate, and that we will thereby be able to explain the nature of the innate linguistic knowledge that all human beings share, whatever specific languages they may know. Chomsky (1976: 29) has referred to this innate knowledge as 'the essence of human language', or **universal grammar**.

Generative grammars, then, see language as a property of the mind, and see a theory that can model our linguistic knowledge as a theory that can model the internal structure of the human mind (Cook 1988: 13). The theory can be thought of as specifying a research programme, setting out hypotheses about language structure that can then be tested against researchers' intuitions concerning well-formed sentences in their own languages. As a result of these tests the theory may be modified, and new models and new hypotheses constructed.

Generative models evolve rapidly: Chomsky's ideas and those of his followers have changed several times since the 1950s, and rival theories to Chomsky's have been developed. Although there are now many different kinds of generative grammar, universal grammar is still the best-known. Not surprisingly, a theory with the ambitious aim of explaining the internal structure of the mind is extremely complex: the theory of universal grammar consists, in fact, of several interacting sub-theories. The best way of giving an idea of this approach to the description of sentence structure is simply to sketch, in the barest of outlines, the development of the theory, from Chomsky's early work until the present time – though since the theory is continually being revised, even this brief account may soon be outdated.

Chomksy's early work attempted to formalize our innate linguistic knowledge in terms of rules. For example, the phrase structures that we described in Section 3.3 could be generated by a set of **rewrite rules** (or **phrase structure rules**) producing rigorous, specific definitions of the elements of a sentence. Thus the rule

S → NP + VP

specified that a sentence consists of a noun phrase and a verb phrase (hence generating the smallest possible sentences in English, such as our earlier examples *Maud laughed* or *The old grey mare was snoring*). The elements NP and VP were then defined by further rewrite rules which added one new element at a time, such as:

NP → (det) + NP
NP → (adj) + N

The parentheses show that the elements within them are optional: these rules can account, therefore, for the elements that appear in noun phrases such as *Maud* or *the old grey mare*. A separate part of the grammar, the **lexicon**, listed individual words for each language, with their word class and other details necessary to generate well-formed sentences: for example, *put* was specified as a verb which had to be followed by both a noun phrase and a prepositional phrase, thereby accounting for the fact mentioned in

Section 3.3 that in English a sentence such as *Maud put the teddy bears in the toy cupboard* is well-formed, but the following are not: **Maud put the teddy bears* (with only a noun phrase), **Maud put in the toy cupboard* (with only a prepositional phrase) and **Maud put* (with neither).

Ambiguous sentences, such as example (25), above, were accounted for by assuming that all sentences are composed of two levels of structure: **deep structure** and **surface structure**. The reason why our sentence is ambiguous is that two different representations in the deep structure can be given the same surface structure. For instance, our example could be derived from a pair of sentences at the deep structure level with forms such as:

(27) The chicken is ready
(28) The chicken eats

or it may be derived from the following pair:

(29) we eat the chicken
(30) the chicken is ready

The first pair contains a sentence in which *the chicken* is the subject of the verb *to eat*; the second one has *the chicken* as the object of *to eat*.

In this early model, **transformational rules** added, deleted or rearranged elements that were generated by the phrase structure rules. This allowed relationships between sentences to be formalized explicitly. For example, our sentences (19) and (20) (*the frogs ate the crickets* and *the crickets were eaten by the frogs*, respectively) could be related by a two-part transformational rule something like this:

Passivization rule

Structural description	NP_1	+	V	+	NP_2			
	1		2		3			
Structural change	3	+	BE	+	*2en*	+	*by*	+	1

The rule states that the second noun phrase (*the crickets*) is moved to the front of the sentence while the first noun phrase appears after the verb, with the preposition *by*. It also states that the auxiliary BE is added to the verb and that the verb appears in the past participle form (conventionally termed the *-en* form). The tense stays the same in both sentences, so the verb BE in the passive version is given the past tense form, *was*. The rule is perfectly explicit and, as long as it is applied completely, it should result in a well-formed sentence. If only part of it is applied, the resulting sentence would be ill-formed: if we leave out the *by*, for example, the result would be **The crickets were eaten the frogs*.

Theories of generative grammar have progressed in the way that all theories do – by making successive generalizations which can cover an ever wider range of phenomena. Publications in the middle and late 1960s, for example, referred to **cyclic NP movements**. These accounted, in part at least, for the relationships between active and passive sentences in English, as we have just seen. But they could also account for other kinds of sentence which, on the face of it, seem rather different. For example, *I gave the cat your dinner* can be derived from *I gave your dinner to the cat* by a process of **dative movement** (*the cat* appears further to the left in the first sentence, just as a passive transformation involves moving the second noun phrase of the active sentence to the left). Sentences related by **subject raising** can be thought of in a similar way: if we compare *It seems that the party is over* with *The party seems to be over*, we can think of the noun phrase *the party* as having moved to the left in the second version (in other words, to have been 'raised' in the surface phrase structure to become the subject of the verb *seem*). It was found that a general transformational rule of **NP movement** could be stated which identified the constraints governing which noun phrases could be moved, and where they could be moved to.

Over the years, it became apparent that still more powerful generalizations were possible. In 1982 Chomsky proposed a more economical model, with one general principle accounting for the movement not only of noun phrases but also of verb phrases and other sentence elements. The research programme then involved specifying the restrictions on movement that exist in different syntactic constructions, in different languages. In English, for example, it is clearly not possible to move just any constituent of a sentence. We would be unlikely to consider as well-formed the sentence **Ate the frogs the crickets*, where the verb phrase can be thought of as having moved to the left of the sentence. When we try to explain why this sentence is ill-formed we are forced to find out which constituents can function as the grammatical subject of a sentence. It is not enough to simply state that a verb phrase cannot function as subject, for a moment's thought produces perfectly acceptable sentences in English where verbs *do* function as the grammatical subject (*To err is human* is one example). In fact, the restrictions on movement that involve grammatical functions of this type are so complex that they are dealt with by a separate sub-theory of the grammar, known as **thematic relations theory**, or Θ-theory, for short. Further restrictions on movement are explored within another sub-theory (**bounding theory**). Yet more sub-theories deal with further aspects of sentence structure: for instance, **X-bar theory** (or X̄-theory, for short) examines hierarchical relations of phrase structure. Overall, the version of universal grammar that is current in the early 1990s can be characterized as consisting of a relatively small number of very general and powerful **principles**, which filter out any unacceptable structures that have been generated by the interaction of the different sub-components of the grammar (see McCloskey 1988). These principles are assumed to apply to all languages even if their patterns of sentence structure appear to be very different from each other.

Chomsky explains the differences that exist in individual languages as due to the setting of **parameters** within which the principles of universal grammar apply. All children, he assumes, are born with an innate knowledge of the general principles of universal grammar, and their acquisition of the language that they hear spoken around them involves fixing the parameter settings for that language.

One such parameter accounts for a basic distinction between those languages that have well-formed sentences without a subject, and those languages that do not. In Italian, for example, *parla* is a well-formed sentence; but the English equivalent, **speaks* or **speaking*, is not. In English and other languages of this type it is necessary to have at least a pronoun as subject (to say, in other words, *She is speaking* or *He is speaking*). Italian and other languages that allow subjectless sentences of this type have been termed **pro-drop** languages, and researchers have found that they share a number of characteristics. For instance, it is possible in pro-drop languages to change the order of subject and verb: in Italian, for example, we can say *Cade la notte* as well as *La notte cade*, whereas in English (and other non-pro-drop languages) we can say *Night is falling* but not **Falls the night* (for discussion, see Cook 1988: 39). It is claimed that these types of facts about language can be explained by assuming that children set the pro-drop parameter when they are acquiring their native language, and all the other characteristics of sentence structure that depend on this parameter then 'fall out' as a result of the setting.

Over the last forty years or so, then, Chomsky's model of grammar has changed from a system of rules that could account for specific constructions in specific languages (such as the English passivization rule) to a 'conspiracy' of very general principles and conditions that affect many different constructions and that, as far as possible, account for facts about particular languages in terms of general, universal principles of grammar (see McCloskey 1988: 20). One of the great achievements of universal grammar has been that it unites a wide range of apparently unrelated syntactic facts, in many different languages, by appealing to a small number of general principles and to the manner in which they interact.

Systemic-functional grammar

Systemic-functional grammar developed within the intellectual traditions of the London school of linguistics – a tradition which, as we explained in Chapter 1, sprang from anthropological research. It is nowadays associated particularly with the work of Michael Halliday, and has been extremely influential in Britain and Australia, though less so in the USA. Linguists working within this tradition see language as essentially a social and cultural phenomenon which has evolved to fulfil our human needs. The primary aim of the grammar is, therefore, to explain how people use language as a resource for 'making meanings' (Halliday 1985: xvii). Since the different meanings that we can communicate are endless in number, the framework that is used for analysing language has to be extravagant rather than economical. Where universal grammar seeks simplicity and economy, and draws on intuition as its main data, systemic-functional grammar (often referred to simply as **systemic grammar**) attempts to be comprehensive and gives much more emphasis to 'real' language that has been spoken or written. It describes such data as a **text** (which refers to any coherent stretch of written or spoken language).

Halliday and his associates suggest that when we create an utterance we are faced at each point in its structure with a restricted set of grammatical options – the kinds of paradigmatic choice which we discussed in Section 3.3. The term systemic grammar refers to the conception of language as a network of relationships (or **systems**) of this kind. Linguists working within this framework usually analyse language at three hierarchical levels, or **ranks**, of structure: the **clause** (which is taken as the largest unit of grammatical analysis, rather than the sentence); the **group** (which is similar to the phrase); and the **word**.

Systemic theory assumes that all languages have developed in response to two very general human needs: the need to express ideas and the need to express our social relationships with other people. Human language thus has a dual function: it communicates what Halliday calls **ideational meaning** and also **interpersonal meaning**. Both kinds of meaning are encoded in grammar. It is not possible, for example, to speak or write without making a statement about social relations: how friendly the speaker is being, or what kind of power difference exists between speaker and addressee. A third component of meaning is **textual**: this refers to the way in which the other two types of meaning can be brought together to form a coherent stretch of speech or writing.

We can give a brief idea of the approach by examining how a simple clause can be analysed in terms of each of these three components of meaning; we will take as our example, once more, *The crickets were eaten by the frogs*. This is a simple sentence consisting of a single main clause.

Analysing the ideational meaning involves examining what we earlier termed the semantic roles of the constituents (see Section 3.3). These can be identifed as follows:

(31) the crickets   were eaten   by the frogs
     goal   **process**   **actor**

A different choice could have been made at each point in the clause, but this would have resulted in the real-world event being represented in a different way. For example, rather than referring to a *process*, a relationship could have been expressed by choosing the verb BE. This in turn would have affected the choice of the following constituent, so that the event would then have been represented as:

(32) the crickets   are   dead
     carrier   **relation** **attribute**

By choosing to position the subject (in this case *the crickets*) before the predicator (*were eaten*) we have given the clause a **declarative** form rather than, for example, an **interrogative** form. (The form *Were the crickets eaten by the frogs?*, with the subject in second position, and the appropriate intonation or punctuation, is described as an interrogative clause.) These choices affect the communicative roles of the speaker and the addressee and hence the interpersonal meaning: the choice of an interrogative structure, for example, normally assigns the role of questioner to the speaker, and the role of respondent to the addressee. The interpersonal aspect of meaning also includes any comments that reveal the speaker's attitudes towards the event: we could have expressed some uncertainty, for example, by choosing *may have been eaten* rather than *were eaten*.

Finally, the textual component of meaning can be analysed by identifying the **theme** and **rheme**. In English the theme is normally the first element in the clause, and signals what the speaker has chosen to single out as being 'talked about'. The remaining part of the clause in the rheme. Our example clause presents *the crickets* as the theme, and thus gives it more importance than *the frogs*. There is thus an important difference between the textual meaning of active and passive versions of the clause in English, with the active version presenting the theme as the frogs rather than *the crickets* (20) the crickets were eaten by the frogs (19) the frogs ate the crickets).

INFORMATION STRUCTURE

In any utterance, at least one part represents new information and forms the **information focus**. Other parts of the utterance may repeat things which have already been mentioned or which can be taken for granted. This distinction is known as that between **given** and **new**. In the following example, the italicized information is *given* – it has already been mentioned.

(33) A: How many litres does the tank take?
B: *The tank* takes 35 litres.

Normally, new information in English clauses is associated with the last lexical item, and any group (i.e. phrase) of which it is head (*35 litres*). This is the unmarked information structure of English clauses. When new information comes earlier in the clause, it will be marked by receiving the main sentence stress (see Section 2.4). Anything which comes after this will be treated as given.

A nominal group (i.e. noun phrase) which provides given information may be repeated from a previous utterance, or it may be abbreviated, very often pronominalized, or even omitted altogether. Look at the following possibilities:

(34) A: The car has a very flat tyre.
B1: The tyre was really old.
B2: It must have picked up a nail.
B3: A broken exhaust, as well.

The labels given and new represent the speaker's interpretation of what can be derived from previous discourse and what is to be regarded as new. In example (33) the italicized information had been mentioned in the preceding question. In other cases something may not have been actually mentioned but may be closely associated with something which has.

(35) A: Park the car in the garage, please.
      B: The tyre is flat.

In ordinary conversation, anything in the immediate physical context can become a focus of joint attention and be treated as given.

(36) A: [Looking through a window] The fire brigade has arrived.

THE ANALYSIS OF SOCIAL CONTEXT

Halliday's view is that language and social context are always closely tied together. This is true from a historical perspective, in the evolution of languages over the centuries; from a developmental perspective, in the development of language in children; and from a situational perspective, whenever people use their language. Unlike universal grammar, then, the premises of systemic grammar require it to analyse the context in which speakers and addressees interact, as well as the language that they produce. Only when the two are taken together can a satisfactory account of meaning be provided. Three different aspects of the context are usually taken into account: field, tenor and mode.

Field refers to the subject matter, or to the activity of which language is a part: we would not expect the syntax and vocabulary of a commentary on the grand prix motorcycle championship to be the same as the syntax and vocabulary used during a prime minister's speech about monetary policy.

Tenor includes the effect of the relationship between speakers and addressees on the language that they use: we are unlikely to speak in the same way, for example, when we are chatting to our friends over dinner and when we are asking the bank manager for an extension of our overdraft facility.

Mode accounts, among other things, for the kinds of difference that result from communicating with an addressee face-to-face, rather than in writing. It refers not only to the physical **channel** used for communication (i.e. acoustic as opposed to visual) but also to the forms of grammar which have become associated with each channel by cultural convention.

The crucial difference between systemic grammar and generative grammar, then, is that systemic approaches focus on the social aspect of language – on the way human beings use language to communicate with each other – while generative approaches focus on the mentalistic aspect of language – on what language reveals about the human mind.

Other theoretical approaches

We have chosen to give brief outlines of universal grammar and systemic grammar, since these illustrate the way in which two very different theoretical grammars can each make important and useful statements about sentence structure. However, there exist a number of other theoretical approaches to the analysis of sentence structure and we will briefly mention some of them.

Generalized phrase structure grammar (or GPSG), **relational grammar** and **lexical-functional grammar** all see themselves as continuing the generative research tradition established by Chomsky's early work (see McCloskey 1988), but they give priority to different aspects of our linguistic knowledge. GPSG, as the name suggests, emphasizes hierarchical phrase structure, seeing this as a way of producing a more elegant and economical theory. There are no transformational rules in this model of language; instead, the phrase structures are fully specified, and linked to a rigorous, explicit semantic theory. Linguists working within this framework give even more emphasis to mathematical precision than Chomsky and his followers.

Relational grammar takes a different starting-point, focusing on grammatical relations such as subject or object, and on relations that we described earlier in terms of semantic roles (Section 3.3). Thus an analysis of the sentence

(37) Josephine went to the mountains by train

would identify *to the mountains* as a **locative** construction and *by train* as an **instrumental** construction. Sentences are analysed as networks of relations of this kind, rather than in traditional phrase structure terms. The relationship between active and passive sentences, which we discussed earlier, is therefore described with a focus on the grammatical relations of subject and object. The analysis is less concerned with the changes in word order that exist between the two sentences, and more concerned with the point that the direct object in an active sentence functions as subject in the corresponding passive sentence, with the preposition *by* indicating that the actor is no longer the grammatical subject of the sentence. It seems that in all languages where there are passive structures, the passive structure involves a relational change between the direct object and the subject of the corresponding active sentence. Focusing on these relationships therefore allows us to make generalizations about language as an abstract phenomenon as well as about the structure of specific languages (see Perlmutter and Postal 1983).

We mentioned in Section 3.3 that the syntactic requirements of particular verbs varies, giving the example of the verb *put*, which needs to be followed by both a noun phrase and an adverbial phrase in order to form part of a well-formed sentence. Since the late 1970s all linguists working within the framework of generative grammar have given increasing importance to this aspect of syntactic structure. Lexical-functional grammar gives the role of specific words a particularly central position, considering the extent to which the form of sentences can be explained in terms of the words that are part of them. Dative movement, for example, which we mentioned in the description of generative grammars, above, is possible with the verb GIVE but not with the verb DONATE (*Herbert donated his money to the cats' home* is well formed but **Herbert donated the cat's home his salary* is not). Some verbs allow passive constructions whereas others, such as LAST, do not: we can say *The lecture lasted one hour* but not **One hour was lasted by the lecture.*

Generative approaches to analysing syntax are often termed **formalist** grammars, since they give particular attention to specifying their analytic procedures in a rigorous, precise way. There are other theories that take a **functionalist** approach, trying instead to relate the form of language to its 'ecological setting – the communicative, social and physiological properties of the human user' (Thompson 1991: 37). Functionalists assume that language structure can be explained in terms of general human cognitive constraints such as memory limitations and attention span, or the ways in which we choose to present information to our addressees. Whereas generativists tend to see our linguistic knowledge as a special, separate part of our intelligence, functionalists see it as part of our general knowledge, subject to the same constraints as all our cognitive faculties.

Systemic-functional grammar can be considered to be a functionalist theory, since it analyses grammatical systems within the context of the functions for which language is used. It is by no means the case, however, that all theories of language can be categorized neatly as either formalist approach or functionalist. **Word grammar** (Hudson 1984a), and **cognitive grammar** (Lakoff and Thompson 1975) seem to straddle the two traditions, sharing with the functionalists the view that our linguistic knowledge is similar to our general non-linguistic knowledge, but sharing with the formalists the aim of constructing a rigorous explanatory model of language.

3.5 Applications of grammars

Introduction

Some people – usually professional linguists or students of linguistics – delight in comparing and contrasting the many different theories of grammar that exist, to see which grammar gives a better account of language. Other people – again, usually professional linguists or students of linguistics – work single-mindedly within the framework of a particular theory, often fervent in their conviction that their preferred theory is the best way to make worthwhile discoveries about the nature of human language. However, there is a third, very large, group of people who turn to linguistics because they have a specific professional interest in language or a particular problem concerning language that they need to examine in a

principled manner. Language teachers, for example, may need to identify
the main errors made by a group of learners, in order to devise a relevant
syllabus for that group; counsellors may wish to record and then analyse
their counselling sessions, to decide on the effectiveness of the different
strategies that they use to elicit speech from their clients; and translators
may need systematically to compare the structures of the languages with
which they are working. People whose interest in language stems from
practical concerns such as these may not have the time or the inclination
to familiarize themselves with more than one approach to the analysis of
sentence and word structure. It is with this in mind, therefore, that we now
review some of the applications of different kinds of grammar. Of the four
types of grammar which we mentioned in Section 3.2, pedagogic and
prescriptive grammars have clear-cut, specialized aims, and there seems no
need to discuss them further. We focus below on descriptive and theoretical grammars.

Descriptive grammars

Descriptive grammars, as might be expected, can be useful when what is
needed is simply an analysis of the words or sentences that have been used
in a particular context. For example, *A Comprehensive Grammar of English* (Quirk *et al.* 1985) provides a framework of analysis that can be used
to transcribe sentence and word structure, in much the same way that the
IPA can be used to transcribe language at the phonetic level (see Garman
1988). Using Quirk *et al.*'s framework, any utterance can be analysed into
its constituent elements at clause level, at phrase level, at word level, or at
all three of these levels. In this way the utterance

(38) Maisie buys the latest books

can be analysed into its structural elements at various levels from clause
to morpheme, in the way we described in Section 3.3:

clause	S	V	O_d		
phrase	NP	VP	NP		
word class	noun	verb	det	adj	noun
word	Maisie	buys	the	latest	books
morpheme	Maisie	buy -s	the	late -est	book -s

Lyons (1990) used this framework to describe the syntactic structure of
some letters she had received from Katy, a nine-year-old child. Lyons
wanted to give a systematic account of Katy's unconscious knowledge of
English syntax, to show how much she knew about language without
having been explicitly taught. In one of Katy's letters was the following
sentence:

(39) What Mum has been doing is giving us spellings which I've never
     heard of, and then my sister and I have to look in a dictionary how
     to spell the word.

The first clause can be analysed into the following elements (see the discussion of functional categories in 3.3): subject (*what Mum has been doing*), a verb (*is*) and a complement (*giving us spellings which I've never heard of*). Analysing these elements at phrase level shows that the subject is itself composed of a clause, consisting of a subject (*Mum*) and a verb (*has been doing*). Similarly, the complement contains a verb (*giving*), an indirect object (*us*) and a direct object (*spellings which I've never heard of*). The direct object consists of a noun phrase with *spellings* as its head and a relative clause, *which I've never heard of,* as a further constituent of the noun phrase, modifying the head constituent. The relative clause can itself be analysed as composed of a subject (*I*) and a verb (*heard of*), with *never* used to express negation.

This description of Katy's sentence at clause level and phrase level shows clearly that she has a sophisticated knowledge of the English clause, for she manipulates with ease some quite complex English structures.

Activity 3.4

Construct either a table (like the one above shown for sentence (38), or a tree diagram (like the ones shown in Section 3.3) for Katy's sentence, using the description we have given above as a guide.

Another application of Quirk *et al.*'s framework is in speech therapy clinics, where it can provide systematic information about a patient's range of linguistic constructions at clause, phrase and word level. This information can be useful in diagnosing language disability as well as for other tasks performed during speech therapy, including screening, assessment and remediation (the language assessment, remediation and screening procedure, or LARSP, is described in Crystal *et al.* 1976; see also Crystal 1991: 221). The same framework has been successfully and usefully applied to language produced in educational settings, such as language units and schools for the deaf.

Crystal (1991) discusses the extension of this framework to the analysis of style: by carrying out syntactic 'transcriptions' it is possible to determine, in a principled manner, the most salient characteristics of different varieties of English. Thus the distinctive grammatical characteristics of legal English occur, in part, at phrase level, particularly in the structure of noun phrases, while the distinctive characteristics of newspaper English appear instead at the level of clause structure and in the kinds of connection that are made between clauses. Crystal points out that because profiles provide a standard grid of features to be observed, they show clearly what is not present, as well as what is. A trivial example is the absence of 'jocular' terms in the legal texts.

Finally, Quirk *et al.*'s reference grammar of English has been used by specialists in English language teaching to produce teaching materials with a sound linguistic basis. Leech and Svartvik's *A Communicative Grammar of English* (1975) is designed for students of English as a foreign language who need a reference grammar that is based on the use of English in everyday communication. Bowers *et al.* (1987) provide exercises based on this reference grammar, which are designed to be used in the classroom in order to stimulate discussion about English syntax. Close (1974) contains more traditional exercises based specifically on the syntactic structure of English.

Theoretical grammars

Of the theoretical grammars discussed in the previous section, systemic grammar has had the widest practical applications. This is consistent with Halliday's aim to construct a grammar that can, in his words, 'say something useful' about texts, whether spoken or written. As Christie (1990: 238) points out, 'the skill is in identifying those elements of the grammar which most usefully illuminate the nature of the particular text in hand'. Christie's analysis provides a critical account of the quality of the language used in a primary school activity known as 'writing negotiation'. She analyses a lesson during which the teacher read out a children's book, then set out and discussed with her pupils a writing task based on the story they had heard. Christie analyses each clause in terms of the three kinds of meaning identified by systemic grammar – ideational, interpersonal, and textual – and examined how these different kinds of meaning were distributed across the theme and the rheme, focusing particularly on the theme. As we saw in Section 3.4, the theme is the clause element that serves as the 'point of departure' of the clause (what the speaker has chosen to signal as being 'talked about'). The following example shows how themes can carry different kinds of meaning:

(40) **theme**   **rheme**
     textual   ideational
     well, now   *these people are back*

The textual element of the above theme is what Christie calls **continuative**. Such themes have the function of carrying the discourse forward, linking different elements together. Another common type of textual theme is called **structural**. These themes also link clauses together, but in a way which establishes a logical connection between them – often using a conjunction such as *then* or *because*. The simple conjunction *and* is also a common element in structural themes, particularly in spoken narrative.
Christie (1990: 239) observes:

> In general, whoever controls structural Theme directs the course the discourse takes, determining in particular the kinds of patterns of reasoning encoded in those patterns. Overwhelmingly, it is the teacher

in this, as in many curriculum genres, who controls the structural Themes, and the children in fact produce very few.

Table 3.1 shows the extent to which the teacher dominates the text. This domination is noteworthy, since the teacher's intention was that in this part of the lesson the teacher and the pupils would negotiate together an understanding of the writing task. For this reason, it was expected that the pupils would contribute substantially to the discussion.

Table 3.1 The distribution of structural and topical themes in the task specification phase of a lesson

Structural themes		Topical themes	
Teacher discourse	*Pupil discourse*	*Teacher discourse*	*Pupil discourse*
39	1	51	7

Source: Christie (1990: 243)

A more detailed analysis of the structural themes in this text showed that a large number were realized by the conjunction *and*, as the following extract demonstrates:

Teacher: Have you ever had a day when you've had no lunch to eat? Jodie? (Jodie nods) What happened Jodie, when you had no lunch to eat?

Jodie: Mum didn't bring it up. She left it at home.

Teacher: Left your lunch at home on the bench, and her mum didn't bring it to school, and she had no lunch. And what happened?

Jodie: Found no lunch.

Teacher: And then what happened? Who had to ring up your mum and dad?

Jodie: Mr. H.

Teacher: And then what happened?

Jodie: My mum brought my lunch.

Teacher: And who else brought your lunch?

Jodie: Dad.

Teacher: She had no lunch to start with, because it was left at home, and she thought her mum was going to bring it at lunch time and when her mum didn't bring it, Mrs S. rang her mum, and she wasn't at home, so her dad brought her lunch and then her mum remembered she hadn't brought her lunch, and she brought her lunch too, so she ended up with two lunches. She ate the lot.

Using *and* to connect clauses is typical of spontaneous unplanned speech, as research by Chafe has demonstrated (see, for example, Chafe 1986).

Christie argues, however, that the teacher's frequent use of *and* as a clausal connective contributes to the setting up of a pattern for a type of reasoning that is essentially anecdotal, requiring children to do little more than reason in terms of simple sequences of events.

As for the topical themes, in the teacher's speech these were mainly confined to people in the classroom (consisting mainly of the pronouns *I* and *you*), whereas in the children's speech they mainly referred to personal relatives (for example, *mum, she, my sister, dad*). While recognizing the value of building on personal experience in classroom discourse, Christie points out that children are not led to speculate and enquire about their world, partly as a consequence of the patterns of reasoning used in the classroom and of the personal anecdotes that form the content of the classroom discussion. Furthermore, the children's writing reflected the structure of the classroom discourse, using the same patterns of personal anecdote and simple sequencing of events. She argues that the classroom discourse which, as Table 3.1 showed, was created essentially by the teacher, failed to provide a model that could help the children. In fact, this group of children showed little development in their ability to use different written genres during their early years of schooling.

Christie's analysis, then, shows how the linguistic analysis of classroom discourse can point to the intimate relationship that exists between classroom discourse and the development of children's writing ability and, more importantly, how teachers might make critical linguistic analyses of this kind in order to decide whether alternative methods of structuring their classroom discourse would be beneficial to their pupils.

The classroom discourse which Christie studied is a type which is sometimes referred to as **asymmetric discourse**: that is, a kind in which one participant is more powerful than another and is consequently able to control the direction which the discussion takes. Systemic grammar has been used by a number of scholars to investigate the way power relations manifest themselves in language use, and, more generally, in how ideological biases and commitments are embodied in particular texts or discourses. We examine this application of grammar more fully in Chapter 7.

Finally, a further application of systemic grammar is in the computer simulation of human language production and perception (see, for example, Winograd 1972; 1983). For those interested in this field the attraction of systemic grammar is that it focuses on language as a system for communicating meaning: in principle, therefore, it is able to integrate both syntactic and semantic processing. In practice, however, formalist generative grammars have been used far more extensively in computational linguistics, since both generative linguists and those working with computers share an analytic approach that emphasizes formalization within a rigorous and explicit framework. Some researchers working within generalized phrase structure grammar have paid particular attention to the computability of their proposals, assigning grammatical structure to sentences in a series of logical steps. Not surprisingly, therefore, it is this theoretical grammar that has been most widely used in computational linguistics so far.

It would not be surprising to find that theoretical grammars were of interest to psychologists, and especially to those psychologists attempting to discover the relationship between language and cognition. Early work in Chomskyan transformational grammar inspired a number of experiments designed to test the psychological reality of transformational rules (see Greene 1972), but more recent developments in grammatical theory have had relatively little impact on psychology. Miller (1990: 321) sees one reason for this as a conflict of research methods, with psychologists irritated by the grammarians' interest in what *could* be said rather than in what *is* said, and linguists irritated by the psychologists' insistence on supplementing intuition with evidence gathered from experiments. Psychologists and linguists have different views about what constitutes an explanation: a linguist's preoccupation is often with formulating successive generalizations, which appear to simplify the data that are being explained, while a psychologist frequently attempts to give explanations in terms of causes and effects.

The theory of universal grammar has given rise to some interesting research questions concerning the acquisition of language. For example Chomsky argues that children acquire language as a result of the interaction between their innate language faculty and the particular linguistic environment in which they find themselves. How then, does the innate language faculty cope when a potentially bilingual child finds itself in an environment where two languages are spoken, particularly when these two languages appear to be very different in structure from each other? How do adult learners of a second language acquire their new language, assuming that their language faculty is now mature? A considerable amount of research has investigated questions such as these – see, for example, White (1985; 1986) on second language acquisition – but this research is likely to be of more interest to those with an interest in the theory of universal grammar than to those whose interest is primarily in language acquisition. This is because in most cases the results of the research feed back into the theory, sometimes seeking to confirm the theoretical principles and sometimes suggesting modifications to them.

A problem with all theoretical grammars, for anyone who is primarily interested in more practical issues, is that the grammars can be quite impenetrable to those without a sound linguistic background in that particular theory. This makes it necessary to devote a very considerable amount of time and intellectual energy to becoming familiar with the technical apparatus and descriptive framework of a theory, and then to keeping up to date with the changes that will inevitably be made to the theory. Furthermore, people who are trying to find a way of coping with a real-world linguistic problem may find it difficult to understand the fervour with which some linguists espouse a particular theory – a fervour which in some cases can seem more like an act of faith than an intellectual position.

It is important to bear in mind, also, that all theories account for only a partial range of linguistic phenomena: some areas of syntax, such as relative clause constructions and 'embedded' questions as in, *I wonder what he wants to do now* have been particularly well researched as part of the phenomenon known as NP movement, while other areas of syntax have received relatively little attention. It is difficult to make use of a specific theory without taking on board the aims of that theory; this means that, despite the allure of a potential explanatory theory, a simple descriptive approach may often be more suitable, for this will allow a stretch of language to be accurately described, or a problem to be set out in a principled way. The nature of the problem and the nature of the language concerned will determine those aspects of sentence and word structure that should be the focus of the analysis, and it is ultimately the nature of the linguistic problem, together with the inclination of the researcher, that will determine the analytic approach to be taken.

4 Meaning

4.1 Introduction

The branch of linguistics that is concerned with how meaning is expressed in language is called **semantics**. The analysis of meaning has proved one of the most difficult and elusive tasks in linguistic description. This is hardly surprising, since it involves investigating the relationship between language and everything that we use language to talk about: and this amounts to the entire world! Yet an understanding of how we use language to talk about the world is fundamental to appreciating how communication works. We shall start by outlining some of the ways in which the meaning of individual words in a language can be analysed, then turn to the analysis of words in context and finally to an analysis that tries to take account of the knowledge that we have to use in order to interpret words in context.

4.2 Word meaning

Words as symbols

Words can be regarded as **symbols**. For example, the word *cat* in English, or *chat* in French, or *Katze* in German, functions as a symbol of the real-world animal; or rather, it might be more prudent to say, as a symbol of the mental concept that we have of a cat. It can do this because there are agreed conventions among language users about the interpretation of the word, though we may not necessarily be conscious of these conventions unless we stop and think about them. Without these conventions, communication could not take place.

The relationship between a word and the entity that it symbolizes, however, is much more complex than for other symbols. Words may well be symbols, but they are very flexible symbols, whose meaning shifts in different contexts – sometimes a considerable distance from what we might think of as their 'usual' meaning. This is particularly true of poetry, to give an extreme example. Yet it is because of their flexibility that we are able to use the words in the vocabulary of a language to talk about anything in the world, and to do so in all kinds of different ways – jokingly or sarcastically, for instance, as well as straightforwardly. Semantic analysis has to try to account for how we can do this.

REFERENCE, DENOTATION AND CONNOTATION

A very simple approach to the analysis of word meaning sees words as 'naming' or 'labelling' things in the world. A distinction can then be drawn between **denotation** and **reference**. 'Denotation' is used for the class of things indicated by a word, whereas 'reference' is used for a particular thing that is indicated when the word is used. For example, the word *cat* denotes the class of all cats in the sentence *A cat makes a good pet*, but it refers to a particular cat in the sentence *A cat scratched her arm*.

This approach, however, takes no account of the flexibility of word meaning. *Cat* in the (admittedly rather dated) phrase *cool for cats* denotes a different class of things from *cat* in the two examples above, and a different class of things again in *that girl's a real cat* (meaning that she's spiteful). It is difficult, too, to see how this approach can apply to all the words in the vocabulary: what, for example, could the words *until, is* or *thus* denote? Abstract words are also harder to deal with in terms of denotation. We undoubtedly have a concept of *power, love* or *job*, but this is less easy to specify than for concrete entities such as *cat* and *gatepost*. The approach does, however, allow a useful distinction to be made between these 'naming' types of meaning (which together can be termed **referential meaning**) and a second type of meaning referred to as **connotation**.

Connotation refers to the associations that words have for us. Psychologists have long been aware that in addition to 'naming things', words carry overtones of meaning which colour our reaction to them. Even the most innocent of words can conjure up associations that may affect our attitude and our response to an utterance which contains them. Table 4.1 shows the words which first came to mind to 1000 people who were given the stimulus word *chair* in an early word-association experiment (Kent and Rosenoff 1910). The stimulus word seemed to tap a cultural, experiential and contextual knowledge of the object. Perhaps, in view of the (by and large) shared functional and cultural significance of the object, it is not surprising that there is a consensus among speakers in their first associations: nearly 60 per cent of the sample answered with *table, seat, furniture, sit* or *sitting*.

It may seem that all this kind of study shows is what speakers know about chairs and how they are used, but at least one interesting, and perhaps surprising, thing comes to light. Of the subjects 107 gave as their *first* response words which seem to indicate some evaluatory association. *Comfort, convenience, rest* and *idle pleasure* were evoked for some subjects, whereas others responded with *hard*. The number of respondents who

Table 4.1 First responses in a word-association test for the stimulus word *chair*

Frequency of response	Response
191	table
127	seat
108	sit
83	furniture
56	sitting
49	wood
45	rest
38	stool
21	comfort
17	rocker
15	rocking
13	bench
12	cushion
11	legs
10	floor
9	desk, room
8	comfortable
7	ease, leg
6	easy, sofa, wooden
5	couch, hard, Morris, seated, soft
4	arm, article, brown, high
3	cane, convenience, house, large, low, lounge, mahogany, person, resting, rug, settee, useful
2	broken, hickory, home, necessity, oak, rounds, seating, use
1	back, beauty, bed, book, boy, bureau, caning, careful, carpet, cart, colour, crooked, cushions, feet, foot, footstool, form, Governor Winthrop, hair, implement, joiner, lunch, massive, mission, myself, object, occupy, office, people, place, placed, plant, idleness, platform, pleasant, pleasure, posture, reading, rubber, size, spooning, stand, stoop, study, support, tables, talk, teacher, timber, tool, upholstered, upholstery, white

Source: Kent and Rosenoff (1910)

associated pleasant sensations with the stimulus word outnumbered those who found the chair *hard* by 102 to 5. We find that there is some degree of agreement within the sample over **connotative meaning**.

If people react to lexical items in this way, with value judgements, sensations of like and dislike and so on, then it is important to know both in what ways they respond to words and the degree to which it may influence them in their reaction to speakers who use them. A much more direct way of getting at such connotative or associative meaning is to ask speakers to rate words on scales such as good–bad, pleasant–unpleasant, strong–weak, fast–slow, etc. Even where such evaluations appear bizarre or inappropriate, subjects manage to perform this task remarkably well, and find it possible to indicate how 'rough', 'tasty', or 'hot' they perceive a word such as *sin*.

Activity 4.1

You can try out this technique yourself. Think of the word *natural* and mark it on the scales below, indicating how close or far from each polar extreme you judge the word to be:

```
       good ——————— bad
       hard ——————— soft
      happy ——————— wretched
      light ——————— dark
  worthless ——————— valuable
     strong ——————— weak
  beautiful ——————— ugly
    sincere ——————— insincere
  masculine ——————— feminine
    violent ——————— gentle
```

Although subjects' responses are in some ways idiosyncratic and may tell us more about their backgrounds, anxieties and personalities than about the word itself – indeed, the technique has been used in diagnosing psychiatric disorders – yet there are areas of consensus which reflect, minimally, culture-wide reactions. Those who have a sensitivity for such things may use it with effect. Such are the professional persuaders – skilled orators, politicians, advertisers – but the art is also found in the best novelists and prose writers. Indeed, at times words may be chosen entirely for their connotative value – whether political or emotive – apparently without regard to their referential meanings. An advertisement in the *New York Times* read: '100 per cent sudsable *natural* acrylic'.

DICTIONARY ENTRIES

In highly literate societies, dictionaries are produced as part of the process of language standardization. Besides giving syntactic, phonetic and (sometimes) historical information, dictionary-makers, or **lexicographers**, try to make explicit the conventions that language users share about the meanings of the words in the language. They do not normally try to deal with connotative meaning, for although there may be a high consensus among language users about the associations that individual words have for them, there are also differences, which reflect the different life experiences that individual language users have had. It is denotative meaning that dictionaries try to describe; but since the meaning that individual words can have is very flexible, it can be surprisingly difficult to describe word meaning in the form of a dictionary entry. It is instructive to see how compilers of dictionaries have tried to capture the flexibility of word meanings, and to see how different lexicographers have often made different decisions about their organization of entries for the same word.

Activity 4.2

Taking the noun *mug* as an example, consult two different dictionaries to see how the entries are set out (ignore the verb *mug* for the purposes of this activity). Try to specify the principles that have been used to classify the different meanings.

The two dictionaries that we discuss here are *Collins English Dictionary* and the *Shorter Oxford English Dictionary (SOED)*. *Collins English Dictionary* has two main entries for *mug*, with the second entry subdivided into three further entries, as follows:

mug 1. a drinking vessel with a handle, usually cylindrical and made of earthenware.

mug 2. **1**. *slang*. A person's face or mouth. **2**. *slang*. A grimace. **3**. *slang*. A gullible person, especially one who is swindled easily.

The *Shorter Oxford English Dictionary*, on the other hand, has four main entries for the noun *mug*, with the first entry subdivided into three further entries and the fourth into two further entries:

mug 1. *dialect*. Any (large) earthenware vessel or bowl; also a pot, jug, or ewer. **2**. A drinking-vessel, usually cylindrical, with or without a handle. **3**. A cooling drink.

mug *slang*. The face or mouth.

mug *slang*. A stupid person: a muff, duffer; a card-sharper's dupe.

mug *slang*. **1**. An examination. **2**. One who mugs or reads hard.

There is a difference in the actual meanings that are given in the two dictionaries: the *SOED* gives the meaning 'examination' or 'someone who reads hard', whereas *Collins* does not. It is the organization of the entries that is interesting, though, rather than the actual meanings that are given. Both dictionaries have decided that *mug* with the sense of 'drinking vessel' is a different word from *mug* with the sense of 'face or mouth' or 'a gullible or stupid person'. They both give *mug* as a 'drinking vessel' as a separate entry; and they both give this meaning first, perhaps because they take into account the history of the word. They differ, however, in the way that they organize the other meanings of *mug*.

To simplify, we shall look at just the entries for *mug* = 'a person's face or mouth' and *mug* = 'a gullible person' (*Collins*) or 'a stupid person' (*SOED*). (We shall ignore the possible different nuances of meaning between 'a stupid person' and 'a gullible person'!) *Collins* has decided that these are two different meanings of a single word, and lists them as two of the three meanings of *mug* 2:

The *SOED*, on the other hand, has decided that these are two separate words, and gives them as separate entries:

We can say that *Collins* treats the relationship of meaning to word form as an example of **polysemy** (where a single word has two or more separate meanings), whereas the *SOED* treats it as an example of **homonymy** (where two or more separate words, with separate meanings, have the same form). Neither dictionary is necessarily more correct than the other: they have simply chosen different ways of representing the meanings that the word *mug* can have – which, like all words, is flexible and not easy to pin down. If you consulted a different dictionary from our two, it will be interesting to see which aspects of the meaning of *mug* your dictionary considers important, and to see how it organizes its entries.

Sometimes, as Palmer (1981) points out, looking for a 'central' or 'core' meaning among the different meanings that we might want to include in a dictionary entry can help in deciding whether to treat these meanings as belonging to a single word or as belonging to different words. For example, the compilers of *Collins English Dictionary* may have decided that mug 2 meaning 'face' and mug 2 meaning 'a gullible person' both have the central meaning of referring to a person, whereas mug 1 has the central meaning of referring to a drinking vessel. These central meanings may reflect the shared conventions of language users (among whom we can, of course, include lexicographers!) However, if these are the 'core' meanings, then it seems from the dictionary entries given above that these core meanings are decidedly fuzzy. Take, for example, the 'drinking vessel' meaning. Both dictionaries consider that the purpose of the vessel is important ('drinking') and so is its shape ('cylindrical'), but *Collins* considers that it has a handle, whereas for the *SOED* this is optional, and *Collins* considers that what it is made of is important ('usually earthenware') whereas the *SOED* does not.

The lack of precise boundaries for the meaning of words is normal, and accounts for their flexibility. It is often possible to specify a central component of meaning for a word, such as 'drinking vessel' for *mug*, and to then specify a number of additional meanings that have different probabilities of applying, depending on the context in which the word is used. The existence of a handle, or being made of earthenware, are perhaps rather less central aspects of the meaning of *mug* in most contexts.

We shall return to this point below. For the time being, we shall simply repeat what we hope this section has shown: that although words can be seen as symbols, the relationship between a word and the aspects of the world that it symbolizes is extremely complex.

Sense relations

So far, we have been discussing the meaning of words in terms of their relationship to the entities or concepts that they symbolize. This type of relationship can be termed 'reference', as we saw above. Like all symbols, however, the meaning of a word is determined (in part, at least) by the syntagmatic and paradigmatic relationships that the word enters into with other words in the language. (*Syntagmatic* and *paradigmatic* relationships were discussed in Section 3.3; if you have not yet read that section, look at it now.) The meaning relationships that different words in the vocabulary of a language have with each other are termed **sense relations**. The rest of this section will describe this aspect of word meaning.

SEMANTIC FIELDS

Just as the meaning of a yellow traffic light is determined by its place in the three-term system of red, yellow and green traffic lights, so the meanings of many words are determined by their place in different **word systems**. We can see this very clearly if we consider the meaning of *good* in different areas of our culture. In an examination system there might be four grades – *poor, fair, good* and *excellent*. In a grading system for hotels in a tourist brochure, on the other hand, the grades are more likely to be *good, very good, excellent* and *outstanding*. The relative meaning of *good* is different in these two instances, because of the relationships that it enters into with the other words in the **semantic fields** of examination grades and hotel classifications.

Sometimes a semantic field is divided up differently by different varieties of the same language, to reflect distinctions that are important in a particular community. In some sheep-farming communities in mid-Wales, for instance (and probably in other parts of Britain, too), the semantic field of 'sheep' includes the words *tup, ewe, wether* and *hoggart* – distinctions that are not usually made in non-farming communities, where they have no cultural relevance.

The way the vocabulary of a language divides up semantic 'space' can often be clearly seen when we try to translate words from one language to another. The English word *cousin*, for example, has to be translated into French by either *cousin* or *cousine*, depending on whether the cousin is male or female. The French kinship terms make a distinction that the English term does not; and the precise meaning of the French word *cousin* is therefore different from its English counterpart, because it stands in a different relationship to other words in the semantic field of kinship terms.

The distinctions that are made by the vocabulary of a language very often reflect a society's beliefs and values. In ancient Greece the words for *carpenter, physician, shoemaker* and *teacher*, for example, all fell within a semantic field of 'occupations that require specialized knowledge'. These were all included in the term *demiourgos*. We usually translate this as *artisan* or *craftsman*, but in modern English there is no term that is exactly equivalent in scope to the Greek *demiourgos* – we tend instead to think in terms of *the professions* and *trades*, and our vocabulary reflects this distinction (Lyons 1977).

The way in which a word fits into different semantic fields can be illustrated by substituting it for other words in a fixed linguistic context. Gannon and Czerniewska (1980) give the following example for the word *struck*, which can be considered as contributing a different meaning to each of the sentences below:

$$
\text{the clock} \left\{ \begin{array}{l} \text{struck} \\ \text{chimed} \\ \text{tolled} \end{array} \right\} \text{twelve}
$$

$$
\text{the miner} \left\{ \begin{array}{l} \text{hit} \\ \text{struck} \\ \text{found} \\ \text{discovered} \end{array} \right\} \text{gold}
$$

$$
\text{the umpire} \left\{ \begin{array}{l} \text{struck} \\ \text{hit} \\ \text{punched} \\ \text{slapped} \end{array} \right\} \text{the spectator}
$$

Where a semantic field seems to be a naturally occurring one, such as, perhaps, the colour continuum, then its scope can be precisely stated. The exact nature of the 'semantic space' that our vocabulary divides up for us, however, is not always so easily formulated (consider, for example, the nature of the semantic space that is divided up by the words that *struck* relates to, in the three examples above – 'announcing time'? 'discovery'? 'physical violence'?). In view of the fuzziness in our beliefs about word meaning, some vagueness in the formulation of the scope of a semantic field is inevitable.

Despite the difficulty of delimiting a semantic field, this approach to the analysis of word meaning has been very useful for some areas of the vocabulary. At the very least, it shows clearly how the meaning of a word depends in part on the syntagmatic and paradigmatic relationships that it enters into with other words in the language.

Syntagmatic relationships are particularly important in determining word meaning, since the linguistic context in which a word occurs often identifies which of several related meanings is intended. Dictionaries often give a context in order to help define a meaning, as you may have noticed during Activity 4.2. A clear example is the meaning of the word *white*, which refers to a different colour in the phrases *white coffee, white wine, white paint* and *white skin*, and to a different semantic field altogether in the phrases *white light* or *white noise*.

Languages differ in the **collocational** ranges of their words. In English we distinguish between wiping our nose, brushing our teeth and polishing our shoes, whereas in German the term *putzen* can be used for all these activities (Stork and Widdowson 1974).

Clichés are born when a word occurs very frequently in a particular collocation. The word may then lose some of its semantic 'force', because we become used to thinking of the phrase as a single unit. Some examples from everyday English are 'last but not least' and 'the more the merrier'. Different professions tend to coin their own clichés: estate agents, for example, talk of 'a wealth of exposed beams' and 'tastefully decorated throughout'.

Habitual collocations often reflect social conventions and social attitudes: the collocations of the words *pretty* and *handsome*, for example, indicate that we categorize good looks for men and women separately. This is one way that language can perpetuate social divisions.

One of the techniques employed by corpus linguistics (which we described in Chapter 1) involves locating every incidence of a target word in a text or collection of texts and printing it out together with the words occurring on either side. Such an approach to analysing patterns of collocation is known as a **concordance** and has been used for centuries in the analysis and interpretation of biblical texts. More recently a kind of concordance known as **Key Word In Context** (or KWIC) has been applied to large-scale corpora of texts in English and other languages to help create modern dictionary entries. A KWIC concordance helps establish the senses in which a word is used in particular genres, or in the language as a whole, and which are the main and which are subsidiary uses of a word.

An example of a KWIC concordance for the word *grammar* is shown in Figure 4.1. The corpus in this case was every article appearing in *The Times* and *Sunday Times* during 1992 and hence shows every instance of the word (or its derivatives) during that year. The concordance shows how often the word is collocated with notions of *spelling*, *punctuation* and *correctness*. The example demonstrates clearly how the word *grammar* is used and understood outside academic linguistics and suggests that linguists will have an uphill struggle in persuading readers of *The Times* that non-standard dialects possess a grammar.

OPPOSITES

Another structural relationship that helps to determine word meaning is the relationship of 'opposites'. This is a paradigmatic relationship, as is the relationship between words in a semantic field, but it is between only two items. There are, however, various kinds of opposite relationship.

Complementarity   Take the pairs *alive* and *dead*, and *asleep* and *awake*. If someone is alive, then, by definition, they are not dead; similarly, if someone is awake, then they cannot also be asleep. The term used to describe this type of relationship is **complementarity**.

Antonymy   As with all our attempts to impose order on language, there are various difficulties even with this apparently straightforward relationship. Although strictly speaking the real-world relationship between *awake* and *asleep* is one of incompatibility, we do sometimes use the words as though they were not incompatible. We talk of someone as being 'half-awake' or 'half-asleep', or even 'three-quarters asleep', or as being 'more dead than alive'. When we do this we are using the words as if their relationship were one of **antonymy**. Like complementarity, antonymy is a paradigmatic relationship of opposites in a two-term system, but this time we can imagine the words in the pairs as being at opposite ends of a continuum. For this reason, they are said to be **gradable**. For example, the pairs *old/young*, *high/low*, *clever/stupid*, or *dark/light* are incompatible (if we are young, then we are not old) but there are intervening degrees between the polar opposites (we can be very young, fairly young, not so young, and so on).

Antonyms can be explicitly graded by using words such as *very*, *fairly* or *not so*, but in fact they can be thought of as always being implicitly graded. We only interpret words such as *old*, *wide* or *big* in terms of being older, wider or bigger than something else. The 'norm' against which we interpret them, however, varies depending on what is being described. The 'young businesswoman of the year', for example, may be in her forties.

Figure 4.1 A KWIC concordance

```
         Essays on Spanish: Words and  Grammar      (1991), a collection of previously-published
              by past generations of male  grammarians  . A case in point was
                    a book that will give  grammar      a good name. The Times
           A gathering of university post-  grammarians  and anti-pedants met on Monday
               to have his Hebrew Bible,  grammar      and dictionary while he was
               him have his Hebrew Bible,  grammar      and dictionary. His death for
           be penalised for poor spelling,  grammar      and punctuation this summer for
          when he published evidence that  grammar      and secondary modern schools got
                    14 to be tested in  grammar      and Shakespeare. What kinds of
             Disputes over the teaching of  grammar      and spelling, the identification of
            against the absurdities of English  grammar      and spelling. The spellers want
              office staff for their poor  grammar      and spelling. During the past
           examiners and employers mind about  grammar      and spelling. They may see
            basic skills in reading, writing,  grammar      and spelling. They take over
            on formal teaching of English  grammar      and syntax. A meeting last
              should obey the rules of  grammar      , and that, for example, they
                by the learning of Latin  grammar      and the close parsing of
             said that conventional rules of  grammar      and usage commanded an unthinking
                         only. That is why conventional  grammars     are unreadable. This is a
         ics, to Chomsky and 'transformational-generative  grammar      ', Burgess soon arrives at his
               spelling and punctuation, and, indeed,  grammar      ; but if 14-year-olds do not
                      are moving to a new  grammatical  construction here.' 'Verbal hygiene' is
            the politically (as distinct from  grammatically ) correct world has been convulsed
               read, write and speak with  grammatical  correctness. Small wonder that the
              what was then a standard  grammar-school education. It might come as
          their skills by correcting Shakespeare's  grammatical  errors. Is this what Mr
                general reader. Slimmer guides to  grammatical  grey areas, such as are
          illuminate the idiosyncrasies of Spanish  grammar      , he sought for parallel usages
               emphasis on handwriting, spelling and  grammar      in primary schools. Requirement for
             teaching of handwriting, spelling and  grammar      in primary schools. A 'balanced'
                    to see where. To regard  grammar      in terms of mistakes, the
           published in quantities for the  grammatically  insecure (anyone of sense some
           mis-spell. Shortly hereafter, Glosa, a '  grammar-free  ' international language based on Latin
                      as mere pedantry. But bad  grammar      is a sign of carelessness
             as 'a series of options'.  Grammar      is not a series of
            also define more precisely the  grammatical  knowledge expected of children and
           English, define more precisely the  grammatical  knowledge expected of children, and
                     /4/92 p11 Logic of  grammar      ;Leading Article Progressive child-centred tea
            form correctly or write a  grammatical  letter? The report suppressed by
           grammar, such as A Comprehensive  Grammar      of the English Language, is
              with the higher reaches of  grammar      . 'Only one person has ever
              pupils need to know about  grammar      or language,' he said. Griffiths
           unable to spell correctly, write  grammatically  or punctuate properly, according to
             might serve to illustrate a  grammatical  or stylistic argument, and an
           possible? In the 18th century  grammarians  practised their skills by correcting
            children need to know about  grammar      , punctuation and spelling. 'English is
                emphasis on basics such as  grammar      , punctuation, spelling and handwriting. It
             silence to a lecture on  grammar      . Quietly, they move on to
             of prejudice: rote learning, phonics,  grammar      , received pronunciation, the essay form
               provocation to read. This is  grammar      restored to its old connotation
           and pink custard, then the  grammar      school and advancement by further
              was educated at a girls'  grammar      school in Streatham. She hated
                    that he ever went to  grammar      school or university, and in
           successful English teaching? Although the  grammar      school to which I transferred
                 to Wigton primary school, Wigton  grammar      school, and if Wigton had
             English literature. Even at Manchester  grammar      school, Geoffrey Parker, the high
                     36 years at the Royal  Grammar      School, Newcastle upon Tyne, said:
                numbers of the great city  grammar      schools which provided the backbone
         report recommended, was 'unhelpful'. Rather,  grammar      should be seen as 'a
              the morphology, inflection and the  grammar      , spelling and meaning of written
              return to formal teaching of  grammar      , spelling and punctuation. Confidential propos
               for a review to emphasise  grammar      , spelling, classic literature and traditional
           to a professional concern with  grammatical  structures; to illuminate the idiosyncrasie
              and Saussure. A proper English  grammar      , such as A Comprehensive Grammar
                changing all the time, in  grammar      , syntax, vocabulary, spelling, and all
                   five (18%) could not write  grammatically  . The handwriting of more than
             bother with the nuances of  grammar      . There is nothing very new
           for poor spelling, punctuation and  grammar      to include coursework by GCSE
               who last week was explaining  grammar      to seven-year-old pupils at Ecole
                  are going to teach me  grammar      . What Elastoplast is is a
               in the heated debate over  grammar      when the national curriculum was
                language can be free of  grammar      , which is merely the way
           asking for old-fashioned vocabulary or  grammar      which the children are right
            should teach it today. Systematic  grammarians  will find this book absurd,
```

This implicit grading can be made use of in advertising: products are often described as *new*, *good*, *clean* or *bright*, which are all adjectives that imply a favourable comparison with other products.

Markedness   Another characteristic of antonyms is that one member of the pair functions as the **semantically unmarked** or 'neutral' member. For example, if we want to ask about someone's age, we ask them how *old* they are; if we want to know if there is headroom for our bus to pass under a bridge we ask how *high* the bridge is. No assumptions are implied about the height of the bridge or the age of the person. In the same way, we can use the word *dog* to refer to an animal that is female as well as to one that is male.

If the other member of the pair is used, however, then assumptions *are* made. If we ask how young someone is, then the implication is either that they are not young, or that they are too young; if we ask how low a bridge is, then we imply that it is low rather than high. Similarly, a *bitch* is unquestionably a female animal; people sometimes speak of a *female dog*, but they would be most unlikely to speak of a *male bitch*. Often there is a noun derived from the unmarked term, but not from the marked term. In English, for example, we have a noun *height*, but no corresponding term derived from *low*. The term that is used as the unmarked member of the pair seems to vary in different languages; where English speaks of a *thickness gauge*, Japanese has a *thinness gauge* (see Palmer 1981). It can be very revealing of society's values to consider which of a pair of antonyms is used as the unmarked one.

Some pairs of words that are 'opposite' in meaning are **formally marked**. For example, *truthful* and *untruthful* can be analysed as complementary in meaning (though they are often used as antonyms, like other examples mentioned above); and in this case the opposition is formally marked by the prefix *un-*. This prefix is often used as a formal marker of 'oppositeness' (some other examples that come to mind are *helpful/unhelpful* and *happy/unhappy*). In English *in-* and *dis-* are used in a similar way, as formal markers of oppositeness, so that we have pairs such as *appropriate/inappropriate*, *eligible/ineligible*, *like/dislike* and *approve/disapprove*. These prefixes do not always mark a relationship of oppositeness, of course: for example, the words *disappoint* and *dismay* do not have corresponding opposite forms **appoint* or **may*. Sometimes a marked member of a pair is formally marked by a suffix, such as the *-ess* suffix in the pairs *host/hostess*, or *lion/lioness*, or the *-ette* suffix in *usher/usherette*. Prefixes and suffixes of this type are described in more detail in Section 3.3, on word structure.

Converses   A further relationship of opposites involves pairs of words where one implies the reversal of the other. In English this includes terms such as *husband/wife* and *borrow/lend*. For instance, if Paul is June's husband, then this implies that June is Paul's wife; if we say that Ann has borrowed £5 from her mother, then this implies that her mother has lent Ann £5. Of course, it is possible to use the word *borrow* in a way that does not imply a converse relationship; we could be speaking loosely, and be trying to make light of the fact that Ann has stolen £5 from her mother (in which case her mother would not, of course, have lent Ann the money!). The possibility of using words in many different ways is always there, as part of the flexibility of word meaning.

In some languages the same word may express both aspects of the relationship; in fact, this may even be the case in different varieties of the same language. In many parts of the British Isles, for example, people use the word *lend* in phrases such as *Can I lend £5?* (meaning 'Please give me a loan of £5') as well as in phrases such as *I'll lend you £5* (meaning 'I'll give you a loan of £5').

On the other hand, there are some languages that make distinctions where English does not. For example, English uses the same word *marry* whether the person who is the subject of the verb is the husband or the wife. In many languages, though, there are two words – one that is used when the subject is the wife (as in *Mary married John*) and another that is used when the subject is the husband (as in *John married Mary*). Italian, for example, would use the verb *maritarsi* in the first case and *ammogliarsi* in the second. Again, the relationships that the language specifies in its vocabulary (or that it **lexicalizes**) can often be very revealing of cultural attitudes.

HYPONYMY

A paradigmatic relationship of a different kind is **hyponymy**. This is a relationship of 'inclusion'. The meaning of the word *flower*, for example, is included in the meaning of the word *daisy*, since daisies are flowers; similarly, the meaning of the word *emotion* could be said to be included in the meaning of *joy* or of *sadness*. Hyponymous relationships are hierarchical, and can be displayed in the form of a tree, as in the diagram below:

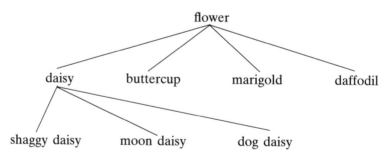

The upper term is called the **superordinate** (in the diagram this is *flower*) and the lower term is called the **hyponym**. In the diagram, *daisy, buttercup, marigold* and *daffodil* are all hyponyms of *flower*, and we have given *shaggy daisy, moon daisy* and *dog daisy* as hyponyms of *daisy*. Someone with a better knowledge of different species of flowers could also give hyponyms of *buttercup, marigold* and *daffodil*. Tree diagrams for hyponymy reflect the way in which language users attempt to organize their world, categorizing things in order to make sense of them. It is often very revealing, therefore, to analyse the different hyponymous relationships in different languages. We mentioned earlier an example from ancient Greek, where there was a superordinate term to include a variety of professions and crafts, such as carpenter, doctor and flute player. English has no such superordinate term. These differences in semantic structure seem to be related to differences in the way that the two cultures have evaluated various occupations.

It can be equally revealing to analyse the different hyponymous relationships for 'pairs' of words in the same language. Todasco (1973) found 89 nouns and 120 adjectives to refer to a promiscuous woman, but only a few to refer to a promiscuous man.

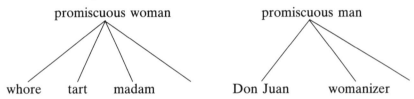

The categories that are reflected in the language can be refined as required by the occasion. In everyday English, for example, we use *beetle* as a hyponym of the superordinate *insect*, but in entomology the term *beetle* is itself a superordinate for over 200 000 different species of what a layperson might call a beetle (Eco 1984).

Some of the words that we mentioned earlier as examples of semantic markedness can also be usefully analysed as examples of hyponymy. *Dog*, for example, is the unmarked member of the pair of words *dog* and *bitch*, in that it can be used to refer to the animal when its sex is not known, or when there is no need to mention its sex. The word *dog*, therefore, is both a superordinate and a hyponym:

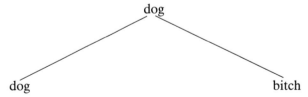

Similarly, the word *man* may function as both a hyponym and a superordinate, and it is not surprising that this can give rise to difficulties of interpretation.

COMPONENTIAL ANALYSIS

Another useful way of analysing word meaning is in terms of **semantic features**, by trying to specify the different components of meaning that make up a word. This approach can be used to analyse several of the meaning relationships that have been discussed so far. Components are usually treated as binary, so that meanings can be economically represented as (+) a feature or (–) the feature. For example, hyponyms can be said to contain the more general, superordinate concept, so that *daisy, buttercup* and *marigold* all have as one of their components [+ flower]; similarly, antonyms and complementaries can be analysed as differing from each other by the presence or absence of a component feature, so that *alive* could be analysed as containing the component feature [+ alive], and *dead* as containing the feature [– alive] (though, as we saw above, this type of analysis will not work in normal everyday language, where the flexibility of words is often fully exploited and where people can be 'half alive' or 'half dead').

When this approach to the analysis of word meaning is used, features are often set up in an *ad hoc* way, so that in theory there would be no limit to the number of components used in an analysis of meaning. Some linguists, however, have searched for a small number of semantic components that can provide definitions for a large number of words, hoping to establish **semantic primitives**, of universals of meaning. These semantic primitives (sometimes called 'primes') would be components that are essential to the word's meaning. For example, we might decide that *animal* has the component [+ animate] as an essential component of its meaning, but not, perhaps, the component [+ furry]. Many animals *are* furry, but some (pigs, for instance) are not; there are no animals, however, that are not animate – though, as always, it is possible to think of occasions when the word could be used without this apparently essential aspect of its meaning. This approach has something in common with the concept of 'core' meaning, mentioned earlier. The idea of core meanings, however, does not necessarily assume that the core meaning is a semantic universal.

This approach to the analysis of word meaning has sometimes been used to describe semantic development in the language of young children. Very often children will learn a word such as *dog*, but use it to refer not only to dogs but also to other animals – cats, perhaps, and horses, sheep and cows. The difference between the child's word *dog* and an adult's word *dog* can then be conveniently described in terms of the semantic components of the word. We could say that for the child, *dog* has the component [+ animal]; whereas for the adult it has the two components [+ animal] [+ canine], and the second component differentiates it from other words in the adult's vocabulary that share the feature [+ animal]. Similarly, some children use the words *mummy* and *daddy* interchangeably; for them, both words seem to have a component such as [+ parent], and in time they will presumably acquire the additional components [+ female] and [+ male] which the adult words *mummy* and *daddy* can be said to have.

Componential analysis can analyse **underextended** meanings as well as the **overextensions** we have just described. For example, a young child may use the word *bottle* to refer to its own drinking bottle but not to any other kinds of bottle; in this case the word could be said to have the components [+ container] [+ drink], whereas for the adult the word could be said to lack the [+ drink] component. Of course, we cannot claim to have given an adequate account of the meaning of *bottle* by simply saying that it contains the components [+ container] [+ drink]. It can often be difficult to know which components to specify as the essential features of a word's meaning. Nevertheless, this approach to the analysis of word meaning can be a neat way of representing the meaning relationships that exist between some words in the vocabulary, and it has had a useful application in describing some of the differences between children's and adults' uses of certain words.

Activity 4.3

If you know a child of about two years old, look through a picture book with the child and ask it to name some everyday things that are in the pictures. Note the words that seem to be underextensions or overextensions of adult usage, and try to specify the semantic features that the child has but that adults do not have, or that adults have but that the child does not.

Although componential analysis has its uses as an *ad hoc* descriptive device, it has several problems. We said above that it is economical to treat components as binary, so that certain words can be said to differ from each other by the simple presence or absence of a semantic feature. Binary relationships of meaning are important in the vocabulary of a language (as we have already seen in the analysis of opposites) but there are other types of relationship that are equally important and that cannot be analysed in this way. For example, words such as colour terms and days of the week cannot be analysed as differing from each other by the simple presence or absence of a particular semantic feature. Furthermore, it is not necessarily particularly revealing simply to list the semantic components of a word, as we saw earlier with *bottle*; and even if it does seem that this can be done, we may need to say how the components are combined. An example that is often given is the word *kill*, which can be analysed into the components [cause], [become], [– alive] but for which we need, in addition, to specify that the components are ordered in a hierarchical relationship:

[cause]
   ↓
[become]
   ↓
[– alive]

and to specify the participants (for example X [cause] Y → Y [become] → [– alive]).

A further difficulty is that, although it is economical to represent semantic features as being present or absent, it is not necessarily helpful to give the meaning of a word in terms of what it is not, rather than in terms of what it is. The meaning of the word *girl*, for instance, has been analysed in terms of the features [– adult] [– male], which do indeed distinguish it from *boy* ([– adult] [+ male]) and from *woman* ([+ adult], [– male]) but which do not tell us a great deal about the meaning of *girl*! In fact, there is no obvious reason why *girl* should not be analysed as containing the features [+ child] [+ female] and *boy* as [+ child] [– female]. Sometimes it is the semantically unmarked term or the formally unmarked term that is chosen as the positive pole – and this may account for the choice of [+ male] rather than [+ female]. However, the choices that analysts make are unlikely to be arbitrary or objective. Like anyone else, analysts will be influenced by the norms and values of their society.

Activity 4.4

You may find it helpful to test your understanding of the different types of relationships between word meanings mentioned so far. You can do this by deciding which of the different types of structural relationship we have discussed is most helpful in trying to analyse the meanings of the following words:

calf
addled
chaffinch
innocent
buy

There is no right or wrong way to analyse word meaning, but since meaning relationships are of several different kinds, some words may lend themselves to a particular type of analysis better than others. The most helpful forms of analysis for the words above seem to be:

calf Since this is the word used to refer to a young male bull, this can be economically analysed as containing the components [+ cattle], [+ male], [– adult] – if we use the conventional 'positive' features. It then contrasts with

bull   [+ cattle], [+ male], [+ adult]
cow   [+ cattle], [– male], [+ adult]
heifer [+ cattle], [– male], [– adult]

In fact, componential analysis was first used by anthropologists to analyse kinship terminology, and it is often a useful way of representing 'family' relationships such as this one.

addled This word occurs almost exclusively in connection with the words *eggs* and *brains*. Its meaning can, therefore, be usefully analysed in terms of its collocations.

chaffinch Since this is one of the species of bird that we identify as a separate type, its meaning can be represented as a hyponymous relationship, with *chaffinch* a hyponym of the superordinate *bird*.

innocent This can be considered to be in a complementary relationship with *guilty*, since in principle it is not possible to be both innocent of something and guilty of it.

buy This can be considered to be in a converse relationship with *sell*, since the two are reverse activities. In the normal course of events someone can only buy an object if it is sold to them.

4.3 Words in context: sentence and utterance meaning

Analysing word meaning is useful, but there is more involved in communication than simply adding together the meaning of individual words. Linguistic context can be all-important in determining which of a number of meanings of a word is intended: compare, for example, the two phrases *Here's a mug of coffee* and *He's an ugly mug!* The linguistic context alone is still not adequate, however. The phrase *Here's a mug of coffee* can have many different meanings depending on such factors as the way in which it is uttered, what has been said before, and the general situational context. It could be a straightforward piece of information mentioned by a speaker as they pass across a steaming mug; but at the end of a party it could be a polite hint that it is time the guests were leaving; or it could be a not very polite way of telling someone they have had more than enough to drink and that they ought to sober up. Many other interpretations are possible in different contexts.

It can be helpful to make a distinction between **sentence meaning**, which can be described in terms of the words and the syntax of what is said, and **utterance meaning**, which takes account of other features of the linguistic context (such as intonation) and of the situational context. However, it is not always easy to draw a clear-cut distinction in this way, and when we interpret language these two aspects of meaning are usually interrelated. Listeners and readers need actively to interpret what is said – to make **inferences** about the meaning of utterances using both their linguistic and their cultural knowledge. In this section we will not attempt to make a clear distinction between sentence meaning and utterance meaning, but we will discuss approaches to the analysis of meaning which take account of the need to interpret words in context.

Speech acts

Speech act theory focuses on the communicative function that a particular sentence has when it is uttered, or the 'act' that it performs. It is possible to identify sentence types on the basis of their syntactic structure. In their *Comprehensive Grammar of English*, Quirk *et al.* distinguish four sentence types: declarative, interrogative, imperative and exclamative. These are associated with acts of giving information; asking a question; giving an instruction; and exclaiming (1985: 803–4):

declarative   Pauline gave Tom a digital watch for his birthday.
interrogative Did Pauline give Tom a digital watch for his birthday?
imperative   Give me a digital watch for my birthday.
exclamative   What a fine watch he received for his birthday!

The relationship between the form of a sentence and the speech act that it performs is more complex than this, however. Although the four sentence types above do often have these semantic functions (some analysts have argued that they always do, though they may have other functions, too) there is not necessarily always a one-to-one correlation. Consider, for example, the sentence *It's hot in here*. This may have the semantic function of giving information (that the speaker thinks that it is hot), but it could also function as an order or as a question, depending on the circumstances in which it was said. If said by someone in authority it could mean 'Will you open the window?' or even 'Open the window immediately!'. In this case we can say that the sentence is an **indirect speech act**.

There are, of course, more functions than the four mentioned above (giving information, asking questions, giving orders and exclaiming). The same sentence, *It's hot in here*, could be an apology (if said to visitors in your home), a complaint (if said by a visitor in a hotel) or even a warning (for example, if the speakers are in a room where nitroglycerine is stored). It can perform several speech acts at the same time: this same sentence, for instance, could be both an apology to visitors and a complaint that someone had not opened the window, as well as a request that someone should now do so. The philosopher John Austin suggested that there could be as many as 10 000 different functions of sentences and others have suggested the number is infinite! These functions are performed by a relatively small number of syntactic structures.

The sheer number of different speech acts that sentences can perform makes it very difficult to analyse this aspect of language. A further problem is to decide whether to categorize speech acts in terms of the speaker's *intentions*, or in terms of the hearer's *perceptions* of the speech act. These do not always coincide, as the example below, adapted from Gumperz (1982), illustrates. A mother is talking to her 11-year-old son, who is about to go out in the rain:

Mother: Where are your boots?
Son: In the closet.
Mother: I want you to put them on right now!

The mother intended her first sentence to be an order for her son to put his boots on (an indirect speech act). Her son interpreted her sentence not as an order but as a question, to which he responded – or perhaps he only pretended to interpret it in this way, in order to joke with his mother. His statement was then interpreted by his mother as a refusal to obey her order. Alternatively, she may have wanted to communicate that joking was not appropriate at that moment. It is even possible that all of these functions were present. We cannot say exactly what went on in this transaction, since we cannot know the intentions or the emotions of the people involved.

Because of these problems, speech acts are often categorized in terms of the act that is performed by speakers when they say a particular utterance, rather than in terms of the speaker's intentions. This is easiest to see when a sentence contains a **performative verb**. In this case it is the utterance of the sentence that performs the act, and it is less necessary to take into account the speaker's intentions and the hearer's perceptions. Some clear examples are:

act of marriage	I hereby pronounce you man and wife.
act of naming a ship	I name this ship the *Saucy Sue*.
act of closing a meeting	I declare this meeting closed.
act of a wager	I bet you a fiver.
act of apology	I apologize.

In all these sentences there is a first person present tense verb, the sentence has the syntactic structure of a statement, and it would be possible to include the word *hereby*. Of course, for the utterances to fulfil their function the circumstances have to be right: not just anyone can pronounce two people man and wife; one has to have the authority to do this. Even in apparently clear-cut examples such as these, the social circumstances of the participants and the situation have to be taken into account.

When a performative verb is not present, the number of potential functions of an utterance greatly increases. However, the situation in which an utterance occurs helps the communication to go smoothly, for our shared social and cultural knowledge provides us with clues about what to expect. For example, we know that a teacher who says to a class of pupils *I can hear someone talking* is more likely to be giving an order for that person to stop talking than to be simply giving information (though these functions probably overlap to some extent). We know, too, that the sentence *Can you swim a length, Mary?* is likely to be a question if it is said by a teacher to a pupil in a classroom, but that if it is said by a teacher to a pupil at a swimming pool it is more likely to be a command, and to be followed by a splash! (see Coulthard 1977). If the people involved do not have the same social and cultural knowledge, however, problems of interpretation can arise. Some illustrations of miscommunication between people from different cultural backgrounds can be found in Gumperz (1982).

Activity 4.5

Identify both the syntactic form (e.g. the four sentence types identified earlier) and the semantic function (e.g. 'asking a question' or 'giving an order') of each of the following utterances. Where more than one semantic function is possible, think of a context in which each possibility might occur.

1 Be there at four o'clock.
2 I name this child Elizabeth.
3 Are you going to do that washing-up?
4 Come upstairs.
5 I bet you a fiver it snows before Christmas.
6 I sentence you to six years' heavy labour.
7 I run round the block every morning.

Sentences (1) and (4) have the form of an imperative sentence, sentence (3) of an interrogative sentence and the other sentences all have the form of declarative sentences.

The semantic functions of sentences (2), (5) and (6) are unambiguous. They all contain a performative verb (*I name, I bet* and *I sentence*) and they perform, respectively, the acts of baptizing, betting and sentencing (if the social circumstances are right). The semantic functions of the other sentences are potentially very numerous: for example, sentence (1) could be an invitation, if said by one friend to another, a command, if said by an army general to his subordinate, a plea, a warning and many other things.

Note that sentence (7) does not contain a performative verb despite the fact that is has a first person present tense form. To say *I bet* constitutes the act of betting, but in order to perform the act of running we have to do more than say *I run*! A test for performative sentences is to see whether the word *hereby* can be added: it could to *I bet*, but not to *I run*.

Inferential meaning

We now examine three types of inference that may be drawn from utterances: **entailment**, **presupposition** and **conversational implicature**. As you will see, the inferences become progressively more dependent upon the non-linguistic context.

ENTAILMENT

This is perhaps the most straightforward inference. Entailment refers to a logical relationship that holds between a sentence and a proposition that the sentence expresses (this relationship should hold irrespective of the context in which the sentence is actually uttered and it can be considered, therefore, as an aspect of sentence meaning as opposed to utterance meaning). Entailment is often described using logical formulae but, in more everyday language, a sentence *entails* a proposition if, under every condition in which the sentence is true, the proposition is also true. Thus the sentence

S   Mary has a cat and a dog

entails the proposition:

S₁   Mary has a cat

since if S is true, so is S₁.

Note that although entailment here refers to certain propositions that may be deduced from sentences it is also a way of handling many of the *sense relations* discussed in Section 4.2 above. In the relation of *hyponymy*, for instance, *x is a rose* entails *x is a flower*, but *y is a flower* does not entail *y is a rose*.

PRESUPPOSITION

Entailment is of limited use in handling inferences listeners may draw from utterances of a particular sentence. It really only applies to sentences that have a **truth value** (i.e. that are either true or false), which rules out non-declarative sentences such as *Who ate those cherries?*

Someone who heard this uttered might conventionally infer that the speaker believed *someone* had eaten the cherries but the sentence cannot *entail* this proposition as it does not have a truth value (it is not possible to say that a question is either true or false). Such inferences, which depend upon the meanings that a listener would conventionally attach to the utterance of a particular sentence, have been termed **presuppositions**.

There has been some argument over the need to distinguish presupposition and entailment. A classic case concerns the sentence

S   The king of France is bald

Some analyses suggest that this sentence entails the proposition:

S₁   There exists a king of France

If, as nowadays, the proposition S₁ is false, then so is the sentence S. An analysis based upon presupposition, however, would claim S *presupposes* S₁. If S₁ is false S is neither true nor false – it is simply based upon an erroneous presupposition. Unlike entailment, it is argued, presupposition holds good under negation and in question forms:

S   The king of France is not bald
S   Is the king of France bald?

still presuppose S₁.

Presupposition has been used to describe other inferences that derive from the (linguistic) meaning of a sentence – for instance, those that derive from verbs such as *know, realize* and *regret*: *Eve knew Adam's fig leaf was loose* presupposes: *Adam's fig leaf was loose.* (Contrast: *Eve believed Adam's fig leaf was loose.*)

Presupposition does have characteristics in common with entailment – for instance, if a presupposition is overtly contradicted, an utterance will not (normally) make sense: consider *Adam's fig leaf wasn't loose but Eve knew Adam's fig leaf was loose.*

Semantic theorists have often been dissatisfied with the notion of pre-supposition – it has proved very difficult to define in a watertight way which includes everything one intuitively feels is a presupposition while excluding everything else. For instance, it has been argued that presuppo-sitions need not hold constant under negation. One might legitimately say: *Of course the king of France isn't bald: there isn't a king of France.*

Kempson (1977) discusses some of the problems associated with presup-position from a theoretical point of view and argues that it is more straight-forward to handle all such relations in terms of entailment. This, however, seems not to account adequately for a common-sense understanding speakers and listeners may have that a sentence can presuppose something it does not directly assert. An alternative suggestion (see, for example, Lyons 1977) is that we should allow presupposition some measure of **context dependency**. For instance, imagine a conversation between X and Y in which X says that, to her certain knowledge, no reigning European monarch is bald. If Y responds seriously that *The king of France is bald*, X could well retort *That's not true: there isn't a king of France.* What is being denied here is Y's assertion that the class of European monarchs contains the king of France. In other contexts, however, *That's not true* would be taken to deny the assertion that the king was bald. (For a fuller discussion of this and other examples, see Lyons 1977: 601–5.)

CONVERSATIONAL IMPLICATURE

The notion of conversational implicature is based chiefly on the work of Grice (1975). Grice identified two kinds of implicature: **conventional** and **conversational implicature**. The distinction between these is not always straightforward but, roughly, conventional implicature refers to implica-tions in an utterance that depend upon the conventional meanings of words and expressions. (These shared conventions were mentioned in Section 4.2 and we saw there that they can sometimes be decidedly fuzzy.) Conversa-tional implicature, with which we shall be concerned here, takes into ac-count not only the literal meaning of a sentence, but also the context in which it is uttered, the background knowledge of speaker and hearer and general principles governing the conduct of conversation. Grice suggested that each participant's contribution is governed by these four principles (sometimes termed *Grice's maxims*):

quantity	do not provide more or less information than is required for the current purposes of the exchange;
quality	speak the truth;
relevance	be relevant;
manner	be clear.

For instance, the utterance of the sentence *I think the car's still there* might imply that the speaker is not *certain* the car is still there since according to Grice's maxim of *quantity* a speaker would normally be expected to be as informative as was necessary. In most contexts it would be preferable to provide more definite information – *The car's still there* – if one had this information. Similarly, if a motorist tells a passerby that she's nearly out of petrol and asks for directions to the nearest garage the reply *There's one just round the corner on the right* would be taken to imply that, as far as the passerby was aware, the garage was open and had supplies of petrol – since, according to Grice's maxim of relevance one would normally be expected to say something that is relevant to the conversation in hand.

Unlike entailment and presupposition, some implicatures can be cancelled by the speaker. The utterance *I think the car's still there* might imply *I don't know it's still there*, but in response to a question *Do you think the car's still there?* a speaker could quite reasonably reply *Yes – in fact, I know it is*.

The notion of implicature is, as Grice recognizes, often imprecise – and the formulation of the conversational maxims themselves is somewhat vague. The distinction between presupposition and implicature is also not straightforward – and, in fact, it has been suggested that presupposition can be handled in terms of conversational implicature. For instance, the utterance *The king of France is bald* would normally flout Grice's maxim of relevance if there were, in fact, no king of France. However, it does not seem sensible to lump the two categories together, since conversational implicature is distinct from presupposition in assuming a speaker is providing information that is not part of the literal meaning of a sentence.

It may sometimes seem that participants are not conforming to these conversational principles (the first one, particularly, may often seem to be flouted!), but in fact these principles often help in the analysis of conversations that appear at first to be problematic. Consider, for example, this exchange:

A: Are you going to the cinema tonight?
B: Jim's away.

If we assume that both A and B are obeying Grice's four maxims, then B's response must be relevant to A's question, and must provide enough information to answer the question. For example, B could be married to Jim and have two small children and no access to babysitters. A would have to know this background information about B, and B would have to know that A knew it.

INDIRECT SPEECH AND PERSUASIVE LANGUAGE

Persuasive language such as that used in advertising often depends in part for its effectiveness on propositions that are implied in an utterance rather than directly asserted. In a study of 800 video-taped advertisements broadcast on American television between 1978 and 1981, Geis (1982) found several occasions when part of the advertisers' message, which might have been difficult to support by evidence, was put across indirectly – obviously by visual means, since his sample of adverts came from television, but also through indirect uses of language, analysed by Geis in terms of presupposition and conversational implicature. Examples of presuppositions include:

(a) *We're in the appliance department to find out why Sears is where America shops*

which presupposes 'Sears is where America shops', and

(b) *This Atra face-hugging action keeps twin blades at the perfect angle*

which presupposes 'Atra twin blades are at the perfect angle'. (Note: Geis terms these 'conventional implicatures' after Grice (1975), but since in this case they are identical to presuppositions, we shall continue to use this term.)

Geis argues:

> Since conventionally implicated propositions [i.e. presuppositions] are rarely defended in ordinary conversation, I submit that viewers will normally not expect to find them defended in advertising. Therefore, any advertiser who wishes to convey some proposition P but does not want to defend P or cannot defend P can simply use a construction that [presupposes] P with little fear that viewers will question P.

He compares utterance (b) above with the following possibility, in which both propositions are formulated as assertions (Geis 1982: 46):

(c) *Atra twin hugging blades are set at the perfect angle and this Atra face-hugging action keeps them that way*

and suggests that viewers would be much more likely to challenge the truth of the proposition that the Atra twin blades are set at the perfect angle had the advertiser said (c) instead of (b).

Examples of conversational implicatures include:

(d) *They invented fluoride toothpaste to help fight cavities. Why hasn't somebody invented a better toothbrush?*

– which implies 'somebody should have invented a better toothbrush' – we later find out, of course, that somebody has.

(e) *Wet feet? LOOK OUT FOR A COLD – gargle with LISTERINE QUICK*

– an old advert from a study carried out in 1943. Geis argues that the use of language in this advert conversationally implicates that Listerine can prevent colds – why otherwise would there be any need for quick action? Here Geis is using Grice's maxim of relevance, discussed above.

(f) *We are building a reputation, not resting on one*

– an advertisement for Ramada Inn. Geis tried out this claim on a number of respondents, virtually every one of whom took it to be suggesting that some leading competitor of Ramada Inn is resting on its reputation. In fact, most of Geis's respondents assumed the leading competitor must be Holiday Inn. Geis (1982: 50) again argues that this implication can be justified by the maxim of relevance: 'Why say you are not resting on your reputation unless someone has said that you are or you believe someone else is resting on his reputation?'

Geis draws conclusions from his study that have implications for practice – he wants advertisers to be responsible for what their adverts would normally be taken to imply, as well as for explicit assertions. In support of this he argues that, in speaking, people normally make inferences about meanings, and that they do not distinguish between semantic inferences (such as entailment) and pragmatic inferences (such as conversational implicature). This, of course, makes sense in ordinary conversation but can be played upon by users of persuasive language.

Activity 4.6

You may like to compare advertisements in your own country with Geis's American sample. Record a sample of television adverts (say, five or six) broadcast during one evening. Listen to each carefully (you may need to replay your recording two or three times) and try to identify how many use 'indirect' language to convey their message. Can you analyse this usage in terms of presupposition and conversational implicature?

Note that this exercise is only a 'taster': to be able to say anything about advertising in general you would need to analyse a representative sample, as Geis did in the USA.

RELEVANCE THEORY

Sperber and Wilson (1986) attempt to develop a theoretical account of communication by focusing on just one of the principles discussed above – the principle of **relevance**. They see this principle rather differently from Grice, however, defining it as a generalisation that can explain the cognitive procedures underlying communication. When we set out to communicate, they say, we attract our addressees' attention and imply that what we are saying is relevant enough to be worth this attention. The task of the addressee is then to infer our intentions. Relevance within communication involves an automatic balance between the processing effort that addressees have to make in order to interpret what is said to them, and the information that they gain as a result of their processing. A simple example. (Sperber and Wilson, 1986: 168)

George has a big cat

In an ordinary situation, Sperber and Wilson claim, the first interpretation to occur to the addressee will be that George has a big domestic cat, rather than a lion or a tiger. If the addressee sees that the hearer can have expected this interpretation to apply, this first inference will be the only one that is drawn, and no further processing of the information will take place. If more processing seemed to be necessary, the theory predicts that this would be compensated for by a gain in information. Thus the repetition in the sentence *we went for a long long walk* necessitates an extra processing effort on the part of the addressee, but this is balanced by an increase in what Sperber and Wilson term 'contextual effects' – here an inference that the walk was longer than might otherwise have been expected.

Relevance theory has been used to try to explain the use of many different kinds of linguistic features as well as more general aspects of language, including metaphor, irony and jokes. Many linguists working on real language data, however, find that the theory requires analysts to rely too much on their own intuitions about the inferences that addressees make and that it treats communication in too mechanical a way, with what people say described as 'a stimulus' and addressees seen as 'individuals whose cognitive environment the communicator is trying to modify'. In its focus on the transmission of information from one individual to another this approach is very much in tune with the traditional models of language that we outlined in Chapter 1 of this book.

4.4 The role of world knowledge

In the previous section we described the types of inference that we draw from the utterances that we hear. In this section we will consider the way in which these inferences are dependent on our knowledge of the world.

Consider, as an example, the following sentences (from Bolinger 1965):

Our store sells alligator shoes
Our store sells horse shoes

It is likely that you will interpret the first sentence as meaning that the store sells shoes that are made of alligator skin, and the second sentence as meaning that the store sells shoes that are for horses to wear. In part it is our knowledge of language that leads us to these interpretations. We can interpret the first sentence by comparing it with sentences such as:

Our store sells leather shoes
                 plastic shoes
                 canvas shoes

and the second sentence by comparing it with:

Our store sells tennis shoes
                 curtain rings
                 dog leads

cat litter
writing paper

In each case we make use of our knowledge of the syntagmatic relation-ships and the paradigmatic relationships in language: syntagmatic, by con-sidering the relationships between the noun *shoes* and the adjectival nouns that describe the nature of the shoes; or between the noun *shoes* and the nouns that describe what the second set of nouns are for; paradigmatic, by comparing *alligator* in the first case, and *horse* in the second case, with other nouns and adjectives that could occur in this phrase. We need to draw on more than our knowledge of language alone, though, for this simply tells us that either interpretation is acceptable in terms of the struc-ture of the language. It is part of our knowledge of the world that horses wear shoes and that alligators do not; and that alligator skins are used to make shoes whereas horse skins are not. We draw inferences from the words in the two sentences, and the inferences result from a combination of our knowledge of language and our knowledge of the world.

If we want to analyse the meaning of words in context, then we need to find a framework that will analyse not only the conventions governing the meaning of words and sentences, and the inferences that are drawn from them, but also our knowledge of the world. This is a daunting prospect. Furthermore, it is not possible to draw a clear line between these two different types of knowledge, for they are interrelated. We could conceiv-ably analyse *horse* as having as one component of its meaning the fact that in certain states of domesticity it is likely to wear metal 'shoes' (see Biggs 1982) but if we take this line of analysis then the amount of information that we would have to include about all the entities in the world that we might like to talk about at some time would be immense. It would also vary from one person to another, since we all have different experiences of the world and we all have different amounts and types of world knowl-edge to draw on when we attempt to interpret language, as well as differ-ent amounts and types of linguistic knowledge.

Eco (1984) gives us a way of analysing how our interpretation of words in context depends on both our knowledge of language and our knowledge of the world. He uses the concept of 'frame', which comes from recent research into artificial intelligence, but which can be usefully applied to real intelligence, too (see also the discussion of 'frame' in Section 7.4). The assumption is that we have an 'encyclopaedic' set of beliefs about the world, which we store in sets of frames. Eco gives as illustration the sen-tences below:

John was sleeping when he was suddenly awakened. Somebody was tearing up the pillow.

When you read these sentences you undoubtedly made the inference that the pillow referred to in the second sentence is the pillow that John was sleeping on. It may seem that this is simply common sense. However, the goal of linguistic analysis is to make explicit the unconscious knowledge that we draw on when we communicate with each other, and so our common-sense interpretation is something that needs to be explained. After all, there is no mention of a pillow in the first of the two sentences. In part, of course, our interpretation depends on our linguistic knowledge: we know (unconsciously, perhaps, rather than consciously) that to say *the pillow* rather than *a pillow* implies that the speaker has a particular pillow in mind. This could be a pillow that had been mentioned in a previous sentence, in which case it is the linguistic context that provides us with the correct interpretation; or it could be simply a pillow that we might expect to be there, since we know that people conventionally go to sleep with their head resting on a pillow. In this case it is our world knowledge that provides us with the correct interpretation – coupled with our linguistic knowledge of the opposition between *the* and *a*.

If we go along with Eco's approach, seeing our knowledge of the world as stored in sets of frames, then we can share his view of the process that you may have used to make the inference that the pillow in his example sentence was the pillow that John was sleeping on (assume, in the quotation that follows, that you are his addressee):

> By resorting to this storage of competence, the addressee knows that human beings usually sleep in bedrooms and that bedrooms are furnished with beds, beds with pillows, and so on. By amalgamation of two or more frames, the addressee realizes that the pillow just mentioned can only be the one John was resting his head on.
>
> (Eco 1984: 71)

Eco gives a further example of the way in which we might use 'frames' in communication. He asks us to imagine that during the night, looking out of the window of her home in the countryside, a (presumably American) wife tells her husband: 'Honey, there is a man on the lawn near the fence!' The word *man* enters into a number of different meaning relationships with other words in the vocabulary. Some of these can be analysed using componential analysis: for example, *man* is related to *boy* (man is [+ adult], boy is [– adult]), to *tree* (*man* is [+ animate], *tree* is [– animate]), and to *dog* (*man* is [+ human], *dog* is [– human]). It also enters into relationships with other words, which cannot be analysed so neatly: if we imagine a 'semantic field' of 'strange things in the garden at night', for example, we might include in the semantic field such words and phrases as *alien invader*, *giant teddy bear* (left there by their children), *shadow of a tree*, and so on. The husband has to make a conjecture about the semantic properties of the word *man* that are important to his wife on this particular occasion. In this case it seems most likely that the woman was interested in the man as a possible threat to their safety. As Eco (1984: 79) says:

> Probably the wife was not interested in the fact that men are mortal or hot-blooded animals; she was interested in their being rational

only insofar as to be rational means to conceive evil intentions. In other words, a man was to her something potentially aggressive, able to move inside. If the thing were a child, it would be felt as non-potentially aggressive; if it were a dog, it would be felt as unable to intrude; if it were a tree or a giant teddy bear, it would be felt as unable to move. On the contrary, a spatial alien would be viewed as a moving and potentially aggressive being. We can also suppose that each alternative elicits the retrieval of a given frame such as 'burglars in the night', 'lost child', 'space invaders', . . . and so on.

Eco's point is that each time we use a word we 'blow up' certain properties of the word, and 'narcoticize' other properties. In this case, as Eco says, the woman had presumably 'narcoticized' the component of the meaning of *man* that is [+ mortal] (i.e. *man* as the complementary of *god*), as well as various other possible components of the word's meaning. Instead, she had 'blown up' the component of [+ dangerous]. We would probably not consider this aspect of the meaning of *man* to be a central aspect of its meaning (unless, perhaps, we had had some particularly unfortunate experiences, which had given the word this connotation for us). It is certainly unlikely to be listed in a dictionary as part of the meaning of the word. However, if we think of words as having various components of meaning, both central and more peripheral, with each component having a probability of applying (as discussed in Section 4.2) then we can see that in the situation that Eco describes – late at night, looking out into a dark garden – there is a higher than usual probability of this aspect of the meaning of *man* applying.

If the husband in this scenario wants to reassure his wife, it is not enough for him to answer 'No, honey, it's not a man', since this would leave open the other potentially threatening meanings of the word. Eco's suggestion is that the husband who interprets his wife's utterance correctly will make a spur of the moment 'hyponymy' tree for himself, to see how the word *man* fits into his wife's own current classification of things. He does this using his knowledge of the world (and this will include his knowledge of what he thinks his wife's knowledge of the world is). The result may be something like the hyponymy tree below:

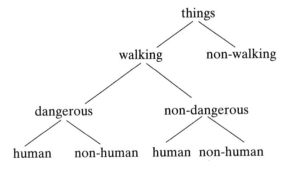

He can then look out of the window to see which of the objects in this *ad hoc* classification the object most resembles. This may then lead him to say something like 'No honey, it's not a man, it's a child' or 'a dog' or 'a teddy bear', so that he can exclude the [+ dangerous] component of meaning. Alternatively, if he wishes to scare his wife, he could say simply. 'No, honey, it's not a man', leaving open the possibility that the thing is, perhaps, a creature from Mars!

Eco's analysis gives us a way of analysing the flexibility of word meaning, and of describing the way in which our interpretation of meaning depends on both our knowledge of language and our knowledge of the world. In his own words: 'language is a flexible system of signification'. We still have not managed to give a framework that will allow us to systematize our knowledge of the world, though. Most linguists and philosophers would agree that this is an impossible task.

We can, however, take a view of human culture that has much in common with Eco's view of word meaning. The philosopher Quine gives an analysis of beliefs and their relation to language which fits in very well with this approach. Quine (1953; 1960) proposes that we share a tightly organized central set of beliefs and a more fuzzy periphery of beliefs. We have recourse to these beliefs when we draw inferences from what people say. Many of the conventions that we share about the meanings of words (their core meanings, for example, or the connotations that they have for us) are part of the central area of our 'world view'. Eco suggests that many of the superordinate terms that we use in our classifications of hyponyms (see Section 4.2) are central beliefs: they have been part of the world view of our culture for millennia, and as a result they are taken for granted as true, and are very resistant to change.

For Quine, our beliefs about the world are similarly part of an interwoven network of inferences or beliefs. It is possible for the central beliefs to change, but for this to happen radical social changes are necessary.

5 Writing systems

5.1 Introduction

Linguists have long demonstrated an ambiguous position with regard to the study of written and spoken language. Halliday (1987: 55–6) has remarked:

> One learnt in the first year of a linguistics course that speech was logically and historically prior to writing. The somewhat aggressive tone with which linguists often proclaimed this commitment did not endear them to educators, who sensed that it undermined their authority as guardians of literacy and felt threatened by a scale of values they did not understand, according to which English spelling was out of harmony with the facts of the English language – whereas for them it was the pronunciation that was out of step, being a distorted reflection of the reality which lay in writing.

When it comes to the analysis of the smaller linguistic units and lower levels of linguistic structure – such as phonetics and phonology – linguists have focused on spoken language. When it comes to larger structures – such as grammatical analysis – linguists have, despite the rhetoric of 'primacy of speech', reflected the dominant cultural values of the modern age and studied almost exclusively written forms of language. This asymmetry is only recently becoming addressed, with studies of the grammatical structures of spoken language, on the one hand, and more detailed studies of the materiality of written texts, on the other.

Figure 5.1 Letter from an Ojibwa girl to her lover

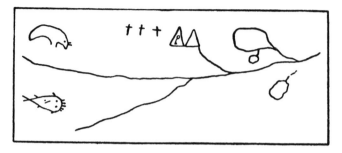

Source: Reproduced in Gelb (1963)

5.2 The development of writing systems

The notion of 'the primacy of speech' which Halliday refers to is the idea that speech is the primary medium of linguistic expression – both in the sense that it evolved long before writing, and in the sense that children learn how to talk before they learn how to write. However, the ways in which humans first learned to communicate with each other – by sounds and gestures – were ephemeral. There was no way of recording communications for archive purposes, or for transmitting messages to a person who was out of sight or earshot. It is easy to see why alternative ways were sought to inscribe messages in a more permanent form.

A variety of techniques were used in early times to convey messages at a distance. Such implements as notched message sticks, or knotted cords, were used in many parts of the world as a mnemonic device to help a messenger remember important details of the message being carried. These message devices were essentially **numerical** in nature.

The earliest known written messages of a more explicit kind were **pictographic**. That is, they sought to convey their meaning through the use of drawings in much the same way as a modern cartoon. Thus the picture might conjure up a whole sentence or linked ideas in the reader's mind. Figure 5.1 shows a letter sent in the nineteenth century by a North American Indian girl which is predominantly of this kind. You may well find it difficult to work out exactly what the letter meant, since you do not share the writer's cultural background or the recipient's expectations. This is how it was interpreted by a contemporary American ethnologist, Garnik Mallery (cited in Gelb 1963: 31):

> a letter written by an Ojibwa girl to a favoured lover, requesting him to call at her lodge. The girl is represented by the bear totem, the boy by that of the mud puppy. The trail leads toward the lakes, shown by the three irregular circles, whence it branches off in the direction of the two tents. Three Christian girls, indicated by the crosses, are

encamped there. From one of the tents protrudes the arm of the girl inviting the Indian boy to call on her.

Apart from the cartoon, this kind of pictograph has modern counterparts in illustrated maps or in certain international road signs – such as the one for 'quayside or river bank' which depicts a car falling from a solid surface into water. Although clearly representational, they embody certain conventions and assumptions about how a message is to be read.

Pictographic writing systems, like message sticks and knotted cords, act as mnemonics which help carrier and recipient to remember the message. They also form some kind of assurance that the message which a messenger bears is authentic – the story must at least fit the marks or pictures. One form of North American picture writing is the **wampum belt**: a means of creating pictures by threading coloured beads which are then woven into the shape of a belt. Such artefacts were used for recording important historical events, but could lead to problems of interpretation:

> An American 'wampum' belt records a treaty between William Penn and Indians by showing the figures of two men clasping hands. It shows that one of the men was European by his wearing of a hat. But there is no further indication of their identity, nor of any of the details of the agreement. Clearly the meaning of such a record is lost for ever when once it is forgotten. A French explorer, Capt. Cadillac, reported in 1703 that an Indian chief told him that his tribe had a wampum collar, which they had received from the Iroquois, but that 'the old men had forgotten what it said'. Normally a disaster of this sort was prevented by taking certain precautions. The belts of a tribe were kept together, in a kind of Record Office, under the charge of a 'Keeper of the Wampum' who possessed a good memory. At regular seasons the tribemen would meet, and then pass round the belts from hand to hand, at the same time all repeating aloud the official version of the event which each recorded.
>
> (Moorhouse 1946: 56)

The social practices described by Moorhouse serve various purposes: they keep alive and circulate the knowledge, but they also ensure that a single authoritative interpretation endures, since everyone participates in and witnesses the event. It may seem that the inexplicitness of such early writing and recording systems makes them very different from modern texts, but it is important to remember that no text (despite frequent claims to the contrary) is fully explicit, encoding every aspect of meaning which is conveyed. People still need to use experience, general world knowledge and reasoning when they interpret texts, as we show in Chapter 7.

Ancient writing systems seem to have developed from systems of pictographs by associating stylized drawings with particular words in the writer's language. Certainly, this is what seems to have happened during the development of the oldest known writing system, **Sumerian cuneiform**,

Figure 5.2 Development from pictogram to wedge symbol in Sumerian cuneiform

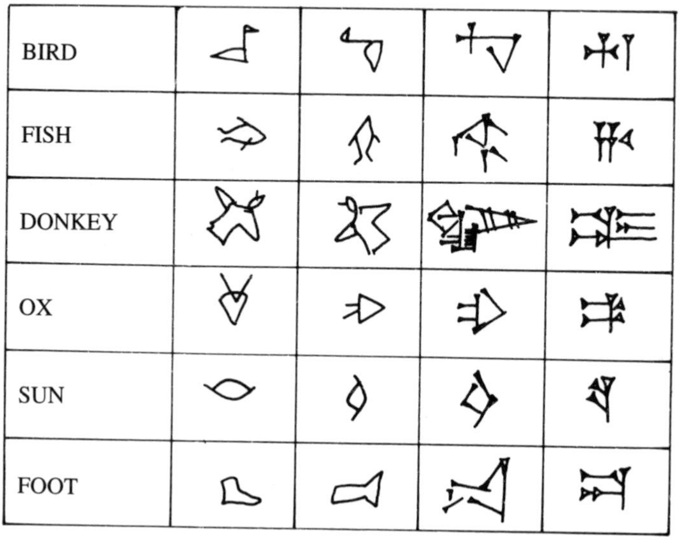

which appeared in southern Mesopotamia towards the end of the fourth millennium BC. Pictographs became more stylized, streamlined, and hence more suited to inscribing on the clay tablets then used. The writing system is called **cuneiform** (from the Latin for 'wedge shape') because of the shape which the signs then acquired (Figures 5.2 and 5.3).

The meaning of the signs also changed as the writing system developed. The writing system was at first a **logographic** one – that is, a single sign denoted a single word – but this had the disadvantage that a new sign had to be learned and remembered for every word in the language. This was obviously not an insuperable problem, however. Indeed, there is at least one major world language – Chinese – whose writing system is still basically logographic in character. (Japanese, which has a mixed script, also uses many logographs borrowed and adapted from the Chinese.) Some of the logographs are highly stylized pictographs. For example, we find not only 木 for a tree but also 林 for a wood and 森 for a forest. It is not difficult to imagine how a picture of a tree gradually turned into the symbol for a tree. But if we give the tree some roots, it becomes 本 which originally meant literally 'a root' but has now come to mean 'origin' or, by extension, 'book' (the source of knowledge). As any reader of Chinese or Japanese will tell you, this is a very simple example. Some complex characters are very metaphorical indeed! But they have the advantage – in a vast country like China, which has a variety of spoken languages – of

Figure 5.3 Fully developed cuneiform found at the Palace of Assourhazirtal, Iraq

being directly comprehensible, without representing the spoken form of any particular language. In principle, if you can understand Chinese script, you can read the words aloud in English or Urdu or whatever spoken language you please. (Naturally, a full understanding of idioms would require greater familiarity with the culture and forms of expression common in specific languages.)

Two kinds of writing system superseded the logographies in most parts of the world: **syllabaries** and **alphabets**. It is believed that an intermediate stage in the transition from logography to syllabary may have been the adoption of **rebus** (Latin for 'by things') principle. This allowed a sign to stand for not only the word it was originally intended to depict, but also for any other **homophone** (a word which is pronounced in the same way).

Thus 👁 might stand not only for 'eye' but also for 'aye' and 'I'; 🐝 not only for 'bee' but also for 'be'. Moreover, monosyllabic symbols could be combined to form polysyllabic words such as 👁 🦌 = eye + deer = 'idea' or 🐝 🍃 = bee + leaf = 'belief'. This represented a fundamental break with the previous principle of a semantic link, however tenuous, between the picture and the word. (It is totally different, for example, from the process at work in the development of Chinese logographs.)

There are still a number of extant syllabaries, notably the **hiragana** and **katakana** scripts used for writing Japanese, which has a very regular syllable structure. They did not prove appropriate for all languages, however, especially those (like English) where syllable structure is more complicated.

The Sumerian cuneiform was not the only writing system used in the ancient world. Although the first to appear, it was soon joined by a number of other more or less independent systems, such as the **hieroglyphics** used in Ancient Egypt. Many of these rival scripts seemed to have developed from a logographic to a syllabic system. But it was not until the ancient Greeks borrowed and modified a Semitic syllabic script that a true alphabetic system was devised. Alphabets require even fewer symbols than syllabaries by using – in an ideal system – only one symbol for each single sound. Most of the world's writing systems are now alphabetic, although there are considerable differences in the shape of the symbols used in different alphabets.

Early writing systems were **nonlinear**. That is, they used the space available in all dimensions, so that the composition of the whole was like a picture or diagram which contained a number of elements. As the pictograms became more stylized, so writing became more linear, and the symbols were strung together in a continuous line. Some of the oldest known examples are actually called **Linear A** and **Linear B**. The linearity might be expressed in various directions, however. Many modern writing systems run from left to right, and from top to bottom on the page, but this is by no means universal. Some forms of ancient Greek, and even some Old English runic inscriptions (see below), employed a bi-directional system similar to the motion of the print head on many computer printers. That is, the writing would run from left to right on one line, then right to left on the next. Sometimes the characters themselves would be reversed, or just the order of the symbols. Such a system is known as **boustrophedon** – from a Greek expression which likens the pattern to that of an ox ploughing a field.

> Some writing systems were what is called boustrophedon
> no tfel ot thgir dna thgir ot tfel morf nar yeht si taht
> successive lines just as an ox turns on a ploughed field.

The evolution of the world's writing systems thus seems to have followed a broadly similar pattern, as shown in Figure 5.4. This may misleadingly suggest, however, that alphabets are inherently superior to other systems, and that they will serve the needs of a literate society better. This is not altogether true. English, for example, makes use of an alphabet, but diverges in many ways from a strict alphabetic principle in the ways it spells words. As Section 5.3 explains, most alphabetic systems are mixed ones, and incorporate some logographic features. What counts as an optimal writing system will very much depend on the structure and internal variety of a given language. There is reason to believe, however, that most systems which work efficiently are mixed ones.

5.3 The pattern of English spelling

If a writing system closely mirrors the spoken word, then differences in written forms will indicate differences in pronunciation and language usage, but anyone familiar with English **orthography** (its spelling system) will know that this is not always the case. Many teachers and learners of English have complained that English spelling seems hopelessly unsystematic. George Bernard Shaw – an ardent supporter of spelling reform – once claimed that it would be quite possible for the word *fish* to be spelled 'ghoti'. His reasoning is given below:

gh as in 'rou*gh*'
o as in 'w*o*men'
ti as in 'na*ti*on'

Shaw was, of course, quite wrong – or, at least, he was being mischievous. The absurdity of his suggestion comes precisely from the fact that we realize that English spelling does not allow such a representation, although we may not be quite able to put our finger on why.

English spelling today can be regarded as containing a number of conventions and systems for representing sounds. Many of these have arisen for historical reasons. In this section, I look briefly at the historical background and then outline several of the subsystems or principles which are inherent in modern English spelling.

Figure 5.4 The development of writing systems

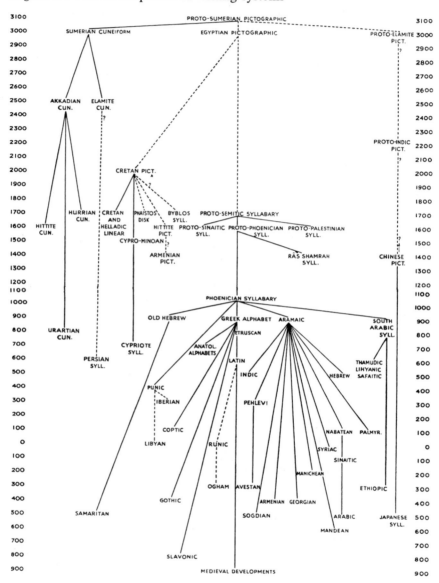

Source: Gelb (1963)

Historical background

The oldest preserved inscriptions in English date from the early eighth century and, like Scandinavian inscriptions at that time, used the **futhorc**, or **runic** alphabet which was based on an early Roman one, modified to make it more suitable for inscribing on stone or grained surfaces with an axe. The manuscript alphabet used in later Old English was not a direct development from the runic, though it retained one or two extra symbols, such as þ (thorn) and ð (eth).

By the end of the eleventh century, Old English spelling had become very close to being **phonemic** (see Chapter 2), and there was considerable agreement between scribes in various parts of England about the conventions to be employed, but this situation changed dramatically during the Middle Ages. The scribes who copied the works of Chaucer, Lydgate or the Gawain poet seemed to spell words in various ways, often spelling the same word differently on the same page. English spelling became destabilized during this period for several reasons. Most scribes were trained in French and Latin, which used rather different conventions for representing sounds, and they often used these conventions when copying or writing in English. (Hence þ became *th*.) There was very little original material being produced in English – most official documents were in French and Latin. Hence it was difficult to maintain a proper tradition of English spelling. The very stability of the Old English spelling system contributed to its own undoing. The pronunciation of English was undergoing great changes, partly as a result of contact with French. This meant that fixed spellings were becoming less and less accurate as representations of speech.

Under these various pressures, medieval scribes began to spell words roughly as they pronounced them in their varied dialects, and according to a variety of conventions. A number of other minor considerations also influenced scribal practice. One was the way certain spellings were modified to make words more legible in particular forms of handwriting. One common practice was to avoid the use of *u* when it was followed by *m* or *n* as this gave rise to a long series of identical vertical strokes, making it difficult to distinguish the individual letters. The problem was simply solved by closing the top of the *u* to make it like an *o*. To this habit we owe modern-day spellings like *son* and *some*. But perhaps the most extraordinary practice was the habit of many lawyers' clerks to add superfluous letters in order to make words longer, because their work was paid for by the inch.

It was not until the advent of printing, that real attempts at recodifying English spelling were made, but the trend to fix English spelling by Caxton and his successors had a somewhat similar result to the fixing in Old English times. That is, the pronunciation of English continued to change – indeed some dramatic changes to the vowel system have occurred since Caxton's period – but the spelling remained static. For this reason, many English spellings reflect a medieval pronunciation better than a modern one. English 'writing retains a regretful memory of its earlier days' (Bradley 1913).

The lack of regularity in spelling was a continual source of grievance to learned men, many of whom tried to reform the system. One of the first was John Hart who, in 1569, published *An orthographic containing the due order and reason how to write or painte the image of Manne's voice, most like to the life or nature*. Hart argued strongly that 'the writing should have so many letters as the pronunciation neadeth of voices and no more or less'. Little impact was made, however, by either Hart or his contemporaries. A century later, Bishop Wilkins in his *Essay towards a real Character and a Philosophical Language* (1668) admitted that 'so invariable is custom, that we still retain the same errors and incongruities in writing, which our forefathers taught us'.

Indeed, some attempts at reform merely made matters worse. Further confusion arose from the over-enthusiastic attempts at respelling certain words by learned Renaissance men, who wished to make words look like their supposed classical origins. *Debt* and *subtle* acquired their *b* through this means, in spite of the fact that it is not pronounced to this day. Such respellings were more extensive than might appear – in many cases the word has since changed pronunciation in order to conform to its new spelling. Hence the *l* in words like *false* and *fault* is now pronounced. Ironically, those who attempted to straighten out the spelling system were largely thwarted by the growing demand for fixing and codifying the language and ascertaining a 'correct' form which would last for all time. The eighteenth century was a period in which England narrowly avoided the setting up of an Academy (like the Académie française) – much to the disappointment of literary figures such as Jonathan Swift. In such a context, little sympathy was found for people who wanted to meddle further with the system.

Attempts at reform have continued, however, in both Britain and the United States. One of the most recent occurred in 1949 when Sir James Pitman and Mr Mont Follick introduced a private member's Bill in the British House of Commons. This measure failed (by a narrow margin) but a revised and more modest proposal in 1953, The Simplified Spelling Bill – which promoted a new orthography suitable for use in schools – was successful. The new simplified spelling was called *Augmented Roman* – it later became known as the *Initial Teaching Alphabet* (i.t.a.).

The structure of modern English orthography

The history of English spelling may help explain some of the features we find today, but it does not provide a proper basis for describing present-day English orthography. People today are, by and large, unaware of the etymological origins of words and of medieval scribal practices. For modern users, therefore, the orthography has a particular structure which can be described entirely in its own terms.

Nearly all the complaints made through the ages about English spelling have been to the effect that it departs radically from a phonemic principle. A simple representation of speech is seen as being the optimal writing system. This, however, is probably short-sighted. It is a mistake to think that writing should necessarily reflect speech. This point has always been made, from the Middle Ages onwards, but has been very much a minority view:

> Many of the advocates of spelling reform are in the habit of asserting, as if it were an axiom admitting of no dispute, that the sole function of writing is to represent sounds. It appears to me that this is one of those spurious truisms that are not intelligently believed by any one, but which continue to be repeated because nobody takes the trouble to consider what they really mean.
>
> (Bradley 1913: 1)

The historical discussion above has highlighted a basic dilemma with writing systems. Adherence to strict phonemic principles will mean that the spelling of words will necessarily change as the language changes, and spelling will vary according to the dialect of the speaker. On the other hand, a fixed spelling system, however regular it is at first, causes a gradual change in the way spelling relates to sound. Furthermore, speakers of different dialects will have to use different sets of correspondence rules to map pronunciation on to written forms. Where one has variety in language (whether socially, geograhically or historically) one must also have either variety in spelling *or* variety in the correspondence rules which relate sound to spelling. Hence one drawback with a strictly phonemic writing system is that it can only represent *one* variety of a language, and disenfranchises readers and writers who do not speak the chosen form. A further problem with too literal a representation of pronunciation is that it may not be the most suitable system for rapid and efficient reading. Psychologists have shown that readers process words broadly in two ways. When their eye falls upon a word, they may form a mental representation of its pronunciation and use this to locate the meaning of the word in their mind. It has been shown that words which are spelled regularly are processed faster than irregularly spelled ones. Very fast and fluent readers, however, and nearly everyone when confronted by a very familiar word, use a different strategy. The whole word will be recognized as a single entity from its orthographic shape, and its meaning located without the intermediate process involving pronunciation. This strategy has been shown to be faster and more efficient. It could be argued, then, that the optimal writing system is one which maintains a distinct and easily recognizable visual shape to words, even at the cost of irregularity in spelling.

For whatever reasons, it is very common for alphabetic writing systems to depart from strict phonemic principles and become systems which are patterned visually. This, then, is a key to understanding the structure of English spelling today. It is partly based on representations of pronunciation, and partly based on graphic regularities.

Representation of sound

An ideal phonemic alphabet would contain one symbol for each phoneme in the language. There are, however, around 44 phonemes in English (the exact number varies from variety to variety) and only 26 letters in the currently used alphabet. Clearly, then, the spelling system must incorporate a more complex way of relating spellings to sounds than on the basis of one symbol, one sound. These relationships are described in terms of **grapheme to phoneme correspondence rules**. Whole books (see, for example, Venezky 1970) have been devoted to the analysis of such rules, but the basic principles are easily described.

1 Certain new symbols can be constructed by putting together two of the existing ones. This forms a **digraph** such as *th* or *ch*, which are used to represent single phonemes. This may lead to a minor problem, since readers need to distinguish between the digraph and the sequence, for example, of *t* and *h* (as in *lighthouse*), but these confusions rarely occur, and it is usually possible to recognize them on other grounds – such as the fact they occur over a **morpheme boundary**.
2 One symbol may be used to represent more than one phoneme. For example, *th* variously represents [ð] (as in *th*is) and [θ] (as in *th*eatre).
3 One symbol is made to represent more than one phoneme, but exactly *which* phoneme will depend on the context of other letters. One of the most familiar examples of this is the so-called 'magic *e*' which influences the quality of a preceding vowel, but which is not sounded itself. Examples are *pane* versus *pan*, or *pine* versus *pin*.

This last principle is the most widespread of all in English, and most of the attempts at describing the correspondence rules have been devoted to identifying the different contexts and sequences which affect the way letters represent sounds. It can be shown through such studies that, although the correspondence rules for English spelling are extremely complex (partly because of the variety of historical changes in pronunciation which created them), they do at least exist. There is also some evidence that although people are not consciously aware of them, they may make use of such knowledge when reading (Smith and Baker 1976).

For example, if we return to Shaw's problem with the word 'ghoti', we can rapidly establish that very few words indeed begin with this sequence of letters in English. Furthermore, initial *gh* sequences are never pronounced as /f/. The correspondence between *o* and /ɪ/ is also extremely rare. Since it results from the medieval scribal practice mentioned above, it could not occur before *t*, but only before *m* or *n*. Lastly, the correspondence between *ti* and /ʃ/ is also contextually determined, and only occurs in certain places where *ti* begins a syllable. In fact, it might be better to think of the whole unit *-tion* = /ʃən/ as a frequent but indivisible sequence.

Context-sensitive correspondence rules, such as these, may not always guarantee a single possible pronunciation. They will, however, usually limit the possibilities to two or three, of which one will be by far the commonest.

Graphic representations

It could be claimed that an ideal writing system should not focus exclusively on phonemes, but should preserve intact higher-level linguistic units. This is, in fact, an important principle in English spelling and it often resolves apparent difficulties in grapheme to phoneme correspondences.

One important higher-level unit is the **morpheme.** The plural morpheme in English is variously pronounced as /s/, /z/ or /ɪz/ (as in *cats and dogs and houses*), but the spelling ignores this alternation and always uses -*s*. Words like *sign* and *signal* or *medicine* and *medical* retain the shape of their shared stem morpheme, which would be obscured by a strictly phonemic system.

In some respects, the English writing system incorporates a logographic principle. We have already mentioned the fact that some words are processed as single units by readers (i.e. as logographs), but there are a number of words in English, often very common ones, where there is no attempt to represent pronunciation. Examples are abbreviations such as *Mrs* or *St* which in the house style of many publishers (including the one which published this book) are not even given a full stop. There are also some words which are so irregular that they can be treated as logographs (e.g. *yacht*).

Conclusion

The English spelling system is not by any means transparent in the way it operates, but it contains a great deal more structure and regularity than might be supposed. Some linguists (Chomsky and Halle 1968) have deemed it as near-optimal in the way it represents underlying linguistic regularities rather than superficial ones. This seems perhaps an overstatement of the case. Nevertheless, English spelling represents a balance between the various competing demands which any writing system must satisfy, and the solutions which have been found are common in other languages. As Stubbs (1980: 49) observes:

> All alphabetic systems which have evolved naturally are mixed systems which involve compromises between phoneme–grapheme correspondence and the correspondence of graphemes to higher morphological and syntactic levels. There must be powerful reasons why the end point of the development of writing systems in the five or six thousand years or so since true writing was invented, and over the many languages to which it has been applied, is alphabetic systems with an admixture of morphological and/or syntactic information.

6 Face-to-face interaction

6.1 Introduction

This chapter is concerned with various aspects of spontaneous communication in face-to-face interaction. Ordinary conversation, by its very nature, is extremely *ad hoc*, but people send out and receive an immense amount of systematic non-verbal information. Some of this is quite independent of what is being said, but much is in support of it and helps the smooth flow of conversation.

Section 6.2 reviews the research literature on non-verbal behaviour. This literature is surprisingly vast, but rather fragmented. Here we restrict ourselves to an overview of the basic areas and functions of non-verbal communication.

Section 6.3 examines various aspects of the 'management' of spontaneous talk – which might be described as how to get a word in edgeways without interrupting. The detailed mechanism which allows people to synchronize their turns is examined, together with the ways in which turns are allocated to different speakers.

Section 6.4 provides a practical introduction to methods of transcribing spontaneous talk – in preparation for the kinds of analysis described in Chapter 7.

6.2 Non-verbal communication

Non-verbal communication (often abbreviated to NVC) includes all means of human communication *other* than words (in fact, other than what we conventionally regard as language). We include the topic in this book because NVC is often intimately bound up with spoken language – our understanding of face-to-face conversation, for instance, may be impoverished if we do not take account of the non-verbal component. Despite its importance, the literature on NVC is rather fragmented and results from research are sometimes inconclusive – even contradictory. Our survey here covers some of the more important functions of NVC in interpersonal interaction and looks at interpretations that may be made of different non-verbal signs. It does not, however, attempt to impose a consensus in those areas where none exists.

When looking at the contribution of non-verbal systems of communication to the meaning of an interaction it is difficult to know where to stop. Clothing, for example, is relevant and may combine with posture, patterns of eye contact and verbal language to convey social meanings about speakers and the relationships between them. But what of other non-verbal signs such as the layout of a room? (For instance, the way the chairs are arranged around a committee room table). Such features have been traditionally regarded as a part of the context of an interaction in analyses that privilege the verbal component, but the distinction between verbal language and context is not always straightforward, as we have already seen in earlier chapters.

In this section we restrict ourselves to a consideration of people's non-verbal behaviour – mainly body movement – which is closely associated with speech in face-to-face communication. NVC, in this sense, performs three rather different communicative functions. First, it can communicate quite specific meanings through the use of conventional gestures and movement. Second, it serves as a complex channel of communication which enables people to let others know their emotional disposition. Information from either kind of non-verbal behaviour may be duplicated by the spoken channel (as when someone smiles and says *Hello* or pulls a face and says *Ooh no, I don't like that*) but such messages may, in principle, stand on their own. Third, NVC may play an important supporting role in speech – it helps speakers coordinate their turns, for example, or allows speakers to add emphasis (as when the preacher thumps the pulpit at a shaky point). This third function of NVC is dealt with more fully in Section 6.3.

If we restrict the term non-verbal communication to those aspects of body movement which have been shown to carry meaning, we can identify six areas of specific interest: gesture; proxemics; body contact; posture and body orientation; facial expression; and gaze.

Gesture

Gesture, is perhaps the most obvious and familiar way in which people convey meanings without using words. Morris *et al.* (1979) made an intensive study of 20 ritual gestures which are used in various parts of Europe, often with different meanings. For example, the V-sign (made with the palm facing inwards towards the signer) forms an obscene gesture in Britain, but is taken elsewhere to be a sign of victory. Such gestures are made intentionally and apparently with specific meanings. Like words in verbal language, their meanings are essentially arbitrary and symbolic (Morris *et al.* 1979: xvii):

If a man taps his temple with the tip of his forefinger, it can mean one of two things, either 'crazy' or 'intelligent' – two opposing meanings, but both relevant to this particular gesture. There is no mimicry involved. A simple hand action stands for – symbolizes – an abstract quality – craziness or intelligence. In a culture where this particular symbolic convention is totally absent, the gesture might well be meaningless.

This rather simple view of the relationship between gestures contrasts with that presented in less popular research literature. A hand salute, for example, might be regarded as a symbolic gesture with a well-defined meaning, but Birdwhistell (1970: 119) argued that it was far more complex a phenomenon than this view allows:

> Although they [gestures] have an apparent unitary and discrete quality, they prove consistently to carry the instruction to look elsewhere in the body behavioral stream for their modification or interpretation. A salute, for example, depending on the integrally associated total body or facial behavior, may convey a range of messages from ridicule and rebellion to subservience or respect.

Birdwhistell favoured a close analogy between the way gestures worked and the way spoken language worked. A small number of movement types combined to form larger structural units (Birdwhistell 1970: 119):

> Gestures are forms which are incapable of standing alone – except of course, where the structural context is provided by the questioner. Just as there is no 'cept' in isolation in American English, an informant may be taught how to produce it together with pre- or con- and -tion.

Not all gestures have such clear intentional status, but they may have communicative significance nevertheless. People often gesture with their hands when talking – even when on the telephone. Such movements may be mannered rhetorical devices (see Figure 6.1) or they may be less obtrusive and spontaneous gestures. In each case, the function is the same – to add emphasis and help identify the structural units of utterances in much the same way as intonation or stress in the spoken channel.

Schegloff (1984) observed that 'Hand gesturing is largely, if not entirely, a speaker's phenomenon'. That is, people listening tend not to gesture with their hands. 'This close relationship between speakership and gesturing with the hands does not extend in quite the same way to other gesturing body parts, like the head' (Schegloff 1984: 273). Schegloff demonstrated that the timing of gestures was intimately synchronized with the spoken delivery, a fact which has been repeatedly observed by researchers in nonverbal behaviour.

The various kinds of gesture which we have identified here have been classified in many different ways by different authors, but most distinguish

Figure 6.1 Victorian recommendations for rhetorical gestures

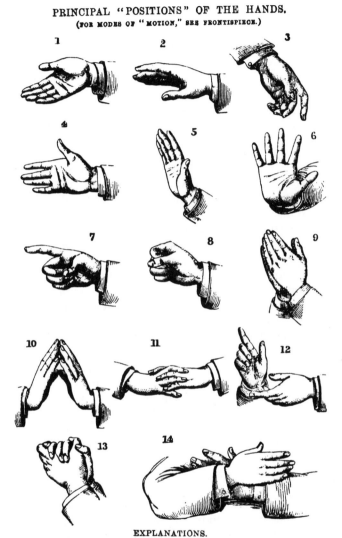

PRINCIPAL "POSITIONS" OF THE HANDS.
(FOR MODES OF "MOTION," SEE FRONTISPIECE.)

EXPLANATIONS.
1. Simple affirmation.   2. Emphatic declaration.   3. Apathy or prostration.
4. Energetic appeal.   5. Negation or denial.   6. Violent repulsion.   7. Indexing
or cautioning.   8. Determination or anger.   9. Supplication.   10. Gentle entreaty.
11. Carelessness.   12. Argumentativeness.   13. Earnest entreaty.   14. Resignation.

Source: Bell and Bell (1892)

between those which seem relatively autonomous from speech and those which support speech. Salutes and V-signs belong to the first category and depend on an observer's construing the gesture as a deliberate communicative act. Speech-supportive gestures seem to depend less on intentionality for their communicative function.

Proxemics

The term **proxemics** was first used by the anthropologist, E.T. Hall, to describe the way people use and interpret physical distance when they interact. Certain distances, within a given culture or sub-culture, are appropriate for certain activities, and a movement from one zone to another will be interpreted as an attempt to change the nature of the interaction. Hall (1963) described the North American proxemic system as embracing four major positions, each with a 'close' and a 'far' subdivision (see Figure 6.2). The most distant was the *public* (12 ft. upwards from hearers) and the nearest *intimate* (from full body contact to around 18 in.). In practice, the two most commonly used distances were *social-consultative* (close being 4–7 ft.: far being 7–12 ft.) and *casual-personal* (close is 18–30 in.; far is 30–48 in.). While people's behaviour may not conform neatly to these zones, it certainly seems to be the case that interactants can be extremely sensitive to distance as an indicator of intimacy or threat. It also seems true that the significance of distance is culturally variable. Hall claimed that the distance at which many Arabs feel comfortable at conducting business may be felt by Americans as invasive and uncomfortably intimate. Distances adopted by people depend also on many contextual factors. Sommer (1962) found that people stood closer together in large rooms than they did in small rooms. Different people also seem to require different amounts of personal space. Male pairs seem to interact at greater distances in Britain and America than female pairs, for example (Addis 1966). Big people seem to need more personal space than small people.

Body contact (haptics)

Body contact includes both intentional and unintentional touching of various kinds. To some extent, body contact is related to proximity – one can only touch if one is within close enough range of the other person – and the significance of certain proximities may derive, in part, from the potential each affords for certain kinds of body contact.

Touching may either occur accidentally, as when one brushes against another person in a queue, or it may be an intentional and perhaps conventional gesture, as when one shakes hands. In many instances, however, it is less clear quite what the status of a touch is. It has been found, however, that people do not have to be even conscious that touch has occurred in order to be affected by it. Fisher *et al.* (1976) showed that women, in particular, responded more warmly and positively to a library

Figure 6.2 Hall's analysis of proxemic distances for white North Americans

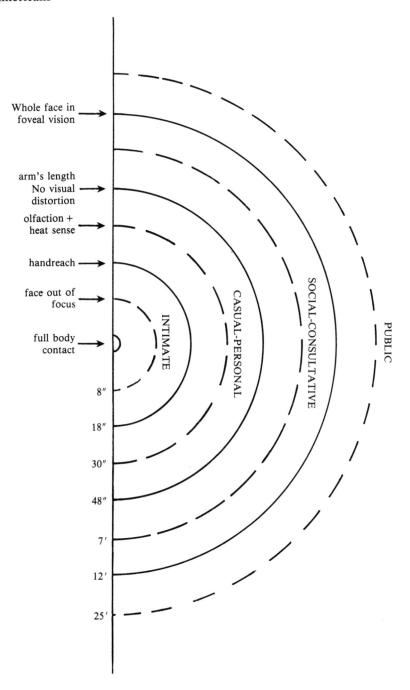

assistant who made hand contact when returning a library card even if they reported being unaware that a touch had occurred.

The amount of touching that can be seen going on in public varies greatly from culture to culture. Jourard (1966) reported observing around 110 touches per hour in Paris, as opposed to none at all in London, and around 2 per hour in the United States. There are also big differences within a culture between the amount of touching which different people give and receive. Several researchers have attempted to explain this in terms of differential status and power. Henley (1973) studied over 60 hours of observations made in public places in Baltimore, examining the socio-economic status, sex, age and race of those involved. She concluded that 'touch may be regarded as a non-verbal equivalent of calling another by first name, that is, used reciprocally it indicates solidarity: when non-reciprocal, it indicates status' (Henley 1973: 93). Overall, the results seemed to support the hypothesis that 'touching is a status variable, with higher status persons having touch "privilege" over lower status persons'. A part of Henley's argument was that women, who received more touch from men than they themselves gave to men, were thereby interactionally placed in a subordinate position to men.

Stier and Hall (1984) were not so impressed with these conclusions when they reviewed 43 studies of touch behaviour. They found no great evidence that men really did initiate touches more frequently than women and, furthermore, the thesis that powerful people initiate touch more than unpowerful people may itself be in doubt: 'at times, the initiation of touch may be more important, and more common, in the less powerful'. Stier and Hall did, however, make the interesting observation that people's beliefs and perceptions may run contrary to observed facts. A number of studies have shown that people really believe that men initiate touch in opposite-gender interactions more than vice versa. This seems, at the very least, to demonstrate that touch is regarded as salient in status and solidarity relationships.

There are several ways of explaining these equivocal results. One is that the meaning of a particular gesture cannot be fully determined without reference to the larger context in which it occurred. It is a commonplace in communication studies that precisely the same gesture or sign will be given different significances in different contexts of use. It is therefore quite possible for touch behaviour to be implicated in the communication of power relationships in spite of the apparently contradictory nature of some of the evidence, simply because very few studies have attempted to distinguish between different contexts of use.

A second reason may simply be that in many of these studies no great attention was paid to the precise *kind* of touch which was involved. Nguyen *et al.* (1975) distinguished between four kinds of touch: a pat; a squeeze; a brush (possibly accidental); and a stroke. They found that a pat was regarded as the most playful and friendly by both men and women, while the stroke was rated most 'loving, sexual and pleasant'. However, subjects also took into account *where* the touch was directed in addition to *how* it was performed, though the relative importance of each seemed to vary. The authors concluded (Nguyen *et al.* 1975: 97): 'subjects relied more on the mode than on the location of a touch to determine how pleasant, playful, and warm/loving a touch was, but they relied more on location to determine whether or not it conveyed sexual desire and friendship/fellowship'. In addition, there seemed to be some evidence that men were, on the whole, rather more attuned to the *kind* of touch involved, whereas women were slightly more concerned with *where* the touch occurred.

Posture and body orientation

The way people hold themselves, how they sit or stand, has long been understood as evidence of their innermost feelings and the state of their relationships with others. Some researchers have attempted to isolate particular postural behaviours, such as direction of lean when seated or openness of arm and leg positions, and assign to them particular interpretations. Scheflen (1964) commented: 'such [postural] behaviors occur in characteristic, standard configurations, whose common recognisability is the basis of their value in communication'. Such postures were, he claimed, governed by rules which determined where and when they could occur: 'a posture such as sitting back in a chair rarely occurs in subordinate males who are engaged in selling an idea to a male of higher status'. Scheflen was keen to establish a parallel between the workings of a supposed 'vocabulary' of postures and verbal language. The repertoire of postures varied from one part of the community to another, and thus identified a person's group membership rather like a dialect. All members of the culture, however, would recognize the various categories of posture being displayed, even if the exact manner of the display varied.

The idea that particular postures can be isolated in this way is an attractive one, but the results of approaches based on this premise have not been very conclusive. Such models are still appealed to in social skills training, however, where patients or clients may be taught to adopt certain postures at certain moments in an interaction in order to gain control or to signal certain meanings.

Probably more important are rather general features of tenseness and relaxation in posture. Mehrabian (1969) concluded that people were most relaxed in the presence of someone of inferior status, and most tense when facing a superior. It remains an interesting question whether such postures reflect a person's anxiety or stress or whether they form part of conventional ways of signalling attention and status.

POSTURAL ORIENTATION

Postural orientation seems to be one exception to this general rule in that specific behavioural changes can be shown to have particular communicative values. At one extreme, people will 'turn their backs' on a person with whom they wish to avoid interaction. People working co-operatively – whether on a joint task or supporting each other in a group discussion – will often be found side by side. An angle of 90 degrees is found by most people to be the most comfortable for casual but friendly interaction. Face-to-face orientations often indicate some more earnest discourse, perhaps between a doctor and patient or between lovers, according to Scheflen (1964).

POSTURAL CONGRUENCE

It has often been observed that when people interact they will fall into postures which are the same or mirror images of each other. If one person in a group leans back, then it is likely that some other member will, without realizing it, move to adopt the same posture. Scheflen (1964: 241) termed this **postural congruence**:

> Since an individual in a given culture can only sit in a limited number of postures, one immediately wonders whether postural congruence is purely coincidental. But even a very few continued observations of a group quickly end any theory of coincidence. Two, four, even six people often sit in postural congruence. When one member of a congruent set shifts posture the others quickly follow suit, so that the congruence is maintained through repeated changes of body positioning.

Congruence, Scheflen argued, often showed who was allied to whom in discussions, even when this was not apparent in what they were saying. Or old friends may shift into congruence when temporarily arguing as if to confirm the ultimate continuity of their relationship. Congruence is also often a sign of peer status (Scheflen 1964: 241):

> When some member of an alliance differs markedly in social status from the others, he may maintain a posture which is quite unlike that of the others . . . In doctor–patient, parent–child or teacher–student reciprocals, where it is important to indicate different status, congruence is unlikely to occur.

A strenuous validation of these findings was undertaken by Beattie and Beattie (1981) who spent five hours a day for a fortnight on a beach on the French Riviera. Observations were made every five seconds of the postural positions of couples lying on the beach. The researchers found that male–female couples spent more than half the time in congruent positions. They concluded (Beattie and Beattie 1981: 51): 'This study has shown conclusively that postural congruence in a naturalistic setting is a very real, common phenomenon, and is not simply the result of the chance coincidence of the relatively small number of postures normally displayed by individuals.'

Figure 6.3 Body movement markers of American syntactic sentences

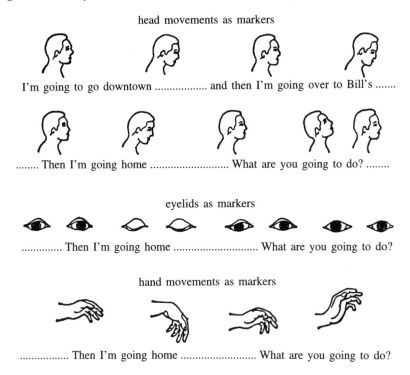

Source: Scheflen (1964)

POSTURAL SHIFTS

It might be thought that a person would shift posture on a fairly random basis, perhaps when feeling uncomfortable or just bored. Scheflen (1964) suggested that posture shifting was far more regular than this and was used to mark important boundary points in an interaction. For example, syntactic boundaries (ends of sentences) were marked by small head movements and gestures, as can be seen in Figure 6.3. A rather larger shift in head posture marked the completion of each point being made in discussion (Scheflen 1964: 231):

> When an American speaker uses a series of syntactic sentences in a conversation, he changes the position of his head and eyes every few sentences. He may turn his head right or left, tilt it, cock it to one side or the other, or flex or extend his neck so as to look toward the floor or ceiling. Regardless of the kind of shift in head posture, the attitude is held for a few sentences, then shifted to another position. Each of these shifts I believe marks the end of a structural unit at the next level higher than the syntactic sentence.

A number of such points might be made in support of what Scheflen termed a 'position'. A shift of gross body position marked the boundaries of such episodes in the interaction.

Facial expression

'As a part of our primate heritage', one researcher observed, '*Homo sapiens* has a mobile, labial visage with which to signal conspecifics' (Mackey 1976: 128). This statement alludes to the two most interesting issues in the poorly researched area of facial expression. The first is the extent to which our facial responses to emotional stimuli are innate and similar to animal behaviour (particularly that of primates). The second is the question of how expressions convey meaning to people. Behind the rather pompous statement lurks the possibility that more than a century of research in the area has yielded very few insights beyond the obvious fact that our faces are capable of betraying our feelings, but that nobody quite knows how it is done.

THE BIOLOGICAL BASIS OF FACIAL EXPRESSION

Darwin's important book, *The Expression of the Emotions in Man and Animals* (1872), was preceded by a couple of centuries of speculation by anatomists and physiognomists which Darwin summarily dismissed as worthless. His main thesis was that emotional displays by animals served various functions which aided species survival. It was therefore possible that certain displays were biologically programmed and subject to processes of natural selection in the same way as other behavioural dispositions which had survival value.

Much more recent research has lent some credence to Darwin's notion that the expression of emotion through facial posture is subject to less cultural variation than other kinds of non-verbal behaviour. Ekman *et al.* (1969) sifted through over 3000 photographs to obtain 'those which showed only the pure display of a single affect' and presented these to people in many cultures, literate and pre-literate, around the world. Each person was asked to identify the emotion being displayed, being allowed to choose from six basic categories: happiness, fear, disgust–contempt, anger, surprise, sadness. The results were sufficiently similar across cultures for the researchers to conclude (Ekman *et al.* 1969: 87) that 'our findings support Darwin's suggestion that facial expressions of emotion are similar among humans, regardless of culture, because of their evolutionary origins'.

THE CLASSIFICATION OF FACIAL EXPRESSION

Such studies beg many questions as to how such 'single emotions' can be identified and labelled. Emotions are rarely signalled by single facial gestures (such as raising an eyebrow or smiling) but by complex muscular responses which may be difficult to describe and analyse. Ekman *et al.* (1972: 1) suggest that 'man's facial muscles are sufficiently complex to allow more than a thousand different facial appearances'. Other authors have hazarded a guess that the figure is nearer 20 000 (Thompson 1973).

There have been two rather different traditions in attempts to describe and classify these possible expressions. The first has tried to isolate a few basic dimensions, such as 'pleasantness' or 'intensity'. Such dimensions are continuous variables which allow any one expression to be coded according to its score on each dimension. By and large, such attempts have met with failure, with different studies of people's reactions to photographs and video tapes arriving at different factors and different numbers of dimensions.

An alternative, and perhaps more obvious, approach has been the establishment of categories such as the ones used in the experiments by Ekman and his associates above. These six categories, which were later increased to seven by the addition of 'interest', were regarded as descriptive of the primary emotions which gave rise to particular expressions, rather than descriptive of the expressions themselves. In some ways, the fact that such categories work at all must be some vindication of the pan-cultural hypothesis. It may not be surprising that the repertoire of facial expressions is similar across cultures since everyone's facial musculature is roughly the same and allows similar expressive possibilities, but a category system based on the motivating emotions can only work if all cultures represent and recognize similar basic emotions in similar ways. The identification of the primary emotions was, in this case, based on earlier independent research on **affect**.

In addition to the primary emotional categories, however, certain expressions were to be regarded as **affect-blends**. 'Smugness', for instance, seemed to be a blend of 'happy' and 'angry' expressions, according to Ekman *et al.* (1972). This suggests that the facial expression is a mixture of those expressions associated with 'happiness' and 'anger' but, in principle, does not suggest that the emotion of 'smugness' is a mixture of happy and angry feelings. In practice, however, the emotional states and facial expressions are too closely connected within such a model to escape this consequence.

THE CULTURAL BASIS OF FACIAL EXPRESSION

Not all researchers have accepted the Darwinian hypothesis about the biological basis of facial expressions. Birdwhistell (1970), for example, argued that they are culturally learned:

> Although we have been searching for 15 years, we have found no gesture or body motion which has the same social meaning in all societies . . . That is, we have been unable to discover any single facial expression . . . which conveys an identical meaning in all societies.

Birdwhistell even suggested that the general facial expressions of those in close relationships will be found to be similar. Such an observation may be no more than folk wisdom (as embodied, for instance, in jokes about old people's faces looking like those of their dogs) but even if true could be explained in various ways. If it is argued that a couple in a close relationship will tend to fall into similar emotional states then the Darwinian hypothesis is left unscathed. A clearly socially motivated explanation, however, might explain the effect as an extreme form of postural congruence.

The issue is not, in fact, a clear-cut one since the proponents of the Darwinian hypothesis accept that there may be a cultural component. Such a hybrid explanation was put forward by Ekman (1973) in his **neurocultural** theory. Displays of emotion had an innate basis, but were filtered by cultural learning. Such cultural learning allowed people to 'manage' their public faces according to socially appropriate display rules (Ekman *et al.* 1969: 87):

> Past impressions of cultural differences in facial displays may represent a failure to distinguish what is pan-cultural (the association of facial muscular movements with each primary affect) from what is culturally variable (learned affect evokers, behavioral consequences of an affect display, and the operation of display rules). Display rules were defined as procedures learned early in life for the management of affect displays and include deintensifying, intensifying, neutralization, or masking affect display. These rules prescribe what to do about the display of each affect in different social settings; they vary with the social role and demographic characteristics, and should vary across cultures.

In other words, one reason why the 'meaning' of a particular facial expression may vary across cultures is that in each culture the social contexts in which such an expression could be freely and appropriately displayed will be very different. The primary affect and facial expression of a bereaved person, say, may be, in principle, similar around the world but some cultures may construe death as an occasion for celebration not distress, or may require the bereaved person to censor or exaggerate their display of emotion.

HOW EXPRESSIONS WORK

The question of how expressions work is perhaps the most interesting of all, and yet it is the least well understood. Two aspects have, however, been identified.

Boucher and Ekman (1975) took photographs of people displaying various emotional states, and cut them into sections. Subjects were then shown one portion of the facial expression and asked to identify the emotion being displayed. The researchers concluded that different parts of the face were important for the display of different emotions. The area around the eyes was important in detecting fear and sadness; happiness was seen more in the cheek and mouth area; surprise from any of the three areas; and anger required more than one area to be visible before it could be reliably recognized.

Ekman and Friesen (1967) suggested that facial expressions were quite good at communicating *how* people felt, but not so good at indicating the *intensity* of the emotion. This was signalled by other aspects of body movement and posture. To get the whole picture, people must take into account the way facial expression was associated with other aspects of non-verbal behaviour.

Gaze

People are remarkably sensitive to what others are doing with their eyes – no other aspect of non-verbal behaviour, except direct physical encounters, is capable of arousing quite the same intensity and subtlety of reaction.

When one person directs gaze at another it is generally termed *looking* in the research literature. When the person looked at simultaneously looks back then a situation of **mutual gaze** or **eye-contact** is reached.

Eye-contact can have an important but simple interactional function in obtaining the attention of someone in order to begin an encounter. It has often been remarked that waiters and officials are very good at avoiding eye-contact, thus avoiding beginning a service encounter until they themselves feel ready to do so. Teachers may silently stare in the direction of a child until eye-contact has been made, or may use eye-contact more subtly during lessons to select a child to answer a question or give permission to speak. In informal interactions, Goodwin (1981) has shown that people will often restart or delay continuing a speaking turn until mutual gaze and hence the attention of the other person is obtained.

Once an interaction has successfully begun, then looking and eye-contact continue to serve important functions, but in a rather complex manner. Kendon (1967) found that people look nearly twice as much when they are listening as when they are speaking, possibly because eye-contact seems to increase the cognitive processing load to an extent that makes it incompatible with simultaneous planning of speech. Whatever the reason, it seems that an increase in looking towards the end of a speaking turn can signal that the speaker is ready to hand over the turn to another. (This is discussed more fully in Section 6.3.)

People are sensitive to changes in this expected pattern of looking and looking away. An increase in looking may be interpreted variously as liking, as sexual interest, or as hostility. Exactly which interpretation is given will depend on other contextual factors and non-verbal behaviour. A reduction in looking may indicate that a person is rejecting the construction of the relationship being proposed.

For example, Jellison and Ickes (1974: 449) argued that an increase in

Figure 6.4 Relation between eye contact and distances for different combinations of confederates and subjects

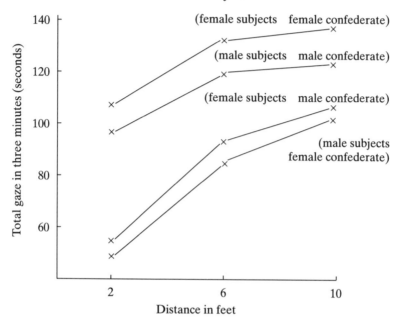

Source: Argyle and Dean (1965)

looking indicated a desire to obtain more personal information about the other person:

> If two people like one another, mutual eye contact may support or validate the mutual liking. On the other hand, if the two people dislike one another, the other's gaze may be interpreted as a desire for information and knowledge to be used against the person.

A more specific extension of the idea that mutual gaze can be threatening is the idea that the person who is first to break gaze is yielding dominance to the other and admitting inferiority.

Another factor which may disturb the pattern of looking and looking away has to do with what is being signalled through other non-verbal channels. As we have seen, information about liking and interpersonal status can be signalled through such things as proximity. Argyle and Dean (1965) have shown that the amount of looking decreases if a speaker stands closer to the listener than would normally be comfortable.

This reduction (see Figure 6.4) was in proportion to the increase in proximity. The two channels thus worked together to signal information about current states of the relationship.

The study of gaze demonstrates several important points which are generally applicable to non-verbal behaviour. One is that the same behaviour may simultaneously be serving several functions. Another is that similar behaviours may serve rather contrary functions, and exactly which will depend on the precise context in which the behaviour occurs. For example, breaking eye-contact may be interpreted as yielding dominance in some contexts, but if it occurs in a listener as a speaker approaches the end of a turn, it may be interpreted as a preparatory gesture to taking over the turn. Finally, gaze behaviour demonstrates the way that non-verbal behaviour must be understood as a series of channels of information which work together to signal meaning.

Integrated descriptions of non-verbal behaviour

Non-verbal behaviour is such a complex phenomenon that it presents many problems of description and analysis to researchers. Much research has attempted to make the task more manageable by examining only one aspect of non-verbal behaviour in isolation, usually in laboratory experiments. It is clear, however, from the descriptions above that in a number of cases the communicative significance of body movement is only apparent when all channels have been taken into account. This then raises the question of how easily we can generalize from the limited kinds of experiment which have been done to a proper and integrated understanding of how people behave in everyday life.

Many scholars would approach this question cautiously, observing that although much is now understood, it is still insufficient to make such an integrated description anything other than speculative. This has not prevented many more popular works on body language from attempting what are essentially caricatures based on behavioural stereotypes and gleanings from unconnected research studies. On the body language of politicians, for example, Wainwright (1985: 121–3) says:

> In sitting position, the politician tends to adopt a forward lean. This indicates a desire to cooperate with the listener in discussion. He often uses more eye contact when he is speaking than is normal . . . Politicians will have a firm, warm handshake. They will nod frequently when listening . . . They will place a protective arm around your shoulder . . . The typical Conservative male wears a dark suit, shirt and tie, has a smart hairstyle and polished shoes. His skin is smooth and he has the air of being well-fed . . . His gestures are restrained and his posture either upright or casually asymmetrical . . . The Labour male is a rougher hewn individual with less of an interest in appearance . . . Posture is more hunched and gestures made with less thought for their effect. They tend to stand closer than their Conservative counterparts and they use the head cock of interest more. The Labour female is more likely than a Conservative to wear

casual clothes and not to wear a bra . . . Gestures will be more like the man as whose equal she rightly regards herself and she makes a great deal of use of the head nod and the head cock.

Such material demonstrates the dangers and limitations of work in non-verbal communication which arise from its fragmentary and partial nature.

6.3 Conversation management

An important feature of ordinary conversation is its improvised nature. If participants make it up as they go along, however, they will need certain basic management skills which will allow them to integrate their perform-ance with those of other speakers and listeners. The ability to get through a conversation without interrupting or overlapping with another speaker but still getting to talk where desired has been likened to the problem of how people walk down a busy street without bumping into one another (Duncan 1972). In other words, the skills involved appear at first sight to be so commonplace that they seem also to be trivial, but a closer inspec-tion shows that listeners and speakers exchange complex signals which guide their behaviour in conversation.

Sacks *et al.* (1974) listed a number of facts which they felt any model of conversational turn-taking would have to accommodate. They included the following:

Speaker change occurs and (usually) recurs.

Only one person usually speaks at a time.

People will take turns which vary in length so a means of identifying when a speaker has completed a turn is needed.

Places where more than one person talks simultaneously are common but do not last long.

Transitions (from one speaker to another) are commonly made without gap or overlap.

The order in which people talk is not fixed in advance but varies. There-fore some means of allocating and distributing turns must be used.

In this section we examine some of the mechanisms which conversation-alists seem to employ to achieve smooth turn-taking and turn allocation.

Turn exchanges

Psychologists and linguists have long been fascinated by the way speakers are able to take over from each other smoothly and rapidly. For example, Beattie (1983) has shown that in over a third of the speaker transitions in his data, the silent gap was equal to or less than a fifth of a second. Such gaps are less than many of the gaps and slight hesitations in normal speech which do not usually give rise to a new speaker taking over the turn. They are also below the reaction time of most people. Hence it is obvious that listeners can recognize whether a speaker is approaching the end of a turn and can anticipate precisely the point at which the turn will finish.

TURN-ANTICIPATION CUES

Sacks *et al.* (1974) invoked a notion of **projectability** to explain prompt turn exchanges. Although turns may consist of a variety of lengths and kinds of structure – from one word to a long monologue – listeners may be able to recognize the type of turn early on. This would then give them a basis for estimating when it will be completed and for recognizing that completion promptly when it does occur. Sacks *et al.* largely left open the question of how such projection was accomplished. Listeners, however, can draw upon various kinds of knowledge allowing them to anticipate with different degrees of precision what kind of utterance will be made next.

General script or frame Participants may recognize the nature of the speech event as one for which they already have a particular **script** (discussed more fully in Section 7.4) which broadly guides who says what. Consider, for instance, the conventional routines associated with buying something from a shop assistant, consulting a doctor about an ailment or being interviewed for a job.

Discourse structures Listeners can draw on their knowledge of discourse structures such as an **adjacency pair** or the **initiation–response–follow-up** pattern found in classroom talk (see Section 7.3). For example, once one part of an adjacency pair (such as a greeting or question-and-answer sequence) is produced then there will be a strong expectation that the second part of the pair will occur next.

Grammatical structure Knowledge of grammatical structure will help the anticipation of the end of a particular turn since it is possible to tell when a sentence is grammatically complete, or potentially complete.

Sometimes, it is the existence of mistakes (interruptions and overlaps) which reveal that such knowledge is being used (Sacks *et al.* 1974: p. 702):

Desk: What is your last name, ⌈ Loraine
Caller: ⌊ Dinnis
Desk: What?
Caller: Dinnis

(Here the square bracket indicates simultaneous speech.) We can note that enquiry desks follow routine patterns of questioning and information-giving which can be anticipated by any caller. Hence the caller anticipated the end of the desk's turn by offering 'Dinnis'. The final address term 'Loraine' was unnecessary either to the grammatical completeness or to the illocutionary force of the desk's turn and it is revealing that the caller came in without waiting to see if the desk actually had anything further to say. Since the caller's name was lost in the overlap, the desk asks for a repetition. The question *What?* now demands a response whose nature and length can safely be predicted. If the caller had continued (by spelling out her name, for instance) then one might hypothesize that the desk would interrupt at this point anyway.

The data thus show how expectations which derive from knowledge of scripts, discourse structure, and grammar can be used by listeners to identify a possible completion of a turn by a speaker. The data also show, by demonstrating an overlap, that there may be more *possible* completion places than are actually used for turn exchange. Such a possible completion point was referred to by Sacks *et al.* (1974) as a **transition-relevance place**.

The notion that turns contain such transition-relevance places is an attractive one, since it allows us to specify more exactly the nature of the co-ordination problem. Listeners must first recognize that a transition-relevance place is coming up (the projection problem) and must then synchronize their entry precisely when the transition-relevance place arrives.

Although the model put forward by Sacks *et al.* (1974) does not go into detail about the precise cues used by listeners when they project a transition-relevance place, it does seem to be assumed that they are broadly of the kind discussed above. In other words, they derive from a listener's monitoring of the discourse and syntax and will be fully visible in written transcripts such as the one above. The model is unsatisfactory, however, in that it fails to explain adequately how it is that listeners can take over a turn almost instantly. Discourse cues of the above kind will allow only an approximate estimation of a turn ending, whereas turn exchanges may be completed within 50 milliseconds of a speaker finishing.

TURN-YIELDING CUES

Some psychologists have suggested that speakers give out complex non-verbal cues to indicate that they are about to finish and wish to yield their turn. Such turn-yielding cues help the prompt recognition of an end of turn, and help participants synchronize their turn exchanges with precision.

GAZE DIRECTION

Kendon (1967) suggested that speakers and listeners use **gaze direction** to co-ordinate turn-changeovers. He noted, in an analysis of seven two-person conversations which were filmed and recorded, that a listener tended to look at the speaker for longer periods of time than the speaker looked at the listener (see Figure 6.5). He suggested that when people are engaged in planning their next utterance (such cognitive planning may not be conscious) they cannot simultaneously deal with the processing load caused by making eye-contact. As speakers came to the end of long utterances,

Figure 6.5 Direction gaze at turn exchanges. At time 0 A
finishes utterance and B begins. Vertical axis shows frequency
of gazes at interlocutor (based on pooled data from 10
individuals and 68 long utterances). Horizontal axis shows
time intervals of half a second before and after turn exchange.

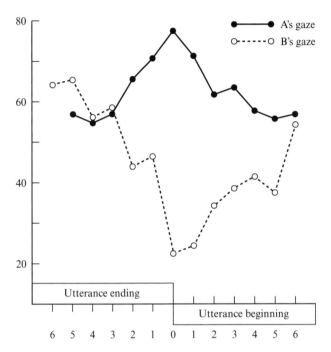

Source: Kendon (1967)

Kendon reported, their looking increased and the utterances were completed with steady gaze directed at the listener. Listeners, on the other
hand, who have been gazing much more at the speaker (possibly to monitor for turn-yielding cues as well as to show attention) looked away as they
began a long utterance, and often a little in advance of it. Kendon showed
that where the speaker failed to look up at the end of a long utterance, the
listener failed to respond immediately in a significant number of cases. In
this way, the changes in speakers' and listeners' gaze behaviour look as if
they might provide cues which help them synchronize the change in turn.

Unfortunately, not all researchers have been able to replicate these gaze
effects, and others have argued that, even though the effects may sometimes occur, they are not necessary to smooth speaker exchange in all
contexts. One of the most convincing demonstrations was by Beattie and
Barnard (1979), who showed that smooth speaker exchanges occurred during telephone conversations between subscribers and directory enquiries.

Although all visual information was lacking, smooth and rapid exchanges were found (Beattie 1983: 96):

> there is no evidence that the absence of visual information adversely affects the management of transitions from speaker to speaker... smooth transitions on the telephone are the rule rather than the exception. The basic temporal characteristics of speaker switches on the telephone are at least comparable with those of face-to-face interaction. In fact... the data suggest that speaker switching... is plausibly executed faster on the telephone.

It may seem paradoxical that speaker exchanges are conducted *more* smoothly when visual cues are absent, but it has been suggested (Rutter and Stephenson 1977: 35) that the availability of gaze information allows participants to take risks which might lead to a breakdown in telephone conversation:

> Face to face, interruption can occur freely because the visual channel allows the communication of nonverbal signals which maintain the interaction and prevent the breakdown which interruptions might otherwise produce. Without the visual channel, such nonverbal signals cannot be communicated and speech assumes greater importance in regulating the interaction.

OTHER VERBAL AND NON-VERBAL CUES

Other cues besides gaze direction must exist if the smoothness of transitions in telephone conversations can be accounted for. Duncan (1972) suggested speakers used a range of techniques to signal that they were about to yield the turn, which are listed below.

Gaze Like Kendon, Duncan recognized the importance of gaze direction. He found that a speaker's head turned towards the listener was associated with a substantial increase in the probability of the listener taking a turn.

Syntax Like Sacks *et al.*, Duncan suggested that grammatical completion of a clause was an important cue.

Intonation Certain changes in pitch were associated with turn endings.

Loudness A drop in loudness occurred at the very end of a turn, sometimes associated with a drop in pitch.

Drawl The final syllable of a turn was often lengthened.

Stereotyped tags Certain formulations such as 'but ah' or 'you know' were typically tagged on to the end of turns.

Gesture Many kinds of gesture were synchronized with speech and completion of a body movement often coincided with turn completion.

Duncan suggested, quite simply, that the more cues displayed simultaneously, the more likely a rapid and smooth exchange would occur. Beattie
(1983) tested this hypothesis but found that most smooth exchanges were
associated with a specific combination of up to three cues. The most frequent case was that where grammatical completion was associated with
intonational cues and drawl (Beattie 1983: 155):

> Clause completion accompanied by a falling intonation with drawl
> on the stressed syllable seems to operate effectively in conversation
> to inform the listener that it is their turn to speak.

Denny (1985) has since suggested that the most rapid and predictable
turn exchanges occur when both listener (through looking behaviour) and
speaker actively co-operate in the manoeuvre. After analysing eight video-
taped dyadic conversations between university students, she concluded
(Denny 1985: 51):

> Turn exchange can be maximally predicted, and virtually ensured,
> by a co-occurrence of elements which consists of both speaker and
> auditor actions.

CONCLUSION

The research which has been described suggests that a complex mechanism
regulates smooth turn exchange. A turn contains a number of transition-
relevance places (potential turn-yielding points) whose arrival can be
projected roughly by a hearer who draws on both discourse and syntactic
knowledge. A variety of non-verbal cues are then used by the speaker
both to indicate at which turn-relevance place he or she intends to yield
the turn, and to synchronize precisely the smooth change.

Turn allocation

So far, the research we have examined has considered only the case of talk
between two people. Where more than two people are involved then a
further problem arises of which person it is who speaks next. Sacks *et al.*
(1974) suggested that on some occasions the choice of next speaker is
effectively predetermined by the nature of the speech event. This would
happen in, say, a formal debate or court proceedings. In fact, Sacks *et al.*
suggested that there existed a continuum of speech events according to
how far turn allocation was predetermined. One of the features of informal conversation, they argued, was that the allocation of next turn was not
predetermined at all but was locally accomplished on a turn-by-turn basis.
Other speech events were intermediate in this respect (Sacks *et al.* 1974:
729):

> In contrast to both debates and conversation, meetings with chair
> persons partially pre-allocate turns, and provide for the allocation of

unallocated turns via the use of the pre-allocated turns. Thus, chair persons have rights to talk first, and to talk after each other speaker, and they can use each such turn to allocate next speakership.

In the case of casual conversation, where turns are not preallocated, one of three situations may arise. The current speaker may select the next speaker by name, by gaze or merely by directing a particular question or comment appropriate to one rather than another hearer. The current speaker seems to have special rights to the selection of the next speaker, perhaps because the alternative of self-selection by a next speaker cannot be done until a transition-relevance place and hence is easily pre-empted by a selection by the current speaker.

Where a speaker gives signs of yielding a turn without selecting a next speaker, someone may self-select. In this case, the maxim seems to be 'first starter gets the floor'. Although brief overlaps are common, it is nearly always the case that whoever comes in second gives up the turn to the first in.

If the speaker has selected no one, and no one self-selects, then the current speaker may continue the turn to another transition-relevance place.

Although the next speaker is, as a general rule, selected on a turn-by-turn basis, this is not by any means random. Turn organization is very sensitive, for instance, to distributions of expertise and experience among the participants. Two people who draw upon a mutual experience will be able to sustain an extended dialogue which excludes a third party from the conversation. There is also a strong bias for the previous speaker to be selected again as the next, thus setting up a pattern of dialogue between two participants which may extend over several turns and which a third person may find difficult to break into. One reason for this pattern is that any queries, requests for clarification and so on (from whatever source) will require the previous speaker to take a further turn. Another is that a speaker may embark upon a discourse structure which is recognizable as requiring several turns to complete, and which therefore reserves speaking rights several turns ahead. Many attention-getting strategies are of this kind. For example, a turn such as:

Julia: Hey, Fred, guess what happened to me today?

immediately removes any third party from the conversation for several turns and ensures the next turn but one will also be Julia's. It has the effect of legitimizing (by obtaining Fred's approval) Julia's bid for an extended turn. Furthermore, Julia can present her next turn in such a way that it will set up the expectation of a further response from Fred. Such devices, therefore, can organize the allocation of turns to both parties several turns ahead.

It is often suggested that 'fair shares for all' is an ideal principle in casual conversation among equals. It can be seen that such a principle is potentially very vulnerable. The dynamics of turn allocation are such that two or more people can collaborate (perhaps unwittingly) to exclude other members from taking turns. Furthermore, the maxim of 'first in gets the turn' which applies to self-selection, implies that there is a certain cut and thrust in ordinary talk. Any member who hesitates or who lacks self-confidence in the slightest degree will lose the turn whenever it is contested or, more embarrassingly, will make a bid to speak and have to withdraw.

Problems of disfluency

Disfluencies in conversation (whether they are hesitations, interruptions or overlaps) constitute potential problems for both conversation participants and conversation analysts: the former, because they may represent a breakdown in the smooth flow of talk which requires remedial action; the latter, because they pose problems of explanation and interpretation.

OVERLAPS AND INTERRUPTIONS
___

Activity 6.1

At this point you might pause to consider:

    a) what you think constitutes an interruption;
    b) why interruptions occur (or, what functions they serve).
___

Brief overlaps between speakers occur quite commonly in conversation. The model presented by Sacks *et al.* explained these in two ways. First, a speaker may wrongly anticipate the arrival of a transition-relevance place because the speaker has unexpectedly delayed it by adding extra material. Second, the 'first in gets the floor' maxim for self-selecting speakers encourages a very rapid entry which may briefly overlap with either the end of the current speaker's turn, or with a competing bid for the next turn by another would-be speaker. Such brief overlaps are, in fact, actually predicted by the model. Sacks *et al.*'s explanation of overlapping speech fits in with their notion of talk as a collaborative activity – but other researchers have identified **interruptions** as a category of overlapping speech that indicates conversational dominance on the part of the perpetrator. While categories of 'simultaneous talk' or 'overlap' are potentially simply and empirically identified, a category such as 'interruption' is in fact far less straightforward. For instance, certain kinds of simultaneous talk are systematically understood (by analysts and, probably, by speakers) not to count as interruptions.

Minimal responses, such as 'mmm' or 'yeah', when contributed by a listener, seem not to be counted as interruptions. The meaning attributed to minimal responses is quite variable, and probably depends as much as anything else upon the intonation pattern with which they are uttered. A speaker can say 'mmm', for instance, in a variety of ways to express a range of meanings from surprise/great interest through to a simple indication

of attention. In general, however, minimal responses are heard as expressing some level of support rather than as a bid for the floor:

> Doctor: If there's any doubt we can always do a blood test
> to ⌈ er confirm the ⌈ situation
> Patient:　⌊ mm　　　　　⌊ mm
> Doctor: but provided you've had the vaccine you can forget it.

These so called **back-channel** cues form one instance where simultaneous
speech is tolerated and does not threaten a current speaker's right to
complete a turn. However, it is not always clear where a minimal response
ceases to be minimal, and longer, but supportive, sequences can occur in
conversations.

There have been several attempts to establish formal criteria for the
identification of interruptions. For instance, Zimmerman and West (1975)
classified as interruptions instances of simultaneous speech (excluding
minimal responses, etc.) that began *before* the word immediately preceding a transition-relevance place in the first speaker's utterance. Overlaps,
on the other hand, began at a transition-relevance place, or the immediately preceding word. This measure seems to take account of the second

Figure 6.6 Classification of interruptions and smooth speaker switches

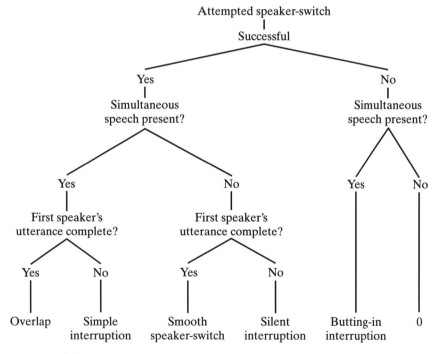

Source: Beattie (1983)

speaker's ability (or willingness) to recognize syntactic cues to a legitimate entry-point and probably reflects Zimmerman and West's concern with interruption as an indicator of conversational dominance.

Beattie (1983), on the other hand, has a more complex model that distinguishes three types of interruption in addition to overlaps and smooth speaker switches (see Figure 6.6). The following are examples of Beattie's classification (adapted from Beattie 1983: 115–16):

1 **Smooth speaker-switch**
Speaker 1: But i-i-i-it's important within (.) within the confines of the figure
(300)
Speaker 2: Within the confines of the figure yes, but not (.) in the general visual field . . .

2 **Simple interruption**
Speaker 1: . . . so he (.) he gives the impression that he he wasn't able to train them up. ⌈Now⌉
Speaker 2:   ⌊He ⌋ didn't try hard enough heh heh heh.

3 **Overlap**
Speaker 1: . . . it doesn't matter where it is, if it's on the edge (.) near near the edge of your periphery (.) or you know right at the centre because you can move your head (.) and it'll move you know
⌈it'll move with it⌉
Speaker 2: ⌊Yes, I   ⌋don't
I don't think we're disagreeing about that, because I think (.) what I interpreted this to mean . . .

4 **Butting-in interruption**
Speaker 1: . . . and you know he said that's rubbish (.) that seems to go back to
Speaker 2:   ⌈ well   ⌉
Speaker 1: that really ⌊ because ⌋I mean why does he say . . . and the right side was on the left and (.) you (.) know
Speaker 2: ⌈oh oh you you still you still⌉
Speaker 1: ⌊and you still keep   ⌋that sort of order you know so I (.) will you know

5 **Silent interruption**
Speaker 1: Yeah I thought you meant its position with respect to everything else not the actual (.)
Speaker 2: You know wherever you've got (.) the parts I mean approximately in the right positions . . .

(Note that (.) indicates a pause of 200 milliseconds or less; (300) means a pause of 300 milliseconds; square brackets indicate overlapping speech.)

It is the criterion of 'completeness' that best distinguishes interruptions from other speaker switches in Beattie's model. Completeness is judged intuitively on the basis of several verbal and non-verbal cues in the first speaker's utterance – but the classification is made at the point at which the first speaker *stopped* speaking, not the point at which the second speaker *began* to speak. Beattie's measure therefore seems to be an indicator of whether the first speaker might 'feel' interrupted but, unlike Zimmerman and West, it does not necessarily take account of those cues present (in the first speaker's utterance) at the point at which a potential interruption begins.

In another study, Beattie (1982) has argued that interruptions may indicate a breakdown in the normal turn-yielding mechanisms. An interruption may occur, for instance, where a listener mistakenly hears the speaker to be giving out turn-yielding signals. Beattie demonstrated that the then British Prime Minister, Margaret Thatcher, was interrupted frequently and unsuccessfully in one television interview at points where she gave out the classic turn-yielding signals (grammatical completion, drop in pitch and drawl) without intending to relinquish the turn.

We have seen that it is possible to establish formal criteria for interruptions, and that different criteria have been adopted in different studies. It is also important to note that the *interpretation* of interruptions depends very much on the context in which they occur. While they are often thought of as an infringement of the original speaker's right to speak, frequent 'interruptions' may occur in the speech of close friends as a form of collaborative talk.

FILLED PAUSES AND RESTARTS

Beattie (1977) showed that **filled pauses** ('mmm's and 'ah's) protected the speaker from interruption for a short while. Another extremely effective tactic identified by Duncan (1972) was an incomplete gesture which indicated that a speaker wished to continue. Even when accompanied by otherwise effective turn-yielding cues, such a turn suppression signal would rarely be associated with a change in speaker. Many political speakers (though not Margaret Thatcher, it seems) use such devices to hold on to the floor. The British Labour politician, Michael Foot, used a more idiosyncratic, but effective, technique of pausing in the middle of clauses where an interruption would be heard as most offensive, and running fast through the transition-relevance place and into the next sentence.

Filled pauses and false starts may also indicate that a speaker is not yet convinced that the full attention of the audience is commanded. Goodwin (1981) has demonstrated that speakers will often restart an utterance when gaze has been obtained from a listener so that the whole utterance is properly attended to. Such restarts can be interpreted as 'requests for gaze attention'. Speakers also use pauses and filled pauses near beginnings of utterances, instead of a restart, to delay the effective beginning of their turn until gaze has been achieved.

A similar effect has been observed (Atkinson 1984) in skilled public speakers, who will repeatedly restart during audience clapping until they can be heard again. Such speakers give the impression that they are battling against unsolicited applause while ensuring that nothing of their message is lost.

In these various ways, behaviour which at first sight seems to be disfluent or incompetent behaviour by speakers, can be seen as part of a systematic and competent mechanism for synchronizing their performance with listeners' behaviour.

Alternative models of turn-taking

The model of turn-taking we have discussed has been highly influential, but it has not been without its critics. It has been developed particularly in relation to conversational data from British and American English, but there are indications that it may work less well in other cultures and contexts. Reisman (1974) has described how public talk by Antiguan villagers may routinely involve loud and simultaneous talk, often repetitive. Basso (1972) has reported that a conversation in Western Apache may in some contexts involve completely silent turns by one of the participants. Such silences, by contrast may be embarrassing in English conversations.

Even within conversations in English, patterns of turn-taking seem to be more variable in practice than the model proposed by Sacks *et al.* would suggest. Several critiques of the model have been derived from analyses of **multi-party** conversations. Carole Edelsky (1981: 396–7) suggests that the traditional one-person-at-a-time model of talk, with a sequential pattern of turn exchange, is based particularly on analyses of talk between two people or from relatively formal contexts (e.g. therapy sessions, classroom talk, conversations between strangers set up by an experimenter). Evidence from such contexts, argues Edelsky, would tend to support a one-person-at-a-time model. Edelsky herself analysed talk from a series of informal university committee meetings. She made use of the concept of 'floor', distinguishing between more formal floors, normally developed by one person at a time; and informal collaboratively developed floors, where there was a lot of overlapping speech. In Edelsky's data, overlapping speech did not necessarily constitute an interruption; and speaking turns often continued beyond an overlap. In the extract below (from Edelsky 1981: 386), for instance, C's speech in lines 3 and 5 is part of the same turn rather than two separate turns:

```
1 R:  OK, let's talk about Tuesday=
2 L:  =Well=
3 C:  =OK, Tuesday
              [
4 S:          as long as we're out by 4:30
              [
```

[

5 C: is my day from from 7:40 in=

6 M: (   )

7 C: =the morning until 6 at night

Edelsky also distinguished between *turns* (talk that is on record) and *side-comments* (off-record talk, normally addressed *sotto voce* to one or a few other participants). Her definition of turn is intuitive; it is also functional and concerned with the exchange of meaning rather than with the formal properties of conversation. A turn is 'an on-record "speaking" (which may include nonverbal activities) behind which lies an intention to convey a message that is both influential and functional' (Edelsky 1981: 403).

Other analyses of conversations have identified the phenomenon of **duetting** (see Falk 1980, cited in Coates 1994) in which two or more speakers jointly construct a speaking turn. Jennifer Coates (1994) found that such patterns of joint construction were common in informal talk between women friends. Overlapping speech, which did not constitute an interruption, was also common in this context. Coates argues that the one-person-at-a-time model of turn-taking described by Sacks *et al.* is the 'base-line', or unmarked form for English speakers. Other forms of organization are, however, possible, and these acquire particular social meanings. In Coates's own data joint construction of speaking turns marked the talk as friendly or intimate (Coates 1994: 189–90).

6.4 Observing and recording conversation

Investigators making observations of spoken language have to contend with the **observer's paradox** (Labov 1972b): while there are ways of lessening the impact, the act of making an observation will itself affect speakers' language use, and so what is observed. Furthermore, there is no 'neutral' way of recording spoken language. Methods will reflect the investigator's interests and the aims of the investigation, as well as the type of interaction being observed. Chapter 7 discusses how spoken language may be analysed. This section focuses on ways of making and recording observations prior to carrying out an analysis, but it will be apparent that the methods chosen themselves presuppose certain forms of analysis (and rule out others).

Live observations

The simplest way to make a record of an interaction is to jot down open-ended **fieldnotes** of the event. Fieldnotes are, necessarily, selective – researchers would tend to focus on particular aspects of the interaction that were of interest (e.g. the topics spoken about; the roles taken by different participants). Fieldnotes tend not to be used, on their own, by linguists, conversation analysts and others whose primary interest is in how conversation is organized because they do not allow talk to be recorded in any detail.

Figure 6.7 is an extract from fieldnotes produced by Janet Maybin. They provide a record of talk in the rather formal context of a school assembly. In this case the talk has also been audio-recorded for closer analysis. The fieldnotes provide complementary information about the behaviour of participants, along with Maybin's initial interpretations of the event.

The layout used for fieldnotes will depend upon the purpose of the investigation and the aspect(s) of the interaction that are of interest. In this case, separate columns are allocated to 'notes' (what actually happened) and 'comments/questions' (the beginnings of an interpretation). This is a useful device – it avoids confusing observations and interpretations – but clearly no observation notes provide a neutral record of events: what is noted down will always depend on an implicit interpretive framework.

Observations can be made more structured by the use of an **observation schedule**, such as that in Figure 6.8. This schedule, like a number of others devised during the 1980s, is designed for those concerned to monitor imbalances in interaction between female and male speakers – though it could also be used by researchers with an interest in the behaviour of individuals.

The schedule in Figure 6.8 identifies certain categories of turn, and each turn must be allocated to one category. It produces information that may be quantified (one could say, for instance, that 30 per cent of male speaking turns 'initiated talk', but that only 10 per cent of female speaking turns fell into this category). But there can be a problem in identifying speaker turns, particularly in informal groups when talk moves rapidly (see also Section 6.3). Nor does the method make any allowance for turns of different lengths – a speaker who produced five or six short turns would be counted as having contributed more than one who produced one or two very long turns. Finally, it is difficult to allocate turns to discrete categories (some researchers would claim this is, at any rate, not legitimate because talk fulfils different functions simultaneously).

PROBLEMS WITH LIVE OBSERVATIONS

Live observations allow an investigator to analyse spoken language at a general level (e.g. to identify large-scale trends or patterns in an interaction). But they do not allow talk to be analysed in any detail. When using an observation schedule, talk is categorized once and for all – there is no opportunity to go back and check the allocation of talk to categories or to discuss this with others.

Researchers whose main interest is in how conversation is organized usually rely on audio or video recordings. These also allow talk to be transcribed for closer analysis.

Figure 6.7 Fieldnotes on interaction in a school assembly

'Sharing assembly' 22/11/90

Tape Counter	Notes	Comments/questions
134	3 children take it in turn to read out poems about animals which they have written. Seated classes quiet and attentive.	I can't hear any of this - neither I suspect can most other children in the assembly. What is being communicated here?
	1 child asks teachers to come and sit on two rows of chairs placed diagonally at the front. Teachers go up to the chairs, acting as if reluctant (sounds of 'oh no').	I immediately realise teachers are being asked to pretend to be pupils, and the child will be their teacher. Air of puzzled anticipation among seated children. Maybe they aren't familiar with this kind of 'role-reversal' sketch?
142	Teachers mess about, pretending to punch each other, pull hair, tip chair etc. Child 'teacher' stands in front looking embarrassed. Seated children laugh and make occasional comments.	Seated children don't seem at ease with this situation and don't quite know how to react. Who exactly is in authority, now? 'Teachers' acting out of pupil unruliness is exaggerated - to make it unreal?
	The child at the front is pretending to try and restore order to his 'class'.	The child 'teacher' in acting out his role is managing to remain respectful to his teacher 'pupils', so he's really acting two roles simultaneously (pupil and teacher)?
	The seated children watching now start to freely imitate the antics of the teachers at the front, and several scuffles break out as the noise level rises.	It's difficult for the watching children to cope with these two conflicting systems - teacher = fonts of authority v. teachers = naughty pupils. They seem very confused.
	Mr. Brown quickly steps out of the role of naughty pupil, and gives the watching children a threatening look as he says 'sh'.	Watching children seem almost relieved that traditional power relations are restored. They settle down very quickly.

Source: Maybin, unpublished data, 1991

Figure 6.8 Schedule to monitor group interaction

Group member (identified by sex)	Initiates talk	Interrupts	Helps another to speak	Supports another's point	Offers opposing view	Adds to what has been said	Challenges	Breaks off	TOTALS
Man[1]									
Woman[1]									
Man[2]									
Man[3]									
Woman[2]									
Woman[3]									
Man[4]									
Man TOTALS									
Woman TOTALS									

Source: NATE Language and Gender Committee (1988: 25); schedule devised Pat Barrett

Audio and video recordings

Audio and video recordings provide a permanent record of spoken language. Recordings can be mulled over at length, and discussed with other researchers and/or with participants. Analyses can identify different categories of talk (as in the observation schedules above) or they can be more open-ended. The different forms of analysis discussed in Chapter 7 will normally have relied on audio- or video-recorded data.

Audio and video recordings necessarily provide a partial record of events. Audio recordings crucially lose all non-verbal information – thus threatening the validity of any study of conversation management. They also lose contextual information, though this can be compensated for to some extent if recordings are supplemented with fieldnotes, as in Figure 6.7. Video recordings are selective. A camera can pick up only a limited amount of information – for instance, it is normally not possible to focus to the same extent on each participant in a group discussion. There is also a danger of introducing bias by focusing selectively on certain speakers or events.

Audio and video recordings are intrusive and will have some effect on the interaction – particularly if speakers are not used to being recorded. Some researchers have made surreptitious recordings (e.g. concealing microphones in flower vases!), though nowadays ethical considerations tend to rule out such practices. In the search for 'naturalistic' data several levels of ethical compromise have been reached, such as obtaining blanket permission to record conversations but not telling participants at the time that they are being recorded; leaving audio recorders and cameras around for a while so that speakers forget about or get used to their presence; getting participants to talk about interesting, exciting or dangerous topics so that their enthusiasm overcomes any wariness about being recorded.

Figure 6.9 shows a very simple **quantitative analysis** of an audio recording of a discussion between four teenagers. In this case the revolution counter on a cassette player was used as a means of **time sampling**. The counter took 2.5 seconds to make one complete revolution. In practice, how long a counter takes to make one revolution will vary slightly from the beginning to the end of the tape, so this method is best suited to making an initial analysis of short extracts rather than a rigorous analysis of longer recordings.

We recorded which participant(s) spoke during each counter revolution. This gave us a rough and ready estimate of the amount spoken – we could say, for instance, that although Lisa was in the chair for this discussion most of the talk came from Tony. Michael spoke least of all the participants. A 'comments' column allowed further information to be added – e.g. that two of Lisa's turns were minimal responses (*mmm* and *yeah*).

Time sampling may well give a different estimate of the amount spoken than counting speaking turns (as in the schedule in Figure 6.8). The method ensures that observers record speech at regular intervals, and may seem to provide a more accurate measure of 'amount of talk'. However, it does not

Figure 6.9 Time sampling of an audio recording

COUNTER	LISA (CHAIR)	STEPHANIE	MICHAEL	TONY	COMMENTS
0				1	
1	1				
2	1	1			S–'Yeah, they can . . .'
3			1	1	M–gives support
4	1		1	1	L–attempts turn, T–interrupts
5				1	
6	1			1	L–'mmm'
7				1	
8	1			1	L–'yeah'
9				1	
10				1	
11	1				
12				1	
13	1				
14	1				
15	1			1	
16					Pause – topic exhausted
17	1		1		L–reads new topic question
18		1		1	S–'no' in resp to Q
19	1			1	T–'no' but gets turn
20				1	L–'Curly do you 'think' – *encouragement*
21		1			
22	1	1			
23	1			1	T–'Yeah' – *Support*
24		1	1		
25				1	T–takes topic 'another thing' . . .
26				1	
27				1	
28				1	
29				1	
30				1	
TOTAL	13	5	4	21	43
%	30%	12%	9%	49%	
	42%		58%		

allow observers to measure separately the frequency and duration of a speaker's turns (very frequent short turns may have a different significance from few long turns). Nor will it allow any detailed analysis of turn-taking (or of other aspects of the interaction). Such analyses require some form of **transcription**.

Transcription

Transcripts provide a permanent and readily accessible record of spoken language, and allow close scrutiny of the data. They may be used to support quantitative analyses, including various forms of computer analysis; they are also frequently used for detailed qualitative analyses (Chapter 7 provides examples of these).

Transcription is time-consuming – Edwards and Westgate (1987) estimate that an hour's recording may take 15 hours to transcribe. But it is possible to make an initial, rough transcript to identify features of interest, and refine parts of this later for closer analysis.

TRANSCRIPTION AS THEORY

In 1979 Elinor Ochs wrote an article about the problems of transcribing children's language, in which she argued that 'transcription is a selective process reflecting theoretical goals and definitions' (Ochs 1979: 44). The point applies to all transcripts, not just those of child language: transcripts select certain phenomena as being of interest and give prominence to them; they embody certain theoretical assumptions, and lead the investigator towards certain interpretations of the data. Kendon (1982) writes of a tension faced by investigators: they need to transcribe talk to perceive its structure at any level of detail, but in transcribing they necessarily impose a particular structure on their data. It is worth quoting Kendon (1982: 478–9) at length:

> The transcription system one adopts itself embodies a set of hypotheses and assumptions that will thereafter structure one's inquiry. It is of the greatest importance to know what these hypotheses are, and whether they are appropriate to the question one is engaged upon, before adopting any system of transcription. It is a mistake to think that there can be a truly neutral transcription system, which, if only we had it, we could then use to produce transcriptions suitable for any kind of investigation . . . transcriptions, thus, embody hypotheses.
>
> As soon as one puts pencil to paper in making a map, as soon as one makes a transcription, one is thereby making a decision, a theoretical decision, about what is important. For no transcription, no matter how fine grained, can ever be complete. One must inevitably make a selection. Thus the map one makes, the transcription one produces, is as much a product of one's investigation as a means of furthering it. But only by laying out on paper a map of the event can

one come to perceive its structure; only in this way can one come to 'see' one's formulation ... One works in a continual dialogue with the specimen.

This point will be illustrated in the examples of transcription that follow.

Transcriptions sometimes use conventions of written language – capital letters, full stops and other forms of punctuation – to represent speech. This in itself is a form of analysis of the data, indicating such features as sentence or clause boundaries, speech acts (question marks) etc. Other researchers would argue that it is inappropriate to impose written conventions on speech. There are also several features of spoken language that are not normally represented in writing but that (depending on the purpose of the investigation) may need to be represented in a transcript. Several sets of transcription conventions have been devised that enable features of spoken language (pauses, overlapping speech, intakes of breath, increased volume, stress, syllable lengthening, etc.) to be recorded (see for instance Sacks *et al.* 1974; Ochs 1979). These are meant to produce more accurate transcriptions – but there is an associated danger that they may lend an appearance of scientific objectivity to what is always an intuitive, impressionistic exercise.

Bearing in mind this caveat, Figure 6.10 illustrates a simplified set of conventions for transcribing spoken language. Numbering lines of a transcript, as in Figure 6.10, allows particular utterances to be referred to easily. Underlining in the text, along with a 'transcription notes' column, allows features of speech, such as increased/decreased volume, to be identified. Depending on the focus of the investigation, additional symbols can be added to record other relevant features such as emphatic stress. An additional column may also be added to record comments, questions, initial interpretations.

Figure 6.10 uses conventional spelling – though note that in line 7 'yeah' is used to indicate Kate's pronunciation (she said 'yeah', not 'yes'). Transcribers sometimes go much further than this, as in the following example from Sacks *et al.* (1974: 732):

J: ... Dass wuhd 'e should of did, // if he – if he's the one thet broke
    it,
V: I'm not intuh this

It is not clear here on what basis special conventions are used for certain features of speech (*wuhd*) but not others (*should*). Sacks *et al.* argue that they have tried to convey as much of the actual sound as possible while still making the transcripts accessible. It is true that using a system such as the International Phonetic Alphabet (see Section 2.2) would make the transcript unreadable for most people, but there is a danger with this

Figure 6.10 Transcript of talk between young people playing a board game

Transcript			**Comment**
1	Lucy:	This girl always wins anyway	
2		she's (brilliant) at losing money	
3		[laugh]	general laughter
4	Kathryn:	I know	quietly
5	Lucy:	Same as me I hate taking money	dice thrown
6		out of my bank account (.)	
7	Kate:	Yeah seven again one two three	several voices
8		four five six seven	join in counting
9		(2 secs)	
10	Lucy:	You and one opponent each	
11		throw a dice high roller gets	
12		50 000 from opponent ( ) I'm	
13		not choosing Kate ⌠ she's good	
14	Kate:	⌡ Just throw	

Key

I know	underlining indicates any feature you wish to comment on
(.)	brief pause
(2 secs)	timed pause – 2 seconds
(brilliant)	transcription uncertain: a guess
( )	unclear speech – something you can't transcribe
⌠She's good ⌡Just throw	overlapping speech
[laugh]	transcription of a sound etc. that forms part of the utterance

Source: Open University (1991: A257)

compromise position of making speech (and speakers?) look somewhat odd while not gaining much in terms of accuracy.

There is no generally agreed system for representing pronunciation features in conversation analysis. Transcribers sometimes home in on readily identifiable features (*yeah, 'cos, wanna, gonna, laughin', innit*). There are obvious problems here if such spellings are adopted for non-standard speech whereas conventional spelling is used for the standard variety. Attempts to represent pronunciation 'accurately' probably say as much about the perceptions of researchers as about the way words are actually pronounced.

LAYING OUT A TRANSCRIPT

Figure 6.10 is set out like a play script, with one speaking turn following another. We shall refer to this as a **standard transcript**, as it is still found

Figure 6.11 Transcript of talk between young people playing a board game, illustrating column format

Lucy	Kathryn	Kate	Transcription notes
1 This girl always			
2 wins anyway she's			
3 (brilliant) at losing			
4 money [laugh]			general laughter
5	I know		quietly
6 Same as me I hate			dice thrown
7 taking money out			
8 of my bank			
9 account (.)			
10		Yeah seven again	several
11		one two three four	voices join in
12		five six seven	counting
13			(2 secs)
14 You and one			
15 opponent each			
16 throw a dice high			
17 roller gets 50 000			
18 from opponent			
19 ( ) I'm not			
20 choosing Kate			
21 she's good		Just throw	

Key Conventions as in Figure 6.10, except that overlapping speech is aligned

very frequently in published sources and is the format most people will be familiar with. An alternative format, particularly useful for group talk, is a **column transcript**. This is illustrated in Figure 6.11. We have retranscribed the data from Figure 6.10 to allow for comparison between the two formats.

The format illustrated in Figure 6.10 assumes that turns follow one from another in a connected sequence, but this is not always the case, particularly in group talk. Column transcripts such as 6.11 preserve the temporal sequence of turns but do not presuppose any direct connection between consecutive turns. (It is worth considering what the relationship is between turns in Figure 6.11.) Column transcripts also make it easier to track different speakers' utterances – for instance, to look at the number, length and type of contributions each speaker produces.

In a column transcript, which column is allocated to which speaker may not be a neutral decision. For instance, there are arguments that, because of factors such as the left–right orientation in European scripts, and associated page layout, we may give priority to information located on the left-hand side. The speaker allocated the left-hand column may appear to be the main initiator in a conversation – or may have been allocated this

Figure 6.12 Transcript of talk showing joint construction of turns

C: I mean in order to accept that idea you're

⎧ C: having to .   ⎡ completely
⎨ E: mhm . completely review your ⎣ view of your
⎩ D: yes

⎧ C: change ⎤ your view of your husband=
⎪ E: husband⎦=   =that's right
⎨ B: =yes
⎩ A: yeah   mhm

Source: Coates (1994: 182)

column through having been perceived by the transcriber as the initiator (this and similar issues are discussed by Ochs 1979).

Transcription layouts may need to be adapted to highlight different aspects of the conversation. We mentioned earlier (Section 6.3) the work of Jennifer Coates and Carole Edelsky, both of whom were concerned with complex patterns of turn-taking in multi-party talk. Jennifer Coates uses a standard layout to transcribe her data, but brackets together turns jointly constructed by more than one speaker (see Figure 6.12).

Carole Edelsky found that a standard transcript could not capture the complexity of talk in informal university meetings. She tried out different forms of transcription to illustrate the ways speakers took/held the floor,

Figure 6.13 Transcript of talk in a meeting, distinguishing turns from side comments

```
 1  R:    (topic is scheduling)
 2        other than that


 3        in stays where it is        | L: Is there a doctor here?
                          ↑_____|    ↑
 4  S: Awright                        | MA: (laugh)
 5                                     | R: (to L) It's OK
 6                                     |    I've tried mine.
 7                                     |    It works well=
 8  R: = Uh in this lab, this         | S: (to C) I need
 9       lab is going to be           |    one of those
10       name the Hudson              |    cookies


11       Room
```

Source: Edelsky (1981: 403)

and to illustrate her distinction between on record 'turns' and off-record 'side comments'. Figure 6.13 shows one of Edelsky's transcripts where turns are set down the left-hand side of the page and simultaneous side comments are set in a box on the right. Note that in this case one speaker (speaker R) switches from a side comment to a turn (lines 7–8).

Any number of complex layouts could, in principle, be devised in an attempt to provide a more valid account of interactions, although there will always be something of a tension between validity and ease of reading.

INCLUDING NON-VERBAL AND CONTEXTUAL INFORMATION

Transcripts are intended to focus on the verbal component of an interaction, but researchers often wish to provide information about non-verbal

Figure 6.14 Transcript of an interview showing non-verbal information

Client	Counsellor	Comments
I've got three certificates on the parts that we had to take exams on. One's operations		
	So, wait a minute, you've got one in operations	*Counsellor writing as she speaks*
One practical		
	Yeah	
And one basic mechanics		
	Basic mechanics. Do you know what certificates they are, are they like?	
I don't remember		
	Right. That's fine. So you like travel then as a hobby, and listening to music and sports. Now, do you play any sports or do you just?	*Counsellor refers to papers*
I watch, I used to play football but I can't because I've had an operation on both me knees.		
	Right, so watching sports.	

Source: Longman and Mercer (1993: 101–2)

Figure 6.15 Transcript showing the contribution of verbal and non-verbal behaviour to turn-taking

─ ─

Teacher: How did they know that those men were
[K J M E A]
─ ─ ─ ─ ──────

alive? (.) Yes

──────────────

Kate: Miss they were knocking

──────────────

Teacher: They were knocking . . .

Key
Superscript letters indicate order of handraising:
K = Kate; J = John; M = Mark; E = Emma; A = Anne
─ ─ ─ ─ ─ = teacher's gaze towards boys
────── = teacher's gaze towards girls

Note: Teacher looking at boys but can see girls. As K's hand goes up, teacher turns to look at girls. By the time boys' hands are raised, teacher has already begun to turn to girls. By the time E's hand rises, teacher's gaze is already directed towards K.

Source: Swann and Graddol (1988: 57)

or contextual features that contribute to the meaning of what is going on. In this respect, as in others, transcripts will be selective: what is included will depend upon what researchers perceive as salient and relevant to their own research interests. Figure 6.14 is a column transcript of talk between a client and a counsellor in an employment training interview. The researchers, Jo Longman and Neil Mercer, were interested in the relationship between written and spoken modes of language use. In this case, then, it was relevant to note, alongside the spoken text, the counsellor's reference to a form she needed to complete. A third column has been added for this information.

The transcript in Figure 6.15 comes from a study of turn-taking between teachers and primary school pupils. This group of pupils normally obtained speaking turns by raising their hands and being nominated by the teacher, either verbally or by the use of gaze. The transcript is an attempt to represent the interplay between speech, gaze towards either girl or boy pupils and order of handraising. While it implies a (relatively) integrated model of verbal and non-verbal behaviour it is still selective. Several features that might have contributed to turn-taking but were not the focus of the study (e.g. posture, gesture, teacher's intonation) are not represented.

Fig 6.16 Transcription of a young child's spoken language

Mark (27 months) is in the lounge with his mother.

Mark	*Mother*
'ot Mummy	[standing by central heating radiator]
	Hot?
	Yes, that's the radiator.
Been? ... (? = burn)	
Burn?	
	Burn?
Yeh.	
	Yes you know it'll burn don't you?
Oh [putting his hand on radiator?]	
Ooh	
	Take your hand off it.
Uh?	
	What about the other shoe? [Mother is asking whether he needs his other shoelace tied]
a all done Mummy.	
	Mm?
It done Mummy.	
	It's done is it?
Yeh.	

Source: Wells (1985)

TRANSCRIBING YOUNG CHILDREN'S LANGUAGE

The extent to which a transcription system imposes certain assumptions and categories on the data is nowhere more apparent than when dealing with data from young children. The basic dialogic structure assumed by 'standard' transcripts such as that in Figure 6.10 is unlikely to be appropriate to young children – it is not always clear, for instance, to whom their speech is directed. Most researchers transcribing children's language therefore use a column transcript, as in Figure 6.16.

Conventions of transcription impose linguistic categories (some so familiar that they pass unnoticed) at all levels of analysis. Quite often it will be found that the vocabulary of adult English is insufficient to record children's talk. In the case of problematic utterances analysts normally use a phonemic or phonetic script to record more faithfully what the child actually uttered, leaving open its status as a word or phrase. Even the IPA alphabet, however, imposes adult articulation categories on the data. In fact, most transcripts of child language proceed on the tacit assumption that children are behaving like adults except in those respects of particular interest to the investigator. Ochs (1979) and MacWhinney and Snow (1985) give a fuller account of the problems of transcribing data from children.

Activity 6.2 Recording talk

Section 6.4 has shown several ways in which talk may be recorded. We have tried to present examples with enough information to enable them to be tried out and adapted, where necessary. As a starting-point we suggest you try out different methods of working with an audio recording.

First, make an audio recording of a conversation between a small number of participants (say two or three). It is best to record your group while they are engaged in an activity they would normally do together – e.g. you could record an informal meeting; or children may be recorded playing a game. You should first obtain permission to make a recording. You will need to select up to 10 minutes of the conversation to work on, but you may need to leave your recorder running for much longer than this, or to record on more than one occasion, particularly if your participants are not used to being recorded.

If you are not used to making audio recordings, you should practise with your machine first. Points to bear in mind include:

- a small, battery-operated cassette recorder with a built-in microphone will be relatively unobtrusive;
- it is also advisable to use a machine that is simple to operate, particularly if you have not made many recordings before;
- on the other hand, more sophisticated equipment will produce a better-quality recording;
- background noise (scraping chairs, other people talking) can spoil your recording: try to find a quiet area, preferably carpeted, where you will not be disturbed.

Next, play through your recording and select an extract of 7–10 minutes when the conversation is running fairly smoothly and participants are no longer showing obvious signs of awkwardness about the cassette recorder. Play your extract through once or twice so that you become familiar with it. Make a brief summary and jot down the first few words so that you can locate it easily (you could also use the revolution counter to help you locate the extract).

Now, try out the sampling method illustrated in Figure 6.9 to gain a general picture of the amount contributed by each participant. It is easiest if you use lined paper to construct a chart like that in Figure 6.9, allocating one line to each revolution of the tape counter. For this part of the activity you should also ensure your counter is set at zero at the start of your extract.

- What can this form of analysis tell you about the amount contributed by participants?
- What are its shortcomings?

Finally, try making a transcript of your extract. You could compare the two formats illustrated in Figures 6.10 and 6.11. Transcription will take you some time: you will need to replay sequences once or twice, particularly if speakers are talking rapidly or if there is overlapping speech. However, do not worry about accuracy too much for this first attempt: you can refine your transcript, or portions of your transcript, later if you wish.

- What was the most difficult part of making a transcript?
- Were the conventions illustrated in Figure 6.10 adequate, or did you find you needed to indicate other features of the talk?
- Is there anything that interests you about your extract? For example, who contributes most? Is this what you would have expected from trying out the sampling exercise? Do different speakers seem to be taking different roles in the interaction? From replaying your tape and looking through the transcript how can you tell when a speaker's turn is near completion (you will, of course, have access only to certain cues since you won't have any visual information)? Do speakers mainly speak one at a time or is there a lot of overlapping speech?

7 Discourse and text

7.1 Introduction

This chapter is concerned with the description of *discourse* and *text*. Traditionally, the distinction between discourse and text was similar to that between 'spoken' and 'written', but this simple correspondence has been eroded over the years by two things. One is the increasing range of forms which written and spoken material may take in modern media; the other is the way theoretical perspectives have evolved. Let us take each in turn.

Written texts traditionally came in a limited range of forms and implied both a limited range of linguistic styles and particular relationships with the reader. A reader, for example, was usually remote from the writer and had limited, if any, possibilities for interacting and responding to the writer. Spoken language, on the other hand, usually implied the actual presence of a listener who was able to intervene in the flow of discourse and help determine later utterances. One can easily think of exceptions to this simple distinction – even in classical times – and the Greek and Roman rhetoricians were not entirely blind to the theoretical implications. By and large, however, whether something was written or spoken implied a particular relationship with a reader or hearer, a particular range of linguistic styles and communicative functions.

Such a simple distinction is now impossible, rather than merely difficult, to sustain as we demonstrate in Section 7.2. Virtually the entire language output of television and all that of radio, for example, is spoken rather than written and yet the viewer or listener is usually incapable of intervening and altering the flow of the discourse. At another extreme, a new genre of computer adventure games is appearing in which the player determines the flow of the story by making decisions and responses at critical points. Where once a distinction between 'spoken' and 'written' could be viewed as a shorthand for a cluster of important distinctions, we now need to be more precise about which distinctions are of interest to us.

Theory has also evolved over the years, perhaps partly in response to changing circumstances. Literary theory, for example, which once required students to evaluate works of literature as artefacts with intrinsic qualities, now is prepared to view a work of literature as being generated at the point of consumption, where it results from the interaction between the reader and the text. This has the effect of making texts more like discourse – meanings are negotiated, as it were, between author and reader, even if each plays a rather different role. In other scholarly traditions, ranging from semiotics to artificial intelligence, a similar rehabilitation of the role of the reader has occurred, as is discussed more fully in Section 7.4 below.

Although some authors still use the terms 'text' and 'discourse' in interchangeable or contradictory ways, many have now adopted the term 'text' to refer to the outward material form of a language event, and 'discourse' to refer to the more complex interaction between participants, text and context. In this way, the *text* rather than the *sentence* is regarded by some as the proper unit of linguistic analysis. For example, drawing on a systemic-functional approach to grammatical analysis (which we described in Chapter 3), Kress and Knapp (1992: 6) suggest that: 'In a social theory of language, the most important unit is the text, that is a socially and contextually complete unit of language.' Although Kress and Knapp use the word 'text' here they apply it to spoken as well as written language. They go on, in fact, to give the following conversational exchange as an example of a text (to be spoken, they say, with a full-on Australian accent):

Mike: Oh, g'day John! How's things?
John: Hi, Mike, not too bad. How's things with you? How's work?
Mike: Can't complain, can't complain, be going on holidays soon. By the way, how's Mary and the kids?
John: Good, real good, actually.
Mike: Well, look, got to dash, good seeing you – catch up with you later.
John: Yeah, look, let's have a coffee soon.
Mike: OK, great; see you then.
John: Yeah, see you.

The authors explain:

This exchange constitutes a text. Its origin is entirely social, as is its function. Its characteristics are specific to a particular cultural group, though in an abstract form it is common to many cultures. It is entirely conventional and recognisable; that is, it is a text with a recognisable and often repeated structure, with a particular way of expressing (coding) social relationships – whether of familiarity and solidarity as here, or of formality, distance, and power differences as in other instances of this kind of text. The conventionalised aspect of this interaction is what we recognise as being generic, as making of this text a particular genre.

By conceptualizing this exchange as a text, Kress and Knapp are able to apply various kinds of linguistic analysis which are more usually to be associated with printed texts – we will examine such things as **narrative structure**, for example, below – and to bring the study of spoken and written language within a single unified framework. By using the notion of **genre**, they can talk about the ways in which such transactions are conventionally structured, and the social significance of such conventions.

Texts belong, in this theoretical approach, to the realm of *parole* rather than *langue* (see Chapter 1). That is, they have a somewhat similar status to *utterances* since both are actual manifestations of language use. A *discourse* is a more abstract entity, similar in theoretical terms to a *language*. It is a term which is increasingly used by analysts who regard language use as closely tied to social practices and ideological positions. We can talk about, for instance, such things as the 'discourse of capitalism', or the 'discourse of teaching'.

Fairclough (1989: 24) distingushes between text and discourse in the following way:

> A text is product rather than a process – a product of the process of text production. But I shall use the term discourse to refer to the whole process of social interaction of which a text is just a part. This includes in addition to the text the process of production, of which the text is a product, and the process of interpretation, for which the text is a resource. Text analysis is correspondingly only a part of discourse analysis, which also includes analysis of productive and interpretative processes.

This, then, is how the theoretical distinction between discourse and text is emerging in the 1990s, but many of the ideas about text structure, social practices, and ideology which we discuss in this chapter have a long history. As a consequence, it is difficult to force the range of work neatly into theoretical categories. We have therefore compromised by dividing the chapter into sections dealing primarily with spoken language and written language, respectively. Both these sections internally distinguish between analytical approaches which take a discourse view and those which take a textual view of their subject matter. This reflects the fact that this distinction (however evasive it may be), rather than that between spoken and written, is of greater current theoretical interest.

7.2 Differences between speech and writing

The primacy of speech

There is a view of language, probably derived from traditional (classical) grammars of English but still with wide currency, that speech is somehow an inferior version of writing: less polished, full of errors and hesitations. Many prescriptions about speech imply that this is, in some sense, a derivative of writing – as when a speaker's pronunciation is corrected: ' "las' week" is sloppy: you should pronounce the *t*'. Modern linguistics, on the other hand, has sought to rehabilitate speech (Palmer 1984: 28):

> A moment's reflection will soon make it clear that speech cannot in any serious sense be derived from writing and cannot therefore depend on it for correctness or non-correctness. Not only did the spoken language precede the written language historically (and even with a language like English only in very recent times has writing been at all widespread), but also every one of us learnt to speak long before we learnt to write. All the patterns of our language were quite firmly established before we went to school, and when we learnt to write we learnt only to put into written symbols what we already knew. If there is priority it is in the spoken, not the written, form of language.

Speech quite clearly preceded writing historically: the oldest known writing system, Sumerian cuneiform, appeared only towards 3000 BC. (See the discussion of writing systems in Section 5.1.)

The idea of the 'priority' or 'primacy' of speech is a key notion in contemporary linguistics, which has tended to take spoken language as its major source of data. A debate between linguists (recorded in Hudson 1984) reaffirmed this stand, while recognizing that the relationship between speech and writing was rather more complex than had previously been acknowledged. Although it is clearly wrong to regard speech as derived from writing, it is also misleading to regard writing as simply a derivative of speech. For instance, some constructions found in writing do not occur, or occur rarely, in speech. The 'past historic' verb tense in French occurs only in writing. English has no such major categorical differences but constructions such as *Jane supposes Susan to be happy* are rare in speech. Many educated speakers spend as much time reading and writing as they do listening and talking – and indeed their speech may be influenced by written language; it is even possible for a spoken language to develop from a language that was restricted to writing, as in the case of modern Hebrew.

It is, in fact, not easy to draw a straightforward distinction between speech and writing. The sections below discuss differences between the two channels, and also how they are interrelated.

Speech and writing as different communication channels

Table 7.1 summarizes some of the more obvious differences between speech and writing, due simply to the fact that they operate as different channels of communication. Even here, though, the differences are not absolute. For instance, telephone conversations cannot rely on gestures and eye contact.

Table 7.1 Some differences between speech and writing

The oral channel	The written channel
1 Sounds	Letters
2 Intonation patterns, changes in pitch and stress to convey attitudes and some grammatical distinctions	No direct counterpart, though underlining words, parentheses, punctuation (e.g. exclamation marks) and capital letters can convey similar meanings
3 Non-verbal gestures, eye contact	No direct counterpart, though different types of handwriting might express similar meanings
4 No direct equivalents, though changes in pitch and speed may express equivalent meanings	Punctuation marks such as dashes, question marks and dots; different types of handwriting or typefaces
5 Pauses and silence	Gaps and dashes
6 Expressions to indicate topic changes, e.g. *right then, now*	Headings, new chapters, paragraphs, etc. Words like *firstly; in conclusion*
7 No direct equivalent	Capital letters for names and beginning of sentences
8 Gap-fillers, e.g. *you know, er*	Hesitations not shown in final form of writing
9 Checks on listener attention and to maintain interaction such as *Do you know what I mean?*	Perhaps less common but checks on reader involvement employed, e.g. *try to bear in mind; if you have followed my arguments so far*

Source: Czerniewska (1985)

Differences in structure and function

Activity 7.1

Here are two examples of discourse, one (originally) spoken and one written.

(a) How do they differ?
(b) How far do you think their differences reflect more general differences between spoken and written language?

The first is a conversation between two lecturers:

A: [Picks up book] Jack's this is Jack's
B: Yes he gave it to me (.) he was clearing out (.)
A: Oh (.) well I don't know whether to check through the references or just to leave it (.) for you to do

B: Don't don't leave anything else for me to do (.) can't you do it
A: Will the editors mmh check references
B: They should do
A: I think someone should mmh go through before anyway uhh to check the photocopies of all the quotations (.) can you do that?
B: Yeah (.) OK [takes photocopies]
A: OK I think that's everything then
B: Right
A: OK see you then
B: See you
A: Bye

The second is a description of a university sickness scheme.

An employee is able to insure himself or herself for up to 75 per cent of gross income less the Single Person's State Benefit, at present £1781. Should an employee suffer long term sickness or injury, he or she would receive this amount beginning 26/52 weeks, according to the waiting period selected, from the date of becoming unable to work up until reaching the normal retiring date.

These may perhaps be regarded, in terms of style, as archetypal instances of speech and writing. The conversation is produced by two people. It is spontaneous and informal. Its collaborative nature is evident in its structure – in the way the two speakers need to 'negotiate' the close of the conversation, for example. Similarly, the fact that it is made up on the spot is evident in the short sequences, hestitations and fillers such as *mmh* (which among other things, allow speakers to plan ahead as they speak). The informality of the occasion can also be seen in the use of more 'casual' forms of speech such as *yeah* and *OK*.

The two speakers can see each other and are talking about the here and now. Hence the use of **deictic** expressions such as *this is Jack's* which refer to items in the physical context. Finally, the conversation is ephemeral (or would be, if it had not been recorded for research purposes).

The written extract is from a published document. It has probably been through at least one draft before being finalized and printed. There is no direct contact between the writer, or writers, and reader. In this case the writer is unknown and, while the document is intended for university staff, the actual reader, on any one occasion, cannot be predicted; nor can the specific context in which the document is read. The style is formal, with constructions such as *should an employee suffer*. The second sentence, in particular, is long and complex, with several dependent clauses. The complexity of this sentence is related to the formal style of the passage, but is only possible because the sentence has been preplanned (probably reflected upon at length!). The language is explicit (there are no deictic expressions referring outside the text).

Imp.

Halliday (see, for example, 1989; 1987) contrasts the **grammatical intricacy** of spoken language with the **lexical density** of written language. He has shown that spoken language tends to employ a different clause structure (fewer lexical items per clause, shorter noun phrases, and more verbs). The relationship between clauses in spoken language is also claimed to be different from that in written language – while written language often makes use of subordinate and embedded clauses, spoken language frequently links together clauses whose structural relationship is less well defined. Halliday argues that this is not because spoken language is 'ungrammatical' but because the grammatical descriptions we have available have been developed to describe written language adequately and tend to fail when applied to spoken language.

There are several communicative consequences, according to Halliday, of such differences in grammatical structure. First, spoken language is said to represent the world in a different way from written language: as a series of processes and actions rather than states and objects since actions which might be described as a process in speech are often turned into a noun phrase in writing. For example, in the extract above of the university sickness scheme, the noun phrase *long term sickness or injury* would probably be expressed through a verb in spoken language *if you are sick or get injured for a long time*. Halliday (1987: 74, 79–80) argues that speech and writing construe the world in different ways:

> each one makes the world look like itself. A written text is an object; so what is represented in writing tends to be given the form of an object. But when one talks, one is doing; so when one talks about something, one happens to say that it happened or was done ... Speech and writing will appear, then, as different ways of meaning: speech as spun out, flowing, choreographic, oriented towards events (doing, happening, sensing, saying, being), processlike, intricate, with meanings related serially; writing as dense, structured, crystalline, oriented towards things (entities, objectified processes), productlike, tight, with meanings related as components.

We explained in Chapter 3 that the Hallidayan concept of **mode** relates not only to physical differences in the channel of communication but also to the conventions of grammatical structuring which have become associated with each channel, and we can now see how this occurs. But any real text can (and usually does) show characteristics of more than one mode. For example, a speaker may use phrases or formulations which have either come from printed texts, or might be intended to finish up in printed texts. A politician responding to a newspaper journalist's question, a teacher giving an explanation of something which might ultimately find its way into a piece of a pupil's writing, a job interviewer's rephrasing of a candidate's experience in a way which makes it more suitable for a form; a seminar group in which a research article is being discussed. In all these examples, there is a ghost of written language behind the spoken language

– a knowledge of the conventions of written language, and forms and style of written language, have influenced the form of talk either because the talk derives in part from a written text, or because it is intended to end up in one.

Activity 7.2

Look at the following transcript from a job training interview. Identify any phrases which seem to you to be more 'written' in style.

Int: What job were you doing last?

Client: I was in light engineering, electrical engineering.

Int: And what were you doing there?

Client: Assembling a thing to switch the earth to mains they manufacture that.

[later]

Client: And most of them say that soldering experience is a necessary qualification but they said that we they would have to have a know-how of er how to pack components into a board and manual dexterity for speed.

Int: uhuh.
         []

Int: When you're on Employment Training you don't sign on. The benefits you have before you start remain the same and you're given a 10 premium per week but the first 4 of fares you have to pay yourself and anything else is refunded to you. Is that OK? Erm you'll be given a wee white card as well and if you keep the wee white card if you're going to start with their training the training manager which is Scotwest Training will arrange for you to go along to the benefit office and you hand in this card and they will sort out your benefits so you don't have to sign on.

The speech in this transcript is, in the main, spoken and spontaneous. Nevertheless there are occasional phrases which seem to be more like written language. For example, where the client refers to his experience in terms of *Assembling a thing to switch the earth to mains they manufacture that* we can see many linguistic features which are typical of spontaneous speech. The client's response is elliptical, in that the subject (presumably *I*) is omitted. The structure of the clause and the way information is presented within the clause is also typically spoken. (You might like to look back to Chapter 3 and try to analyse this utterance in terms of its theme–rheme, and given–new structure.) Later, however, when the client notes that for one training opportunity he would need to have a *know-how of how to pack components into a board and manual dexterity for speed*, we can see the intrusion of phrases from the printed texts which he had just been reading. And in the last turn, the interviewer seems almost to be reciting from a benefits leaflet for the first two sentences, albeit a benefits leaflet which already attempts to be clear and fairly informal. When the interviewer asks *Is that OK?*, there is an abrupt shift of voice. This is signalled lexically by words like *wee* as well as by clause structure.

Many spoken texts thus contain elements of the written mode. This reflects the important status given to written language in our culture: much of our day-to-day business which requires talk is shaped by printed texts of some kind. In this extract, for example, there are the forms which the client has already filled in to describe his work experience, the form he will fill in to apply for training, the brochures which describe the various training opportunities available, the official documents which the interviewer draws on to provide information to the client and which guide his conduct of the meeting. Very many written texts are also informed by speech: a school essay which is written after a class discussion, or taking notes from a lecture. And some kinds of written text are special genres for recording such talk: the transcript conventions which we described in Chapter 6, for example, or the minutes taken at a meeting.

Dimensions underlying speech and writing

Comparisons between speech and writing are, then, unlikely to be very fruitful unless one specifies what kind of speech is being compared with what kind of writing. Table 7.2 shows a number of dimensions along which instances of language use can be ranged. Examples of writing (above the lines) and speech (below the lines) are given for the 'extremes' of each dimension.

Relationships between the two channels are highly complex and interact with a range of other factors. However, because of the sets of factors typically associated with each channel, they differ in status. For instance, the university document quoted in Activity 7.1 is probably legally binding – and it is often the case that formulations with legal status are written and not spoken. Lexicographers compiling the *Oxford English Dictionary* gave priority to written sources when collecting citations. One justification for this has been that such sources are 'verifiable' – but clearly a recording of a radio interview is just as verifiable as a written source.

Ironically, despite their protestations about the primacy of speech, exposure to higher-status written forms may also affect linguists' perceptions of language. For instance, the adoption of the sentence as the largest unit of syntactic analysis was probably affected by writing: sentence-like structures are less likely to occur in speech. Even descriptive grammars tend to be biased towards the kind of formal language conventionally associated with writing. The *Grammar of Contemporary English*, the first in a series of grammars produced by Randolph Quirk and his associates (Quirk *et al.* 1972), describes 'the grammar of educated English current in the second half of the twentieth century in the world's major English-speaking

Table 7.2 Some dimensions by which language use can be classified (based on Hudson 1984b)

1 Transitoriness

permanent record	printed book _____ note for milkman	ephemeral
	recording of conversation	
	a parliamentary debate	

2 Degree of formality

formal	Act of Parliament _____ shopping list	informal
	Queen's Speech informal conversation	

3 Use of standard English

	school poem in local	
standard	textbook _____ dialect	non-standard
	BBC News parent–child conversation	

4 Degree of interaction between producer and receiver

	telephone notes passed between	
low interaction	directory _____ children in classroom	high interaction
	radio talk telephone conversation	

5 Type of interaction between producer and receiver

message-oriented	recipe _____ Christmas card	socially-
	football 'How do you do?'	orientated
	commentary	

6 Dependence on context

	instructions for	
context-independent	a story _____ self-assembly kit	context-
	poetry recitation oral directions	dependent

communities'. However, the emphasis is on 'the English of serious exposition' and illustrative examples are normally edited. Examples such as:

A: John gave the girl an apple
B: *Gave the girl an apple*! How kind he is!

and *What a present he had given the girl*! (Quirk *et al.* 1972: 57–8) seem to owe more to written than spoken norms.

7.3 Spoken language

Introduction

In this section we will review briefly two scholarly approaches to the analysis of spoken language which have become particularly important since the early 1970s. In each case only a summary of the main features of each tradition is given. Some aspects of the analysis, such as turn-taking and speech-act analysis, have been of interest to other disciplines and more detailed accounts can be found elsewhere in this book. In such cases, appropriate cross-references are given.

The two approaches discussed in this section are those known, respectively, as **conversation analysis** (CA), which is treated at greater length, and **discourse analysis** (DA). At first glance, there may not appear to be a great difference between the two. Both are empirical traditions concerned with discovering order and structure in naturally occurring spoken data. Conversation analysis grew out of work by American sociologists, and is particularly concerned with how people do things in talk and understand what they are doing. Discourse analysis is in origin a British tradition founded by linguists and provides a formal framework of analysis. There are many differences of emphasis and approach between the two traditions, and yet they also share many concerns. Both agree on the importance of sequencing in structure, for example, yet one insists that no formal framework of analysis can be achieved, and the other sets out to provide one.

The essential difference, perhaps, lies in their respective notions of 'structure'. Discourse analysis conceives of structure as 'linguistic structure' – each stretch of discourse has a particular inherent structure which can be made visible by studying the organization of linguistic units. Conversation analysts, by contrast, claim that in order to make visible the organization of conversation, one needs to know the functions of utterances, and these are more indeterminate than discourse analysis will allow, appearing as a result of negotiation between participants. 'Structure', then, is a more fluid phenomenon which emerges from people's attempts to make sense of each other's utterances. This distinction should become more apparent in the description of each approach given below.

Conversation analysis

Conversation analysis, in the form which we discuss here, began in the United States in the 1970s and grew out of attempts by sociologists (in particular, Harold Garfinkel) to explain how people made sense of ordinary everyday behaviour. It quickly became apparent that conversation was an ideal subject for such analyses. Although people seem to find conversation an easy enough task, a closer examination showed that it was rather difficult to explain exactly how people understand what is going on in a conversation. Conversation analysis recognizes that conversation is not only complex but also fluid in structure. It developed interests in both how that structure manifested itself to participants, and how participants co-ordinate their behaviour in order to allow the interaction to progress smoothly.

The ideas of co-ordination and co-operation are fundamental to conversation analysis and can be illustrated by considering a non-verbal example. If someone wishes to pass an object to another person – whether a ball or a pair of scissors – the success of the manoeuvre depends on co-operation between both people. The person who is passing needs to signal that they are about to pass, and the person receiving must not only get ready to receive but must also demonstrate this in a manner which allows the person passing to synchronize their actions. One way in which such synchronization can be easily accomplished is if the patterns of behaviour are structured in a routine and familiar way. We can then see not only that someone is about to pass us an object, but also predict precisely when the moment of transfer is to come. If we could not do this, then the object would, of course, end up on the floor.

Conversation analysts suggest we do somewhat similar things when talking. We need to make our behaviour familiar and predictable in structure. The person who wishes to tell bad news, or tell a joke, or ask a favour needs to display by some means that they are about to do so. Without such warning, the recipient may not make the correct or timely response and the topic might end, metaphorically speaking, on the floor.

An important claim by conversation analysts, then, is that conversational activity may be fluid, but that it is organized in an orderly way. In particular, certain things are said in a particular order, or said in a particular format.

A second claim is that although conversation is orderly, it is by no means transparent in its structure. Participants constantly need to work at making sense, at checking or clarifying what is going on, and at co-operating with others to produce an orderly structure. In this respect the structure of conversation is very unlike that of a written sentence, say, in that at least two people work together to improvise the finished product.

It will be obvious from this summary that conversation analysts are interested both in detailed management problems, such as the minutiae of smooth turn-taking, and in larger organizing principles and structures in conversation. In this section, we will deal only with the latter. A discussion of turn-taking can be found in Section 6.3.

OVERALL ORGANIZATION

Although conversations may seem to meander without great structure or direction, conversation analysts have noted that they share certain similarities in overall organization. All conversations, for example, need to be started and finished. Starts and finishes happen in a fairly regular manner which partly reflects basic interactional problems (like attracting someone's attention at the beginning, or checking that they have no more to say at the end), and is partly a cultural convention. Rather like a game of chess in which opening moves and endgames are more highly constrained than the middlegame, openings and closings in conversations seem to be ritualized.

Sandwiched, as it were, between the opening and closing sequences, a large range of things may happen. People may give invitations, tell stories, make compliments, tell about troubles, and so on. Each activity, however, has been shown by conversation analysts to have a recognizable and regular organization. We can tell whether someone is offering a compliment or asking a favour, it is argued, not so much from what is said, as from the format in which it is said, and the way in which it has been led up to. Two kinds of organization have been identified: **sequential organization** and **preference organization**.

SEQUENTIAL ORGANIZATION

The closing sequences of a conversation form a good example of an activity which is clearly sequentially organized. Schegloff and Sacks (1973) suggested that how a telephone conversation can be brought jointly and smoothly to a close represents a technical problem of co-ordination. Unexplained silences during telephone calls are generally avoided. If one person stops talking then the other will take over, or at the very least give some minimal response which shows that they are still there and attending. So, the problem is one of 'how to organise the simultaneous arrival of the co-conversationalists at a point where one speaker's completion will not occasion another speaker's talk, and that will not be heard as some speaker's silence'. One way of ensuring this might simply be to say 'goodbye' and to put down the phone. In practice, this very rarely happens. Schegloff and Sacks argued that participants first go through a sequence which establishes that both parties have said all they wish to say. If speaker A finishes a turn, then there is normally an obligation on speaker B to start a new one. If, however, B gives only a minimal response, such as 'OK', then effectively speaker B returns the obligation to speak to A, indicating that he or she has nothing to add at that stage. If A now also gives a minimal response, yielding the turn again, then a situation has arisen in which both participants have indicated a readiness to finish the call. Schegloff and Sacks demonstrated that 'goodbye' sequences were preceded by such reciprocal 'OK's or similar responses.

The following examples illustrate how closings are made. Each call was recorded (with permission) on internal telephones at the Open University.

```
 1   A: the thing is we are receiving pages later this week
 2       um of with all the corrections in
 3   B: yeah
 4   A: but I just wanted to see how many it came to anyway
 5   B: mmm
 6   A: so there's probably an index on top of that then
 7   B: yeah it will be⌈yeah
 8   A:                 ⌊yes right
 9   B: O.K.?
10   A: Thanks very much
11   B: right bye bye
12   A: bye.
```

Note how B is, throughout this extract, giving no more than noises of affirmation. These serve to indicate both that she is still there and listening, and that she has nothing herself to say. Hence discussion of the topic will end when A has nothing more to say himself. This point seems to be reached in line 8 where A gives the first *right*. In line 9, B asks for confirmation that A has finished, which A gives in line 10. At this point, an 'opening for a close' has been made, and one of two things can happen. If B has something to say on another topic, then now is the time for her to introduce it, but she initiates instead the closing sequence. B's *bye* is returned by A and the call is ended.

```
 1   B:  can you still potter on coz I'm actually you know got some-
 2        thing I'd quite like to sort of get on with this morning
 3   A:  O.K.
 4   B:  if that's all right
 5   A:  yeah
 6   B:  I'll I'll come over this afternoon
 7   A:  right O.K. then
 8   B:  right
 9   A:  bye
10   B:  bye
11   A:  bye
```

The structure of this sequence is rather similar to the first, although two different speakers are involved. You may wonder why there are so many turns involved in closing the conversation. This is common in telephone conversations, and probably reflects the fact that participants are going through several stages of closure. At the very least, closure of the topic in hand must be distinguished from the closure of the call itself. The last repeated *bye* by A may be because, in English, it is often the person who initiates the call (A in each case) who gets the last 'goodbye'. This convention is not quite as strict as the one which operates at the beginning of conversations, which requires the person who is called to speak first.

This description of closing sequences assumes that the two parties have equal status. There may be contexts, for instance, where both people do not have equal rights to bring the call to a close. A powerful person may curtail the call more abruptly, without ensuring that the other person had fully finished.

Closure sequences demonstrate a number of features of conversational structure. They show one way in which participants can prepare each other for an upcoming event (in this case closure) and co-ordinate its successful arrival. They also show how, in parts of a conversation, things are said in a particular order.

Elsewhere in the conversation the actual utterances may not be quite so predictable, but nevertheless there are sequential patterns. For example, of the following two hypothetical sequences, (1) sounds more plausible than (2):

(1)   A: It's cold in here
      B: The door's open

(2)   A: It's cold in here
      B: The light's on

The interesting thing about such sequences, however, is not whether they are plausible or not, but how we set about understanding them. In practice, conversations are full of sequences that would look extremely implausible if a researcher produced them as hypothetical examples. Sequence (1), however, seems to have a greater **coherence** than sequence (2). We can see easily how B's utterance follows from A's. In some way or other, we can hear B providing an explanation of A's observation. If sequence (2) seems more implausible then perhaps it is because we have expended more effort in trying to envisage a context in which B's utterance appears relevant to A's.

One pervasive feature of talk is that each contribution should accord with what Grice (1975) has termed **conversational maxims**. (These are discussed more fully in Section 4.3.) One such maxim is the criterion of **relevance**. The criterion of relevance suggests that any utterance will be understood by reference to what has preceded it, but it does not in itself indicate *how* it should be relevant. If, in sequence (1), we hear A as making an indirect *request* to close the door, then we might hear B's response as a refusal of that request. If, on the other hand, we hear A as making a *complaint* that the fire has not been lit, then we might hear B to be explaining why it was not necessary.

Exactly which interpretation we arrive at will normally depend on a number of other aspects of the context not supplied in this extract, which may include the relative status of the speakers and their perceived rights to make complaints or requests. In each case, however, we have traded upon an expectation that certain kinds of utterance follow others. Schegloff and Sacks (1973) suggested that such utterances formed **adjacency pairs**: these are sequences of two utterances that are: (a) adjacent; (b) produced by different speakers; (c) ordered as a first part and a second part; and (d) of particular types, so that a particular first part requires a particular second (or range of second parts). Common adjacency pairs include greetings and questions and answers. If I say 'hello' to someone, then their next utterance or gesture is likely to be interpreted as a response to that greeting; if I ask a question, I will evaluate the speaker's next utterance as a potential answer. Many a politician has given the appearance of answering unwelcome questions simply by responding with bland, irrelevant talk.

The way any utterance is taken in a conversation crucially depends on its location within a recognizable sequence. Whether the utterance *right* is taken to be an agreement or a preclosing manoeuvre will very much depend on what kind of turn preceded it:

The point is that no analysis, grammatical, semantic, pragmatic, etc., of these utterances taken singly and out of sequence, will yield their

import in use, will show what co-participants might make of them
and do about them.

(Atkinson and Heritage 1984)

PREFERENCE ORGANIZATION

Some adjacency pairs may take more than one kind of response, but have
only one as the common pattern. Such a response is said to be a **preferred
response**. The existence of a **preference organization** of this kind sets up
a stronger pattern of expectation and helps reduce uncertainty about how
to take the next utterance. For example, many utterances which seek action on the part of the listener may logically be met with either compliance
or refusal, yet the latter is a strongly dispreferred response. People need
to go on special assertiveness training courses, it seems, in order to 'learn
how to say no'. If a hearer wishes to refuse a request, then he or she is
more likely to accede to a lesser request, or provide the future grounds for
granting it. It is by no means impossible for a speaker to give a dispreferred
response, but if one is given it is likely to be marked in some way
'Dispreferred seconds are typically delivered: (a) after some significant
delay; (b) with some preface marking their dispreferred status, often the
particle *well*; (c) with some account of why the preferred second cannot be
performed' (Levinson 1983: 307). Table 7.3 shows the preference organization of a number of adjacency pairs.

Table 7.3 Preference organization of adjacency pairs

First parts					
	request	offer/invite	assessment	question	blame
Second parts					
Preferred	acceptance	acceptance	agreement	expected answer	denial
Dispreferred	refusal	refusal	disagreement	unexpected answer or non-answer	admission

Source: Levinson (1983: 336)

PRESEQUENCES

It is not just the sequential location which affects how an utterance will be
taken. Precisely the same utterance may function one way in a *blaming*
episode, say, and another way in a *request* episode. Or, to put it another
way, the function of an individual utterance or turn depends very much
on the prior understanding of what kind of activity the participants are
engaged in. This is one reason why it is so important for participants to
approach such activities in an orderly and predictable way.

Presequences are one way of doing this. If someone asks *Are you doing anything tonight?*, it probably heralds some kind of invitation. Such a presequence anticipates the organization of an invitation sequence in which a refusal is dispreferred and must be supported by a reason. The presequence orients to the most likely grounds for a refusal and thus clears the way for the invitation to go ahead. Similarly with requests. If you go into a shop and ask *Do you sell matches?*, the shopkeeper may reach directly to serve you, anticipating the forthcoming request. Such formulations are not routinely taken to be enquiries about the shop's stocking policy.

Presequences, then, help flag the nature of the upcoming activity. They do this by being seen to anticipate the known organization of the particular activity.

PARTICIPANT ORIENTATIONS

Presequences demonstrate that participants are themselves aware of the local organization of particular kinds of conversational activity. Such an awareness allows them to check regularly on each other's understandings of what is going on. A compliment and a blaming both form the first part of an adjacency pair, for example, but they have different second parts. If I say something which is intended as a compliment, I can quickly tell whether it has been misconstrued as a criticism by monitoring the kind of response which it elicits.

Conversation analysts put great stress on the fact that participants are themselves aware of the organizational structure of conversation:

> We have proceeded under the assumption (an assumption borne out by our research) that in so far as the materials we worked with exhibited orderliness, they did so not only to us, indeed not in the first place for us, but for the co-participants who had produced them.
>
> (Schegloff and Sacks 1973: 290)

This is put into methodological practice by insisting that on every occasion a claim is made about how participants understood an event, then a 'warrant' for such a claim must be found in the data. In other words, if an interactional detail or feature of organization is regarded as important by conversation analysts then there is a requirement to show that participants themselves orient to that feature:

> The analyst is not required to speculate upon what the interactants hypothetically or imaginably understood, or the procedures or constraints to which they could conceivably have been oriented. Instead, analysis can emerge from observation of the conduct of the participants.
>
> (Atkinson and Heritage 1984: 1)

Conversational data provide various kinds of evidence for such participant orientation. We have already suggested that the organization of presequences demonstrates an awareness of the organization of the activity which they herald. Another source of evidence comes from misunderstandings which result in a participant's seeking or giving a clarification.

THE ROLE OF EMPIRICAL DATA

Perhaps the most notable feature of conversation analysis is the great emphasis it puts on empirical data. In this it can be contrasted with other traditions in linguistic research which have taken the analyst's recollections or intuitions as data and provided invented examples as illustration. Conversation analysis also differs from other empirical traditions in sociological and psychological research which use either interview or experimental techniques. Conversation analysts set out to discover what people actually do and, restricting themselves to naturally occurring conversations in all their messiness and apparent imperfection, they often find that people do some surprising things.

This empirical emphasis is, in principle, commendable and it guards against premature and speculative theory-building. It also leads to particular insights and observations about people's everyday behaviour which were unobtainable in other ways. Even so, it still gives rise to one or two problems of both a methodological and theoretical kind.

Conversation analysts claim the raw data are precisely that – the actual event as it happened. Recordings and transcriptions are mere mnemonics of that original event. In practice, however, recourse is made to transcriptions and recordings for the purpose of analysis. There is, of course, no way around this. The close detail in which they need to observe interactions – which may include the precise relative timing of a head shake with someone else's interruption, for example – demands a recording which can be played again and again. It is occasionally the case, however, that this requirement for detail proves to be a source of difficulty.

First, it is futile to suppose that there could exist a single and authoritative version of the original event. Different participants will have experienced rather different things. Perhaps one person was looking in the other direction, or simply blinked when the head shake occurred. Again, one must be careful about supposing that interactional nuances which emerge only after hours of painstaking study by a diligent researcher were particularly salient to the original participants. Any explanation of participants' behaviour cannot delve further and further into the detail of the interaction without bearing these things in mind.

Second, there is an important respect in which, at this level of detail, the transcript represents an analysis generated by the transcriber. Given the difficulties which professional linguists experience when trying to notate intonation (see Section 2.4), conversation analysts appear to put remarkable confidence in somewhat crude representations of prosody. The fact such transcriptions appear intimidatingly detailed does not mean they are not already digested. Rather than raw data, the analyst has already selected, organized, and partially analysed the material.

Conversation analysts rightly warn against attempts to provide a definitive and authoritative analysis of 'what is going on' in an interaction. Their own search for an authoritative and immensely detailed transcription may, however, be similarly misguided.

It is not just at the level of detail that a problem about the analyst's relationship to the data appears. As has been seen in the discussion above, the structures and organizations which are described by conversation analysts are not identifiable through independent linguistic or formal criteria. Before the regular organization of, say, an invitation sequence can be perceived, the functions of certain individual utterances must be identified. Conversation analysts often resort to what they call 'member's knowledge' (which seems to be similar to the linguist's 'intuition', see Section 1.5). If *they* can hear something as an invitation, then this requires explanation, and the warrants or cues for that interpretation will lie in the data. This is claimed to be a legitimate exercise, since the analyst is like an ordinary member of the community in this respect, applying 'common-sense' knowledge.

But if analysts generate a text on the basis of their own interpretative skills, then there is a very definite sense in which they are investigating their own, rather than the participants', strategies of understanding. This may not amount to a very important consideration when they investigate data taken from their own speech community. In other instances, in anthropological research or work with child conversation, it may become a much more worrying issue.

It would be wrong to suggest that conversation analysts have no answers to this kind of criticism. It is a canon of conversation analysis that data should not only be given where appropriate to support analyses, but that in principle such data should be made available for public inspection in its most raw form. In principle, then, if colleagues wished to object on the grounds laid out above, they could inspect and analyse the data themselves.

More importantly, conversation analysis guards itself against the charge of constructing its own data through the claim that any organizational structures visible to the analyst must also be available to the participants. It is in order to demonstrate such participant orientations that conversation analysts must rake through so much data in such detail:

> As the analysis proceeds it will become apparent that the search for evidence of participant orientations may involve the analyst in protracted examination of small fragments of data. The claim that one's analysis is more than a purely analytic construct but reproduces and explicates the bases of participants' understandings is a strong one. In view of this, the painstaking, 'inch-by-inch' approach to interactional data that CA recommends becomes understandable not as a matter of quirk or indulgence, but as one of necessity.
>
> (French and Local 1986: 159)

However, it is not always the case that orientations and understandings will be visible in subsequent talk. The evidence provided by conversation analysts often relies more on its plausibility than on provision of proof.

One further problem with a strict and laborious empiricism of this kind is that it makes it very difficult to illuminate the relationship between what happens in individual interactions and larger patterns in social structure, or patterns of social inequality. For example, it might be tempting to explain certain episodes in a conversation between, say, an employer and an employee in terms of differential institutionalized power. Conversational analysis, in its strictest form, would not allow as legitimate any discussion which appealed to abstract notions of power or of social identities except in so far as the workings of such constructs were visible in the empirical data. In this, they may be open to the charge that their explanations of conversational behaviour are, in an important respect, impoverished ones.

We have discussed some of the methodological problems with conversation analysis in order to indicate where the technique can best be used. Many of the apparent limitations can be circumvented by the use of other techniques, and there exist many researchers who employ the techniques of conversation analysis in a flexible and eclectic manner.

Discourse analysis

The *discourse analysis* approach to the analysis of talk is a clear embarrassment for the distinction between 'discourse' and 'text' which we made in Section 7.1. Discourse analysis was devised by two British linguists, John Sinclair and Malcolm Coulthard, and was an attempt to produce a structural linguistic analysis of spontaneous conversation. It can therefore be reasonably regarded as a *textual* approach within the terms we have described, despite its name.

Discourse analysis is based on speech act theory (see Section 4.3) and assumes that, within discourse, there is a finite set of identifiable functions that utterances can perform. Sinclair and Coulthard suggest that these functions can be reliably correlated with specific linguistic items or nonverbal events (that is, it should always be clear exactly how to categorize an utterance); that sequences of functional units occur in a restricted set of possible combinations; and that any discourse can be exhaustively described in terms of its component-functional units and their patterns of combination.

THE HIERARCHICAL ORGANIZATION OF TALK

The system of analysis was meant to handle classroom talk, of the type where a teacher interacts with a group of children. A lesson, like any other example of talk, can be analysed sequentially (as a series of turns) but Sinclair and Coulthard posited a hierarchical organization. A lesson consisted of topically coherent units, termed **transactions**. These could be

Figure 7.1 The hierarchical organization of talk

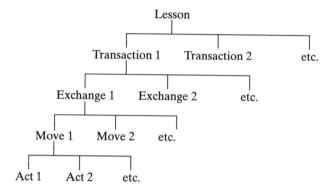

further segmented into sequences of speaker turns or part-turns, termed **exchanges**. Exchanges consisted of **moves** (speaker turns or part-turns). And moves were composed of functional units called **acts**. This hierarchical structure can be represented as a tree diagram (Figure 7.1), rather like those you saw used for sentence analysis in Chapter 3. As an example of Sinclair and Coulthard's analysis, and what it can reveal about classroom discourse, we shall look in more detail at the exchange and its component parts.

EXCHANGES IN CLASSROOM TALK

During a transaction, a teacher can direct a pupil to carry out a task, try to elicit from a pupil some verbal contribution to a discussion, or provide information. Sinclair and Coulthard found that these activities gave rise to characteristic patterns of speaking turn. These different patterns suggested the category 'exchange', which can be defined as a minimal interactive unit of conversation (for example, a question followed by its answer; or a statement followed by an acknowledgement). Four main types of teaching exchange were identified (see Sinclair and Coulthard 1975: 63ff.):

1 **Directive**
   Teacher: The first quiz is this.
   Can you fill in this sentence?
   See if you can do it in your books.
   (The pupils write in their books.)

2 **Check**
   Teacher: Finished Joan?
   (Pupil provides non-verbal response.)

3 **Informative**
   Teacher: And – when I can find my chart – here it is.
   Here are some of the symbols that they used.

4 **Elicitation**
  Teacher: Read us what you've written, Joan.
  Pupil: The cat sat on the rug.
  Teacher: Yes that's right.
          I changed the last word.

The structure of these exchanges can be described in terms of component 'moves', which are respectively *initiating, responding* and *follow-up*
moves (these are often termed I, R and F). The 'elicitation' exchange
above contains all three sorts of move, and can be represented as in Table
7.4. Other exchanges show different (characteristic) sequential patterns.

Table 7.4 The elicitation exchange

Moves	
Initiating	Read us what you've written, Joan.
Responding	The cat sat on the rug.
Follow-up	Yes, that's right. I changed the last word.

Source: Sinclair and Coulthard (1975: 63)

Table 7.5 The elicitation exchange

Moves		Acts
Initiating	Read us what you've written, Joan.	(elicit) (nominate)
Responding	The cat sat on the rug.	(reply)
Follow up	Yes, that's right. I changed the last word.	(evaluate) (comment)

Source: as Table 7.4

The moves that make up exchanges can themselves be segmented into
acts (according to the functions they perform in the discourse). For instance, part of the teacher's initiating move in the exchange above is
concerned to nominate one pupil (from the whole class) to answer. The
constituent acts of this exchange can be represented as in Table 7.5.
    Sinclair and Coulthard identified 22 acts, which they claimed were suf-
ficient to describe all classroom discourse.
    This system of analysis provides a way of describing classroom talk
between teacher and pupils, and the different discourse patterns that this
may contain. Below are two rather differently organized sequences of

classroom talk, the first of which is relatively easy to fit into Sinclair and Coulthard's framework, the second less so. To the right of each transcript is an analysis into moves and exchange types. If you wish to check your understanding of the discussion so far you could cover up the right-hand columns and attempt your own analysis of the data before reading the ones we give.

Extract 1

		Moves	Exchanges	
T:	what do you notice there – what's special about that particular section of tape – what's the child doing – anybody	I	Teacher	1
P:	trying to say something	R	elicitation	
T:	er, right Rosita	F		
	what's he actually trying to say	I	Teacher	2
P:	trying to get a word out of his mouth	R	elicitation	
T:	and what's the word he's trying to get out	(F)I	Teacher	3
P:	mm daddy·	R	elicitation	

In exchange (1) the teacher produces a string of initiations. Teachers often do this, and pupils operate a rule that they only answer the final one. So here the teacher's utterance is just coded once. In exchange (2) one could assume either that there is no F or that I in exchange (3) is simultaneously an F in exchange (2). The IRF patterns evident here occur very frequently in classroom discourse.

Extract 2

		Moves	Exchanges	
P:	and that's er what do you call it – what you have for breakfast	I	Pupil elicitation	1
T:	what you have for breakfast	I	Teacher	2
P:	sometimes	R	check	
	oranges – what do you call them – red things	I	Pupil elicitation	3
T:	what you have for breakfast	I	Teacher	4
P:	sometimes	R	check	
T:	oh – it is – it isn't a living thing this	I	Teacher	5
P:	no	R	check	
T:	strawberry	I	Teacher	6
P:	yes	F	informative	
T:	you have strawberries for breakfast	I	Teacher	7
P:	yeah	R	check	
T:	do you really	F		

This interchange is unusual partly because it is the pupil who is initiating, but also because the teacher is asking genuine questions, not test questions: hence a series of teacher checking exchanges, and not teacher elicitations. The pupil's initiations in (1) and (3) do not get immediate answers. The initiation in (6) could alternatively be taken as an answer to the pupil's question, but separated from it. The pupil appears to evaluate the teacher's remark in (6), giving an uncharacteristic teacher informative exchange: IF. The analysis of Extract 2 is not intended as the 'definitive' version: the point is to show how the organization of the interchange is different from Extract 1, and more difficult to fit into the system.

LIMITATIONS OF DISCOURSE ANALYSIS

Discourse analysis was initially devised for the type of tightly structured talk that is often found between a teacher and pupils in classrooms, where the teacher is in control (normally) of information that has to be conveyed to pupils. While later attempts were made to adapt it to other contexts (see, for instance, Coulthard and Brazil 1979) it is not really suitable for more casual conversation.

Discourse analysis is a general analytical model and, when applied to actual data, some interpretation will be required on the part of the analyst. Although the aim was to produce a system in which the categorization of utterances would be clear and unambiguous, in practice there is unlikely to be agreement about all coding decisions.

The system is comprehensive in that all utterances are coded from beginning to end, but only one level of function is coded (the function of an utterance *within* the discourse); the analysis has nothing to say about the way language is used to convey irony, threats, humour, etc. If one accepts this limited notion of function, it is still unlikely that utterances can be analysed unambiguously in terms of a single function. Consider the following example:

A: What are you doing tonight?
B: Nothing. Why?
A: I was thinking of going to a movie, wanna come?

A's first utterance is undeniably a question but it also functions as a pre-offer (i.e. it signals that an offer is about to be made; A is not really requesting a detailed account of B's planned evening activities). B's response, *nothing*, indicates an awareness of this second function.

A further problem is that, while the analysis relies on the possibility of correlating discourse functions with specific linguistic items or non-verbal events, it is not always possible to identify utterances independently of their functions. For instance, virtually anything can function as a bid at an auction – a call of 'Here!', a wave, even a scratch of the head or a wink. Knowing whether something counts as an 'utterance' (in the sense of being part of the interaction) relies on prior recognition that it has fulfilled a particular function.

Finally, it is not possible to specify general sequencing rules (i.e. to specify what sort of functional units can follow one another). Permissible combinations will be heavily dependent upon particular contexts. For instance, consider the following:

(A is a shopper in search of a pullover to go with a beige jacket; B is a shop assistant serving A)

A: Yes mm. Do you think that blue would stand a chance with mm beige?
B: Well, try that one on (selecting a grey pullover).

A's utterance functions as a question, and it has been supposed that this requires the provision of information as an adequate response. B's response does not do this – it seems, rather, to function more as a suggestion, in imperative form. Yet in this context the sequence seems quite acceptable.

7.4 Written language

Written language has a much longer history of analysis than spoken, and there exists a much wider variety of approaches. Once again, approaches have been distinguished here according to whether they treat the subject as properly an interaction between the written forms and a reader (who applies a knowledge of the world as well as a knowledge of language to the task); or whether they restrict themselves to an analysis of intrinsic structural or more superficial properties of written passages.

Among discourse approaches to written language, undoubtedly the most influential has been that developed by cognitive psychologists. The concepts and framework described here will be found referred to in many apparently unrelated traditions. For comparison, we also include a brief description of a kind of **political discourse analysis** known as **critical linguistics**, which represents a rather different attempt to describe the meaning of discourse as a culturally situated phenomenon. Among the textual approaches, we have described several which have been influential in educational circles. The selection is by no means comprehensive, and, if it appears fragmented, this reflects the fact that many techniques of textual description have been developed for particular, and often very limited, applications.

Discourse approaches to written language

COGNITIVE PSYCHOLOGY

Our understanding of what kinds of things texts are, and how people perceive their internal structure, owes a great deal to work over several decades in cognitive psychology. Much of this research, in principle, could apply equally well to both spoken and written language, and indeed, many of the experimental methods used by psychologists involve reading texts aloud. The contribution of cognitive psychology is discussed here, however (rather than in Section 7.3), for two reasons.

First, nearly all the material investigated has, in practice, been in the form of continuous prose or two or three connected sentences. The reason why experimenters often present such passages by reading them aloud is simply that it helps ensure all subjects have been given exactly the same information and time. Although it might be possible to generalize the findings to elucidate the structure of talk between two or more people, to do so would introduce complexities which have not yet been tackled. The models discussed are therefore particularly applicable to continuous prose.

Second, some of the concepts and terminology developed by cognitive psychologists have been widely taken up by researchers in text linguistics, and an understanding of them is most useful when reading research papers and literature in this area.

Research in cognitive psychology can nevertheless be regarded as a contribution to the study of *discourse* as opposed to *text* in the more abstract sense of the terms outlined in Section 7.1. That is, such research is characterized by a concern for how real people in particular contexts and states of knowledge arrive at understandings through the use of inference and general world knowledge.

Memory for meaning   When people read or hear some piece of continuous prose, they store some kind of representation of it in memory – that is, they can, at some future time, recall things about it. Psychologists have often used experiments on recall to gain insights into the kinds of structure people perceive in text. What has been found is that people do not normally remember words and sentences verbatim. Instead they seem to form a general memory of the objects and happenings referred to in the text, which might be termed a **semantic representation**.

Kintsch (1974) reported an experiment in which, from the same basic story, he constructed two written texts, one syntactically complex and one simple. Although subjects took longer to read and understand the complex version, they could not be distinguished from those who read the simple passage in terms of the kind or speed of their responses to questions made later. Kintsch concluded that subjects from both groups stored the meaning of each paragraph in a similar abstract form which was independent of the form of the original sentences.

The role of world knowledge   In a well-known experiment by Bransford *et al.* (1972), one group of subjects heard sentences such as (1) read aloud, and another group sentences like (2):

(1) Three turtles rested beside a floating log and a fish swam beneath them.
(2) Three turtles rested on a floating log and a fish swam beneath them.

In (2), but not (1), it is possible to infer that the fish swam underneath the log. This inference is arrived at as a result of our general experience and knowledge of how things work in the world. It is not a strict logical entailment (see Section 4.3) in the way propositions (3) and (4) are:

(3) Logs float
(4) Fish can swim

Subjects were later given a list of sentences and asked to pick out those which they had originally heard. The list included new sentences such as (5) and (6):

(5) Three turtles rested beside a floating log and a fish swam beneath it.
(6) Three turtles rested on a floating log and a fish swam beneath it.

The experiment showed that subjects who had heard (2) often claimed, incorrectly, that they had heard (6), but those who had heard (1) did not confuse it with sentence (5) in the same way. The researchers concluded that the semantic representations which people made when reading or hearing a text could only be arrived at by making inferences based on ordinary world knowledge – that is, information which lies outside of the text.

Schemas, frames and scripts   The finding that people apply their knowledge of the world to generate representations of a text in their memory is a most important one. Among other things, it has given rise to a whole new movement in **artificial intelligence** (AI), since it demonstrated that in order to get machines to understand text properly, it was insufficient to build in a grammar and vocabulary which would allow them to recognize the words and the syntactic structure of the sentences. In addition, it is necessary to build in a vast store of world knowledge, and a set of principles for making inferences.

The finding gave rise to a more specific problem, however, of how people actually selected and activated one rather than another segment of their world knowledge when they read a particular text.

An experiment by Bransford and Johnson (1972) showed that it was possible to prevent people from successfully accessing their general knowledge. A text could then appear incoherent and incomprehensible. Subjects were read the following passage:

> The procedure is actually quite simple. First you arrange things into different groups. Of course one pile may be sufficient depending on how much there is to do. If you have to go somewhere else due to lack of facilities that is the next step, otherwise you are pretty well set. It is important not to overdo things. That is, it is better to do too few things at once than too many. In the short run this may not seem important but complications can easily arise. A mistake can be expensive as well. At first the whole procedure will seem complicated.

Soon, however, it will become just another facet of life. It is difficult to foresee any end to the necessity for this task in the immediate future, but then one never can tell. After the procedure is completed one arranges the materials into different groups again. Then they can be put into their appropriate places. Eventually they will be used once more and the whole cycle will then have to be repeated. However, that is a part of life.

Comprehension and recall scores were very low when the passage was presented in this way. Another group of subjects were given a title beforehand, 'washing clothes'. Their scores were very much higher. A third group, who were given the title after hearing the passage, obtained even lower scores than the group who had no title at all.

This experiment showed that a very small clue (that the passage was about washing clothes) seemed to make an enormous difference to the subjects' ability to form representations of the passage in memory. It was as if this single clue acted as the key which gained them access to a whole area of world knowledge and which allowed sense to be made of descriptions such as 'going somewhere else if there is a lack of facilities'. The experiment also showed that people constructed their mental representations of the text as they went along – otherwise the group who were given the title after hearing the passage would have performed as well as those who heard it first. The process of building a representation of text structure was not a retrospective one peculiar to long-term memory.

If it is possible to interfere with the process of accessing relevant world knowledge by withholding a single key, then this suggests that world knowledge is itself structured in some way. It is as if all the relevant information was filed on a single filing card somewhere which could not be located until the reference code had been discovered. Bartlett (1932) proposed a solution rather like this, and which is basically the one adopted in AI today. Human memory, he suggested, organized the various pieces of knowledge and experience into cognitive structures called *schemas*. When people recalled a text, then events and descriptions which could be related to an existing schema were better remembered. If a text related events which were similar to, but not identical to, a familiar schema, then the memory of the text was often distorted so that it became more like the existing schema.

A modern development of schema theory is that of **cognitive frames** proposed by Minsky (1975):

A *frame* is a data-structure for representing a stereotyped situation, like being in a certain kind of living room, or going to a child's birthday party. Attached to each frame are several kinds of information. Some of this information is about how to use the frame. Some is about what one can expect to happen next. Some is about what to do if these expectations are not confirmed.

We can think of a frame as a network of nodes and relations. The 'top levels' of a frame are fixed, and represent things that are always true about the supposed situation. The lower levels have many *terminals* – 'slots' that must be filled by specific instances or data. Each terminal can specify conditions its assignments must meet. (The assignments themselves are usually smaller 'subframes'.) Simple conditions are specified by markers that might require a terminal assignment to be a person, an object of sufficient value, or a pointer to a subframe of a certain type. More complex conditions can specify relations among the things assigned to several terminals.

In practice, the terms 'schema' and 'frame' are now used almost interchangeably in the literature. A frame is essentially a stereotype of a particular object or event which shows those characteristics which are essential, those which are variable, and those which past experience has shown are likely to be present. Figure 7.2 illustrates what a frame for *dog* might look like. Whenever the word *dog* appears in a text, then the reader can fill in the unstated facts that a dog has four legs, ears, etc. Where the text gives information about optional values, these are filled in. If not, they are filled in by the *default values* supplied by the stereotype.

The use of the definite article sometimes betrays the existence of a frame. Normally, one only uses and expects to see the word *the* in connection with something already referred to in the text, or whose existence is otherwise explained. But objects may be used with the definite article when they appear in a familiar and relevant frame even if they have not appeared in the text: *Whenever Joyce walks into a room she opens the window*. All rooms are expected to contain at least one window and hence there is no problem about which window is being referred to.

Schank and Abelson (1977: 422) proposed a further elaboration of the notion of frame to describe our knowledge of sequences of events: 'A *script* is a predetermined, stereotyped sequence of actions that define a well-known situation. A script is, in effect, a very boring little story.' A restaurant frame, for example, might contain information about a door leading off a street, windows, tables, menu cards and so on. A restaurant **script** on the other hand, would include the sequence of actions that a customer might expect to do. These would include 'enter', 'wait', 'be shown seat', 'look at menu', right through to 'pay bill', and 'leave'. Bower *et al.* (1979) have shown that in several cases people do agree on what the main events in particular scripts are, and that in their recall of stories they often erroneously include events which appear in the script but not in the original story.

Cognitive psychologists have shown that people's understanding of texts not only depends on a general knowledge of the world, but also involves strategies of comprehension which are not peculiar to language. Scripts and frames will help us understand people's actions in the world as much as written descriptions about them.

It might be thought that cognitive psychologists' work is more relevant to how people understand prose than to descriptions of the texts they

Figure 7.2 A 'dog' frame

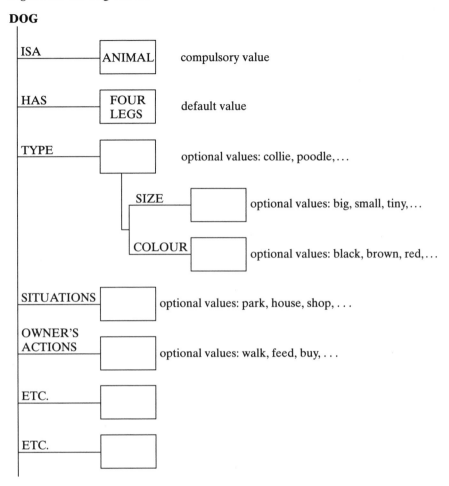

Source: Greene (1986)

attempt to comprehend. This, however, is by no means true. Such research demonstrates that any description of the structure of a text in terms which have psychological reality must take into account the role of an intelligent and informed interpreter. It also suggests that perceived structures will be different for different readers, depending on what knowledge schemas are triggered and what their content might be.

Political discourse analysis

The term **political discourse analysis** has been used (Seidel 1985) to refer to types of analysis that, rather than looking simply for patterns and structures in writing, see it as a form of social practice. For this sort of approach both the immediate and wider social contexts in which language is produced are all-important. Language is seen as reflecting and sustaining the values of a culture. Seidel (1985: 44) discusses the assumptions underlying such an approach:

> It is my contention that discourse of any kind – text as a supra-sentential unit of meaning, an extension of the syntactic and logical structuring of a sentence – is a site of struggle. It is a terrain, a dynamic linguistic, and above all, semantic space in which social meanings are produced or challenged. This is most clearly, but not exclusively, the case with political discourse, since the theory and practice of politics and political talk is seen to be primarily concerned with power. This of course assumes a conflict, not a consensus model of society, and a model of language use seen as part of social action and concerned with the relation between action and structure.

One may compare this with **sociolinguistics**, which also explores the relationship between language and society but often seems to regard both as neutral. Such neutrality would be contested by researchers working within a 'political discourse analysis' tradition. Seidel (1985) gives an overview of these traditions. Here, by way of example, we shall look briefly at one approach that has been termed **critical linguistics**.

CRITICAL LINGUISTICS

Consider the following two extracts from British newspapers, reporting an incident in which police in Rhodesia (as it was in 1975) killed 11 black people:

Rioting Blacks Shot Dead by Police as ANC Leaders Meet
Eleven Africans were shot dead and 15 wounded when Rhodesian police opened fire on a rioting crowd of about 2,000 in the African Highfield township of Salisbury this afternoon.
    The shooting was the climax of a day of some violence and tension during which rival black political factions taunted one another while the African National Council Executive committee met in the township to plan its next move in the settlement issue with the government.

(*The Times*, 2 June 1975)

Police Shoot 11 Dead in Salisbury Riot
Riot police shot and killed 11 African demonstrators and wounded 15 others here today in the Highfield African township on the outskirts of Salisbury. The number of casualties was confirmed by the police. Disturbances had broken out soon after the executive committee of the African National Council (ANC) met in the township to discuss the ultimatum by the Prime Minister, Mr. Ian Smith, to the

ANC to attend a constitutional conference with the government in the near future.

(*Guardian*, 2 June 1975)

Trew (1979) carried out an analysis of these extracts using a number of linguistic categories. His aim, however, was not simply to describe interesting discourse patterns but to see if these could reveal the ideology, or set of values, inherent in the discourse. He argues that police shooting innocent people is not regarded as normal, or legitimate, and therefore needs to be explained. The newspaper articles, therefore, do not simply describe events but offer explanations or interpretations. This is often done implicitly, through the choice of particular words or syntactic structures. Trew sets out as a table his analysis of the first sentence in each article (Table 7.6).

Table 7.6 Analysis of two newspaper extracts

	Agent	Process	Affected	Circumstance
Times Headline	police	PASSIVE shoot dead	rioting blacks	(as) ANC leaders meet
Report	–	shoot dead	eleven Africans	(when) Rhodesian police opened fire on a rioting crowd
Guardian Headline	police	ACTIVE shoot dead	11	(in) Salisbury riots
Report	riot police	shoot and kill	11 African demonstrators	

Source: Trew (1979)

The linguistic features Trew draws attention to include the following:

1 The verbs in the main clause in *The Times* article are passive ('Eleven Africans *were shot*') whereas the *Guardian* uses active verbs ('Riot police *shot* . . . 11 African demonstrators'). Futhermore, in *The Times* article the *agents* (those who did the killing) are placed at some distance from the main verb in a dependent clause ('when Rhodesian police . . .'). The use of the passive, argues Trew, coupled with the displacement of the agent, puts this agent in a less focal position.

2 Both newspapers describe the circumstances in which the shooting took place as a 'riot', which can provide a framework for explaining police action, and makes at least their intervention, if not the actual killing, legitimate.

Trew analyses further developments in the Press treatment of this story, including an editorial in *The Times* of the same day and subsequent articles in both *The Times* and the *Guardian*. While 'riots' continue to be emphasized, the agents of the killing (the police) are not referred to again. Trew argues that it is by this sort of process that a 'favoured' interpretation is offered of events and unpalatable aspects are obscured.

He contrasts *The Times* editorial with one that appeared in the *Tanzanian Daily News*. The first sentence of each gives an impression of the different interpretations placed upon the event:

> The rioting and sad loss of life in Salisbury are warnings that tension in that country is rising as decisive moves about its future seem to be in the offing.
>
> *(The Times)*

> Rhodesia's white supremacist police had a field day on Sunday when they opened fire and killed thirteen unarmed Africans, in two different actions in Salisbury; and wounded many others.
>
> *(Tanzanian Daily News)*

For examples of other work carried out within a critical linguistics framework see Kress and Hodge (1979) and Fowler *et al.* (1979). The overall aim of the method is to identify and describe 'the social, interpersonal and ideological functions' of a range of linguistic constructions used in a variety of contexts. Although we have given an example from a newspaper, in principle any discourse, spoken or written, can be analysed.

An important point to note about this kind of analysis is that the theory underlying it is explicitly *determinist*: it suggests that the (varieties of) language used in a culture affect the way people perceive and interpret events. Linguistic determinism has a chequered history. One of the major early exponents was the anthropological linguist, Whorf, who argued that different languages caused their speakers to interpret the world differently. The argument has since been applied to different varieties within a language, but it is by no means uncontroversial and perhaps merits more detailed and cautious consideration than critical linguists such as Fowler *et al.* are inclined to give it (at least in their 1979 volume).

The method of analysis has other limitations. We mention here one that seems to us to be particularly important. (This is not a criticism of Trew's analysis, which is a good example of its kind, but of the tradition in general.) The researchers are clearly politically committed and this will affect the sort of discourse they choose to analyse, the features they select for study and, arguably, the interpretations they come to. (While this contrasts with the objective intentions of other research on language and society it should be borne in mind that no such research can be absolutely objective. Even if never articulated, the beliefs or sets of values held by researchers are likely to influence what they study – or do not study! – and how their research is conducted.) Fowler *et al.*, however, tend to offer single 'correct' interpretations for the linguistic categories they identify in certain types of discourse – and to imply that these are somehow not apparent to 'lay' readers, who will be deceived by the discourse. So, passivization obscures the agent from lay readers, but not from the professional analyst who, presumably, has been able to escape from the ideological straitjacket of his or her culture.

This criticism could be levelled also at other forms of linguistic analysis where the linguist works directly from his or her own intuitions (see Section 1.5). In practice, the assignation of meaning is rather more complex, with people producing a range of interpretations of discourse, depending upon their previous experience, political commitment, etc. (see also the discussion of 'cognitive frames' above). Some readers, for instance, may accept the 'legitimated' portrayal of police killing offered by *The Times* not so much because they are *deceived* by the passivization as because their political convictions lead them to prefer this interpretation. Others, with different political beliefs, would probably manage to focus on the agency.

This is not to suggest that a particular type of portrayal of an event will have no effect upon how it is perceived (nor that constant exposure to particular uses of language will have no effect in the long term upon a speaker/listener's set of values). It is, however, too crude an analysis to suggest that linguistic structures have one correct interpretation and that those from whom this is hidden are somehow being duped.

More recent attempts to analyse the ideological and political effects of texts take a more complex view of the possible interpretations which a reader might make. Norman Fairclough (1989), for example, describes an approach which he calls **critical language study** (CLS). This adopts many of the insights of critical linguistics but places a greater emphasis on social theory to explain and analyse the social conditions within which texts are read and acted on. Fairclough recognizes that there exists a certain 'ideological diversity' which means that readers may be aware that a text is mobilizing assumptions other than the ones they themselves would want to make. This is one way in which a text is a 'site of struggle', not only over what kinds of belief and political interest should inform the interpretation of the text, but also over the appropriateness of the particular genre or discourse which the text activates.

In any discourse, argues Fairclough, participants are able to take up only certain roles – they are 'positioned' by a text – that is, encouraged to fall into particular relations of power. One example he gives is of classroom discourse where there is a *pupil role* and a *teacher role*. The recognizable structure of classroom discourse depends on participants' agreeing to play these roles, and through the discourse itself they can display their compliance. It is through entering into discourses of this kind, Fairclough argues, and occupying such 'subject positions' that we *become* pupils or teachers. In this way, our experience of discourses helps create important aspects of our identity.

Although we have given an example here of spoken discourse, the difference between speech and writing is not a particularly important one within CLS. We could as well have been discussing advertisements, for example, or the language of the forms which an unemployed person needs to fill in to claim benefit.

Critical language study is a less determinist approach than critical linguistics, since it recognizes that different people will be affected in different ways by texts and allows for a struggle over interpretation. It is a more ambitious approach in that it attempts to explain the role of discourse in the maintenance of the social order and in social change. It assumes that there exists a 'dialectic of structure and practices'. That is, we help maintain social and institutional structures by entering into discourses which require such structures to be understood. Every time a pupil or teacher enters into classroom discourse, the institutional relationship between pupil and teacher is reinforced.

The form of identity which discourses construct is called **subjectivity**, and Fairclough argues that it is created progressively over a lifetime through the 'slow drip' effect of being repeatedly positioned in a range of subject positions. But the diversity of these positions means that subjects become 'composite personalities' and can be played upon by different texts in a variety of ways. This postmodern notion of identity contrasts with that employed in sociolinguistics, where social identities are assumed to be more unified and monolithic. The sociolinguistic approach might regard multilingual speakers, for example, as parcelling out different bits of their social identity via different languages; a postmodern theory of subjectivity might describe multilingual speakers as having composite personalities in which they feel they are a different kind of person, with different kinds of feelings and social values, when speaking each of their languages. In a number of non-Western countries, for instance, young couples use the English language, rather than a local language, because it allows them to escape traditional discourses of marriage and to establish a more Western-style relationship.

Textual approaches to written language

The approaches to the description of text which are described below are all concerned with intrinsic structural or presentational qualities. It may seem strange that so many researchers in such a variety of traditions should attempt to analyse and characterize texts without taking into account the audience or contextual factors, particularly when cognitive psychologists and others have demonstrated the crucial role of the reader. However, not all of the approaches discussed below are incompatible with the view of written language as discourse.

In some cases they simply make certain assumptions about the shared world view, experience and expectations of readers which makes it unnecessary (in their view) to take readers into account when examining distinctive differences between texts. Other approaches are unashamedly concerned with somewhat superficial aspects of texts, simply because their purposes do not seem to require anything more.

An example of this is as follows. Claude Shannon developed a theory of textual properties which allowed him to create a series of texts which bore more or less resemblance to real English. In doing so, he was modelling the statistical probabilities of certain sequences of letters or words occurring in the text. He produced one text (Shannon 1948) which displayed within it all the transitional probabilities of English. That is, if it were repeated many times, it would display the same overall characteristics as a very long sample of any English text:

THE HEAD AND IN FRONTAL ATTACK ON AN ENGLISH WRITER THAT THE CHARACTER OF THIS POINT IS THEREFORE ANOTHER METHOD FOR THE LETTERS THAT THE TIME OF WHO EVER TOLD THE PROBLEM FOR AN UNEXPECTED

The Shannon text, as it is called, is now used as a test routine for electronic typewriters (and other communication links), since it simulates not only the relative frequencies of letters but also the likely rotational operations in the print head which occur when moving from one letter to another. Predictions of failure in the machine under long periods of normal use can be made much more accurately than by using familiar sentences such as *The quick brown fox jumped over the lazy dog*.

This demonstrates that even apparently superficial characterizations of text may have important uses. It follows that in assessing the adequacy of a particular approach one must bear in mind the practical application, which may warrant the use of assumptions which are on theoretical grounds somewhat unsatisfactory.

COHESION

One factor that distinguishes text from a random collection of sentences is the existence of links between one sentence and another. Consider, for example, the following pair of sentences (from Halliday and Hasan 1976: 2):

Wash and core six cooking apples. Put *them* into a fireproof dish.

Them refers to *six cooking apples*: the words form a cohesive relation constituting an **anaphoric tie**. That is to say, the relation is backwards (anaphoric). The tie is grammatical rather than lexical. If, instead of *them* the example had *the apples*, then *apples* would be a **lexical tie** and *the* (defining *which* apples we are talking about) a **grammatical tie**.

Cohesive relations need not require reference to something earlier in the text. **Reference** may be forward (**cataphoric**) as in the first word of this example (from Halliday and Hasan 1976: 17):

This is how to get the best results. You let the berries dry in the sun, till all the moisture has gone out of them. Then you gather them up and chop them very fine.

Sometimes reference is not to the text at all. In that case it is **exophoric** (related to a context or situation) as in 'Here *she* comes', as an isolated

Figure 7.3 Types of reference

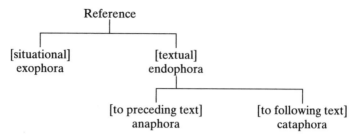

Source: Halliday and Hasan (1976)

statement, rather than **endophoric** (related to the text) as in 'We've been waiting a long time at the bus stop for *Linda*. Here *she* comes at last.' Types of reference are set out by Halliday and Hasan as shown in Figure 7.3. On this basis, Halliday and Hasan build a considerable scheme taking account of personal reference (she, me, etc.), demonstrative reference (this, that, here, etc.) and comparative reference (better, more similar, different, etc.).

To reference they add other cohesive relations. These include **substitution** and **ellipsis**. In substitution, but not in reference, the item substituted is a replacement for an item that must have occurred earlier in the text and whose meaning is not 'recoverable from the environment' as are pronouns. Halliday and Hasan acknowledge that the distinction between reference and substitution is blurred at the edges. However, they contrast the reference items *she* 'some person (female), other than the speaker or addressee, who can be identified by recourse to the environment' with the use of *one* as 'a sort of counter' in, for example, *My axe is too blunt. I must get a sharper one* (Halliday and Hasan 1976: pp. 88–9). They stress that reference is a semantic relation, whereas substitution is grammatical and so is ellipsis (which involves omission, e.g. *Joan bought some carnations, and Catherine some sweet peas* – where the verb is not repeated but the two clauses are linked). Another grammatical relation is **conjunction**, which links in various ways (e.g. by cause and effect relationship, as in *He was knocked down by a car. As a result he spent two months in hospital*). **Lexical cohesion** (already mentioned in the example of the apples) is more complicated because it is established through semantic relations in vocabulary though grammatically constrained.

The full system of cohesive analysis provides a very detailed coding system developed for the analysis and description of text. The book *Cohesion in English* also gives a discussion of the relationship between cohesion and register (roughly, style and tone of language), for Halliday and Hasan (1976: 23) consider that the two taken together 'effectively define a text'. We have given here no more than an introduction to their work in the form of a broad outline of the system of cohesion, a system based on examination of intersentential ties.

Quantitative approaches to text analysis largely disregard both the role of the reader and the importance of conventions that readers and writers share. Their emphasis is on the text itself. However, they tend to have less concern for the overall structure of texts, than for low-level elements, notably words. Nevertheless, quantitative methods possess a rigour less apparent in other approaches and they are fairly readily replicable. The problems come in interpreting the data obtained and in assessing the validity of findings.

Here we consider two quantitative approaches that are related to each other. The oldest and simplest approach involves counting how frequently each word occurs in a text; sometimes a record is made of where each word is used, and these data are the basis for a **concordance**. Concordances for the Bible have been available for several centuries. However, the growth of computing has made the study of word frequencies and the compilation of concordances much less time-consuming and has led to more, and more sophisticated, work. We have already mentioned the use of concordance techniques in the compilation of dictionary entries in Chapter 3. The second approach we discuss is that of readability formulae, which are in fairly widespread use for assessing the difficulty of educational and technical texts.

Word-frequency studies   Texts have been examined to produce word-frequency lists for several purposes. In education, for example, the lists compiled by West (1927) and Thorndike (1932) have been widely used in preparing and assessing reading materials. Such lists are associated with the approach to foreign-language teaching that considered a 'controlled vocabulary' to be of importance. For beginning readers in Britain, the 'Ladybird Reading Series' is based on a word-frequency list (McNally and Murray 1962), so that the most frequent words are learnt first in reading.

Another use of word-frequency studies is to help establish authorship, both in literary studies (such as the 'Who wrote Shakespeare?' controversy) and in historical and criminal investigations. Examples given in a most useful guide to linguistic computing by Susan Hockey (1980) include establishing the authorship of 12 of the 88 *Federalist Papers* written in 1787–8 to persuade New York citizens to ratify the constitution. Here, all but 12 of the 88 papers were known to be by one or other of three authors, though published under one pseudonym. One of the three authors was known not to have written the 12 papers whose attribution was in question. The claims of the other two, Alexander Hamilton and James Madison, were investigated by manual counting of sentence length. Mean sentence lengths and ranges in length were compared, but inconclusively. Subsequent computer analysis revealed that Hamilton always used 'while' but Madison preferred 'whilst' in papers known to be by them, and that relatively frequent use of 'upon' and 'enough' also marked Hamilton's style. This provided strong evidence, which was later corroborated by further detailed work. More recent analyses have been more sophisticated and have taken into account imagery, such items as conjunctions, certain grammatical patterns, and so on. The purpose of this work has been largely to give objective evidence for speculations on an author's work and to compare authors. An interesting application to Open University texts is reported by Whalley (1980) who computed the frequency of conjunctions and related this to the occurrence of new main themes in the OU texts.

Word-frequency analyses need not be restricted to literary texts, of course. One corpus which has been studied consists of the 100 000 words of Richard Nixon's conversations on tape, the so-called 'White House tapes'. As reported by Stokes (1974), a computer concordance program was used to examine what words were used by Nixon in what context. About one-third of the tapes are rehearsals of public speeches, the remainder mostly private conversation. Analysis by Parrish and Shames at Cornell University showed the word 'cooperate' was used 23 times in the public mode but only six times in the private mode, and on two of these occasions Nixon was indicating he preferred not to cooperate in investigations. It was also found that 'I' was used about ten times as often as would be expected in a corpus of contemporary American English such as Kučera and Francis (1967) and that there was a predominant pattern of military and hunting imagery.

Readability formulae   Readability formulae attempt to provide a description of some of the linguistic properties of texts in a very rough and ready manner which obscures syntactic, and particularly semantic, complexities. Nevertheless they have been very influential – at least in education – as predictors of the difficulty which a text will present to a reader. Readability formulae do at least have the virtue of being precisely specified and replicable in use.

Most formulae work on the principle that long sentences and long words make for a difficult text, but they vary on how exactly they take such features into account. Examples of two formulae commonly used, taken from Klare (1974), are given below.

Fog Index

Reading grade level = 0.4 × (average sentence length + percentage of words of 3 or more syllables).

Note that a passage of 100 words of text is usually taken as a sample for convenience. 'Reading grade level' refers to American school grade. Grade 1 = 6 years of age.

Example A passage of 100 words contains $6\frac{2}{3}$ sentences. Average sentence length is therefore: 100 divided by $6\frac{2}{3}$ = 15 words.

The passage contains 18 words of 3 or more syllables. Reading grade level is, therefore: 0.4 of (15 + 18).

that is, $\dfrac{4}{10} \times 33 = 13.2$

Flesch Reading Ease Formula

Reading ease = $206.835 - 0.846 \times wl - 1.015 \times sl$, where wl = number of syllables per 100 words and sl = average number of words per sentence. Samples of 100 words are again taken in applying this formula, as is usually the case.

Example Taking the hypothetical passage of 6 sentences (i.e. $sl = 15$) and, say 210 syllables ($wl = 210$) we substitute as follows:

$$\text{Reading ease} = 206.835 - (0.846 \times 210) - (1.015 \times 15)$$
$$= 206.835 - 177.66 - 15.225 = 13.95$$

Stokes (1978) compared seven readability formulae on samples from 11 British textbooks. He found that the different formulae gave significantly different results and concluded that none could be regarded as more reliable than the others.

There are several reasons why readability formulae are, in practice, poor predictors of the difficulty which children will actually experience. One is that, as Stokes has shown, many textbooks (though not fiction) are extremely inconsistent in readability level from page to page. No single measure could therefore satisfactorily characterize a whole book. A second, and more important reason, is that the difficulty a particular child will experience will depend on many things associated with that child's personal experience, knowledge and motivation. Readability formulae make no attempt to characterize the conceptual difficulty in text.

Rhetorical and narrative structure

Most, if not all, texts have some overall organization or structure which is typical of their **genre**. At its simplest, one can say that most texts have a beginning, middle and end.

Classical rhetoric, a subject of study in schools and universities for over two thousand years, established certain conventions for generic structure, mainly to help in the composition of texts. It provided three things:

1 A means of classifying texts into certain genres according to their internal structure. Examples might be *judicial, deliberative* or *dramatic*.
2 A means of describing the internal structure of such texts. For example, a judicial speech should, according to Cicero, comprise six parts: *exordium, narration, partition, confirmation, refutation* and *conclusion*. Each part may, in turn, be subdivided into smaller sections. The conclusion contained three parts: *summing up, inciting indignation against the opponent* and *arousing sympathy for the client*.
3 A means of classifying the stylistic devices and conceits which comprise each part of the speech. Such devices included speakers saying they will finish and not bother the listener with certain matters (which are thereby introduced and dealt with) and were explicitly taught in Roman times.

Figure 7.4 Partial rhetorical structure of a law court speech according to Cicero

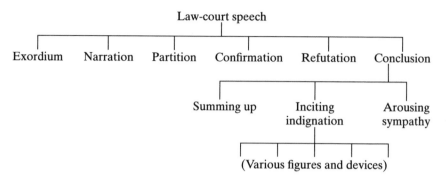

In this way, a law speech might be regarded as having a tree structure as is partially displayed in Figure 7.4.

Nowadays, it is for the stylistic devices which were used to persuade and mislead an audience that rhetoric is most often remembered, but its work on generic structure has also been of importance in the historical development of many kinds of text in the West. The range of genres available to a modern writer and speaker is now much greater than in classical times, and the range of conventional structures consequently wider, but many of the principles set out in classical rhetoric still apply today.

It is from that period that a very common structure for academic essays originated: the statement of a *thesis* (the arguments for some proposal); an *antithesis* (the counter-arguments and disadvantages); the *synthesis* (which proposes elements of both extremes to provide a workable solution). Similar structures may be found in strategy reports compiled within large companies, though increasingly a rival structure is to set out a range of options of which one is seen clearly to be more desirable than others.

Scientific papers and reports also have a well-recognized structure, though it is one which varies from discipline to discipline. Such papers might typically begin with an abstract, followed by an introduction, method, results, discussion and conclusion. As in Cicero's day, each section has its own internal structuring. The method may, in a report of a scientific experiment, be structured chronologically, whereas the discussion will be structured according to some theoretical issues raised by the result. Kress (1985: 143) comments on the institutional interest represented by such generic structures:

> Anyone who reads or writes papers for a scientific journal will know that there are very precise rules to be followed in the construction of a text within that genre. It is equally well-known that the formal requirements of this genre are absolutely tied into and arise out of the practices of the institution of science, and hence are expressions

of the meanings of that institution . . . Genres are not merely empty forms available and waiting to be filled with content; rather they have specific meanings and they produce quite specific effects. That is why being scientific or being a scientist has as much to do with, and is defined as much by, mastery and implementation of the requisite genres as it has to do with any of the other practices that constitute modern science. Effects of factualness or non-factualness are produced by the formal structure of genres: so, for example, the genre of the scientific paper or of a newspaper editorial produces the former, while the genre of the novel or of casual gossip produces the latter.

Fictional narrative is also structured in conventional ways. Propp (1958) analysed a hundred fairy tales and suggested that at an abstract level they contained the same underlying **story structure**. Although fairy tales contain a vast number of characters, Propp identified eight basic character roles: the *villain;* the *donor;* the *helper;* the *princess* (or other sought-for person) and her father; the *dispatcher;* the *hero;* the *false hero.* Similarly, although each tale appeared to tell a different story, Propp identified 32 fixed narrative elements of functions. No one tale contained all elements, but those which were included always appeared in the same order. The set was divided by Propp into six sections: preparation, complication, transference, struggle, return and recognition.

Propp's analysis has been found to work well with modern popular fiction, films and TV programmes. For example, Fiske (1987: 137) claims:

> most popular television narratives conform more or less precisely to this structure. At times the conformity is astonishing in its precision. I tested the structure on *Bionic Woman* and found that the pre-title sequence conformed to preparation. Complication took the narrative to the next commercial break and so on.

The American sociolinguist, William Labov, has applied the technique to narratives of personal experiences told in face-to-face conversation, showing that such narratives (at least in the Western world) conform to a predictable structure. An implication of this is that when someone wishes to relate a personal experience, he or she will have to recast it in terms of a recognized story structure so as to take on the role of hero, perhaps, overcoming some obstacle or complication.

Fiske (1987: 139) describes news stories in newspapers and other media as a social narrative of the conflict between the social order and disruptive forces. Newsworthy events, then, are those that disrupt or restore equilibrium. Just as in Propp's analysis, certain characters (such as unions) may be cast as villains and others (such as management or consumers) as heroes/victims. Allan Bell (1991) compares the story structure of newspaper stories with other kinds of narrative. He argues that newspaper stories do contain most of the elements mentioned by Propp, but concludes that the main difference is that information in news stories is rarely ordered chronologically.

The structuring, rather, is one which reflects news values and the institutional processes involved in creating the stories. 'The ideal news story is one which could be cut to end at any paragraph. It is thus common for cohesion between paragraphs to be unclear or non-existent' (Bell 1991: 172).

Propp's approach to narrative structure has been formalized in terms of a **story grammar**, that is, a set of rewrite rules (see Chapter 3) which construct a narrative in a manner similar to the way a generative grammar constructs sentences. Story grammar has been used in studies of people's ability to remember stories.

Mandler and Johnson (1977) give an analysis which can provide a hierarchical representation, based on a series of rewrite rules. For instance, their first rule is:

Story → setting + event structure

(→ is a symbol conventionally used to mean 'may be expressed as'). They used *states* and *events* as their basic units ('terminal nodes' in their nomenclature) and consider there are three kinds of relationship between these units, namely *and*, *then* and *cause*.

An example of Mandler and Johnson's representation of the structure of a short story is shown in Figure 7.5. The dog story on which it is based (Mandler and Johnson 1977: 119) is given below.

Dog story
1 It happened that a dog had got a piece of meat
2 and was carrying it home in his mouth.
3 Now on his way home he had to cross a plank lying across a stream.
4 As he crossed he looked down
5 and saw his own shadow reflected in the water beneath.
6 Thinking it was another dog with another piece of meat,
7 he made up his mind to have that also.
8 So he made a snap at the shadow,
9 but as he opened his mouth the piece of meat fell out,
10 dropped into the water,
11 and was never seen again.

Cognitive psychologists have shown that where a story conforms to a well-known pattern it is more easily remembered and understood. Such findings seem to lend some validity to story grammars, but they are equally compatible with the schema and script theories discussed in Section 7.2. In other words, a story grammar can be regarded as a cognitive script which people use for certain kinds of text. Van Dijk and Kintsch (1978: 75) comment:

> We have hypothesized that the reader approaches a narrative with a narrative schema in mind, and that part of the process of comprehending the narrative consists of filling in the empty slots in that schema with appropriate information from the text.

Figure 7.5 A representation of the underlying structure of the dog story

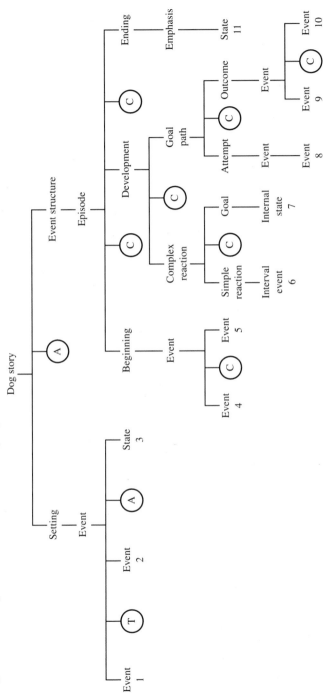

Note: The connections *and*, *then* and *cause* have been abbreviated to A, T, and C, and circled. The numbers under the terminal modes refer to the surface statements of the story.
Source: Mandler and Johnson (1977)

They tested this hypothesis by asking college students to make abstracts of two stories, one from Boccaccio's *Decameron* and a second from an Apache myth. The first had a familiar narrative structure, but the Indian story was regarded as 'weird' by the students. 'The story, of course, does follow a well-developed schema, but known only to Indians and anthropologists.' The researchers found that most students made very similar summaries for the Decameron stories, but gave very varied responses for the Indian story. They concluded that the process of writing a summary is directed by the schema which a person has applied to the text.

Appendix: answers to activities in Chapter 2

Activity 2.2

(a) The sound is voiced.
(b) The tongue makes contact with the soft palate or velum; the sound produced is thus said to be velar.
(c) The manner of articulation would be plosive.
(d) The three-part description of the sound is voiced velar plosive. The symbol for this is [g].
(e) The symbol for a voiceless velar plosive is [k].
(f) The manner of articulation would now be fricative not plosive.
(g) The symbol for a voiced velar fricative is [ɣ]. The symbol for a voiceless velar fricative is [x].
(h) These sounds are not normally used in English. [x] is found in some Scots and, more rarely, in some English dialects. [ɣ] is used in some continental European languages, such as Danish.

Activity 2.3

(a) (i) The tongue is higher in the mouth for [i] than for [ɑ].
    (ii) The highest point of the tongue is nearer the front of the mouth for [i].
(b) (i) The tongue is higher for [u] than for [a].
    (ii) The tongue is highest nearer the front for [a].
(e) (i) [u] is produced with the lips rounded and is hence referred to as a rounded vowel.
    (ii) The other rounded vowels shown in Figure 2.8 are [o] and [ɔ].

References

Aarts, J. (1991) 'Intuition-based and observation-based grammars'. In K. Aijmer and B. Altenberg (eds) *English Corpus Linguistics.* London: Longman.

Addis, B.R. (1966) 'The Relationship of Physical Interpersonal Distance to Sex, Race, and Age', MA thesis: University of Oklahoma.

Alladina, S. and Edwards, V. (eds) (1991) *Multilingualism in the British Isles.* London: Longman.

Andersson, L. and Trudgill, P. (1990) *Bad Language.* Oxford: Basil Blackwell.

Argyle, M. and Dean, J. (1965) 'Eye-contact, distance and affiliation', *Sociometry*, 28: 289–304.

Atkinson, J.M. and Heritage, J. (eds) (1984) *Structures of Social Interaction.* Cambridge: Cambridge University Press.

Atkinson, M. (1984) *Our Masters' Voices: The Language and Body Language of Politics.* London: Methuen.

Bartlett, F.C. (1932) *Remembering.* Cambridge: Cambridge University Press.

Basso, K.H. (1972) ' "To give up on words": silence in western Apache culture'. In P.P. Giglioli (ed.) *Language and Social Context.* Harmondsworth: Penguin.

Beattie, G. (1977) 'The dynamics of interruption and the filled pause', *British Journal of Social and Clinical Psychology*, 16: 283–4.

Beattie, G. (1982) 'Turn-taking and interruption in political interviews: Margaret Thatcher and Jim Callaghan compared and contrasted', *Semiotica*, 39: 93–114.

Beattie, G. (1983) *Talk: An Analysis of Speech and Non-verbal Behaviour in Conversation.* Milton Keynes: Open University Press.

Beattie, G. and Barnard, P.J. (1979) 'The temporal structure of natural telephone conversations', *Linguistics*, 17: 213–30.

Beattie, G. and Beattie, C.A. (1981) 'Postural congruence in a naturalistic setting', *Semiotica*, 35: 41–55.

Bell, A. (1991) *The Language of News Media.* Oxford: Basil Blackwell.

Bell, D.C. and Bell, A.M. (1892) *Ball's Standard Elocutionist.* London: Hodder & Stoughton.

Biggs, C. (1982) 'In a word, meaning'. In D. Crystal (ed.) *Linguistic Controversies.* London: Edward Arnold.

Birdwhistell, R.L. (1970) *Kinesics and Context.* Harmondsworth: Penguin.

Bloomfield, L. (1935) *Language.* London: George Allen & Unwin.

Bolinger, D. (1965) *Aspects of Language.* New York: Harcourt Brace Jovanovich.

Bolinger, D. (1985) *Intonation and its Parts.* London: Edward Arnold.

Boucher, J.D. and Ekman, P. (1975) 'Facial areas of emotional information', *Journal of Communication*, 25: 21–9.

Bower, G.H., Black, J.B. and Turner, T.J. (1979) 'Scripts in text comprehension and memory', *Cognitive Psychology*, 11: 177–220.

Bowers, R.G., Bamber, B., Cook, R.S. and Thomas, A.L. (1987) *Talking about Grammar.* London: Longman.

Bradley, H. (1913) *On the Relations between Spoken and Written Language with Special Reference to English.* London: The British Academy.

Bransford, J.D. and Johnson, M.K. (1972) 'Contextual pre-requisites for understanding: some investigations of comprehension and recall', *Journal of Verbal Learning and Verbal Behaviour*, 11: 717–26.

Bransford, J.D., Barclay, J.R. and Franks, J.S. (1972) 'Sentence memory: a constructive versus interpretive approach', *Cognitive Psychology*, 3: 193–209.

Chafe, W. (1986) 'Writing in the perspective of speaking'. In C.R. Cooper and S. Greenbaum (eds) *Studying Writing: Linguistic Approaches.* Beverly Hills, CA: Sage.

Chomsky, N. (1957) *Syntactic Structures.* The Hague: Mouton.

Chomsky, N. (1965) *Aspects of the Theory of Syntax.* Cambridge, MA: MIT Press.

Chomsky, N. (1976) *Reflections on Language.* London: Temple Smith.

Chomsky, N. and Halle, M. (1968) *The Sound Pattern of English.* New York: Harper and Row.

Christie, F. (1990) 'Young children's writing: from spoken to written genre'. In R. Carter (ed.) *Knowledge about Language and the Curriculum: The LINC Reader.* London: Hodder & Stoughton.

Clark, H.H. and Clark, E.V. (1977) *Psychology and Language.* New York: Harcourt Brace Jovanovich.

Close, R.A. (1974) *A University Grammar of English Workbook.* London: Longman.

Coates, J. (1994) 'No gap, lots of overlap: turn-taking patterns in the talk of women friends'. In D. Graddol, J. Maybin and B. Stierer (eds) *Researching Language and Literacy in Social Context.* Clevedon: Multilingual Matters.

Cook, V. (1988) *Chomsky's Universal Grammar: An Introduction.* Oxford: Blackwell.

Cooper, W.E. and Sorensen, J.M. (1981) *Fundamental Frequency in Sentence Production.* New York: Springer–Verlag.

Coppieters, R. (1987) 'Competence differences between native and near native speakers', *Language*, 63: 544–73.

Coulthard, M. (1977) *An Introduction to Discourse Analysis.* London: Longman.

Coulthard, M. and Brazil, D.C. (1979) *Exchange Structures* (Discourse Analysis Monographs 5). Birmingham: University of Birmingham English Language Research.

Crystal, D. (1969) *Prosodic Systems and Intonation in English.* Cambridge: Cambridge University Press.

Crystal, D. (1985) 'How many millions? The statistics of English today', *English Today*, 1: 7–9.

Crystal, D. (1991) 'Stylistic profiling'. In K. Aijmer and B. Altenberg (eds) *English Corpus Linguistics.* London: Longman.

Crystal, D. (1992) *An Encyclopedic Dictionary of Language and Linguistics*. Oxford: Blackwell.

Crystal, D., Fletcher, P. and Garman, M. (1976) *The Grammatical Analysis of Language Disability*. London: Edward Arnold.

Czerniewska, P. (1985) 'The experience of writing' in Open University (ed.) *Every Child's Language: An In-service Pack for Primary Teachers*. Milton Keynes: Open University Press.

Darwin, C. (1872) *The Expression of Emotions of Man and Animals*. London: Murray.

Davies, A. (1991) *The Native Speaker in Applied Linguistics*. Edinburgh: Edinburgh University Press.

Denny, R. (1985) 'Marking the interaction order: the social constitution of turn exchange and speaking turns', *Language in Society*, 14: 41–62.

Duncan, S. (1972) 'Some signals and rules for taking speaking turns in conversations', *Journal of Personality and Social Psychology*, 23: 283–92.

Eckersley, C.E. (1958) *A Concise English Grammar for Foreign Students*. London: Longman.

Eco, U. (1984) *Semiotics and the Philosophy of Language*. London: Macmillan.

Edelsky, C. (1981) 'Who's got the floor?', *Language in Society*, 10: 383–421.

Edwards, A.D. and Westgate, D.P.G. (1987) *Investigating Classroom Talk*. London: Falmer Press.

Ekman, P. (1973) *Darwin and Facial Expression: A Century of Research in Review*. New York: Academic Press.

Ekman, P. and Friesen, W.V. (1967) 'Head and body cues in the judgment of emotion: a reformulation', *Perceptual and Motor Skills*, 24: 711–24.

Ekman, P., Sorenson, E.R. and Friesen, W.V. (1969) 'Pan-cultural elements in facial displays of emotion', *Science*, 164: 86–8.

Ekman, P., Friesen, W.V. and Ellsworth, P. (1972) *Emotion in the Human Face: Guidelines for Research and an Integration of the Findings*. New York: Pergamon.

Fairclough, N. (1989) *Language and Power*. London: Longman.

Fairclough, N. (ed.) (1992) *Critical Language Awareness*. London: Longman.

Falk, J. (1980) 'The conversational duet'. In *Proceedings of the 6th Annual Meeting of the Berkeley Linguistics Society*, 507–14.

Felix, S.W. (1987) *Cognition and Language Growth*. Dordrecht, Netherlands: Foris Publications.

Fisher, J.D., Ryttine, M. and Hesling, R. (1976) 'Hands touching hands: affective and evaluative effects of an interpersonal touch', *Sociometry*, 39: 416–21.

Fiske, J. (1987) *Television Culture*. London: Routledge.

Fowler, H.W. (1926) *A Dictionary of Modern English Usage*. Oxford: Clarendon Press.

Fowler, R., Hodge, R., Kress, G. and Trew, A. (eds) (1979) *Language and Control*. London: Routledge & Kegan Paul.

French, P. and Local, J. (1986) 'Prosodic features and the management of interruptions'. In C. Johns-Lewis (ed.) *Intonation in Discourse*. London: Croom Helm.

Fry, D.B. (1955) 'Duration and intensity as physical correlates of linguistic stress', *Journal of the Acoustical Society of America*, 27: 765–8.

Fry, D.B. (1958) 'Experiments in the perception of stress', *Language and Speech*, 1: 126–52.

Gannon, P. and Czerniewska, P. (1980) *Using Linguistics: An Educational Focus*. London: Edward Arnold.

Garman, M. (1988) 'Syntax: the structure of English'. In W.F. Bolton and D. Crystal (eds) *The English Language*. London: Sphere.

Geis, M.L. (1982) *The Language of Television Advertising*. London: Academic Press.

Gelb, I.J. (1963) *A Study of Writing* (2nd edn). Chicago: University of Chicago Press.

Goodwin, C. (1981) *Conversational Organization: Interaction between Speakers and Hearers*. New York: Academic Press.

Gowers, Sir Ernest (1986) *The Complete Plain Words* (revised by Sidney Greenbaum and Janet Whitcut). London: HMSO.

Graddol, D. (1994) 'Three models of language description'. In D. Graddol and O. Boyd-Barrett (eds) *Media Texts: Authors and Readers*. Clevedon: Multilingual Matters.

Graddol, D. and Boyd-Barrett, O. (eds) (1994) *Media Texts: Authors and Readers*. Clevedon: Multilingual Matters.

Greene, J. (1972) *Psycholinguistics: Chomsky and Psychology*. Harmondsworth: Penguin.

Greene, J. (1986) *Language Understanding: A Cognitive Approach*. Milton Keynes: Open University Press.

Grice, H.P. (1975) 'Logic and conversation'. In P. Cole and J. Morgan (eds) *Syntax and Semantics, 3: Speech Acts*. New York: Academic Press.

Gumperz, J.J. (1972) 'Introduction'. In J.J. Gumperz and D. Hymes (eds) *Directions in Sociolinguistics*. New York: Holt, Rinehart and Winston.

Gumperz, J.J. (1982) *Discourse Strategies*. Cambridge: Cambridge University Press.

Gussenhoven, C. (1986) 'The intonation of George and Mildred: post-nuclear generalisations'. In C. Johns-Lewis (ed.) *Intonation in Discourse*. London: Croom Helm.

Hall, E.T. (1963) 'A system for the notation of proxemic behavior', *American Anthropologist*, 65: 1003–26.

Halliday, M.A.K. (1978) *Language as Social Semiotic*. London: Edward Arnold.

Halliday, M.A.K. (1985) *An Introduction to Functional Grammar*. London: Edward Arnold.

Halliday, M.A.K. (1987) 'Spoken and written modes of meaning'. In R. Horowitz and S.J. Samuels (eds) *Comprehending Oral and Written Language*. San Diego, CA: Academic Press.

Halliday, M.A.K. (1989) *Spoken and Written Language*. Oxford: Oxford University Press. First published in 1985.

Halliday, M.A.K. and Hasan, R. (1976) *Cohesion in English*. London: Longman.

Harris, J. (1993) 'The grammar of Irish English'. In J. Milroy and L. Milroy (eds) *Real English: The grammar of English dialects in the British Isles*. London: Longman.

Harris, R. (1980) *The Language Makers*. London: Duckworth.

Harris, Z.S. (1946) 'From morpheme to utterance', *Language*, 22: 161–83.

Henley, N.M. (1973) 'Status and sex: some touching observations', *Bulletin of the Psychometry Society*, 2: 91–3.

Hockey, S. (1980) *A Guide to Computer Applications in the Humanities*. London: Duckworth.

Holmes, J. (1992) *An Introduction to Sociolinguistics*. London: Longman.

Huddleston, R. (1984) *Introduction to the Grammar of English*. Cambridge: Cambridge University Press.

Hudson, R. (1980) *Sociolinguistics*. Cambridge: Cambridge University Press.

Hudson, R. (1984a) *Word Grammar*. Oxford: Blackwell.

Hudson, R. (1984b) *Higher Level Differences between Speech and Writing*. London: Committee for Linguistics in Education.

Jellison, J.M. and Ickes, W.J. (1974) 'The power of the glance: desire to see and be seen in competitive situations', *Journal of Experimental Social Psychology*, 10: 444–50.

Jourard, S.M. (1966) 'An exploratory study of body accessibility', *British Journal of Social and Clinical Psychology*, 5: 221–31.

Katzner, K. (1986) *The Languages of the World* (rev. edn). London: Routledge & Kegan Paul.

Kempson, R. (1977) *Presupposition and the Delimitation of Semantics*. Cambridge: Cambridge University Press.

Kendon, A. (1967) 'Some functions of gaze direction in social interaction', *Acta Psychologica*, 26: 22–63.

Kendon, A. (1982) 'The organisation of behaviour in face-to-face interaction: observations on the development of a methodology'. In K.R. Scherer and P. Ekman (eds) *Handbook of Methods in Nonverbal Behavior Research*. Cambridge: Cambridge University Press.

Kent, G.A. and Rosenoff, A.J. (1910) 'A study of association in insanity', *American Journal of Insanity*, 67: 317–90.

Kintsch, W. (1974) *The Representation of Meaning in Memory*. Hillsdale, NJ: Erlbaum-Wiley.

Klare, G.A. (1974) 'Assessing readability'. *Reading Research Quarterly*, 10: 62–102.

Kress, G. (1985) 'Socio-linguistic development and the mature language user: different voices for different occasions'. In G. Wells and J. Nicholls (eds) *Language and Learning: An Interactional Perspective*. London: Falmer Press.

Kress, G. and Hodge, R. (1979) *Language as Ideology*. London: Routledge & Kegan Paul.

Kress, G. and Knapp, P. (1992) 'Genre in a social theory of language', *English in Education*, 26: 4–15.

Kučera, H. and Francis, H.N. (1967) *Computational Analysis of Present-day English*. Providence, R.I.: Brown University Press.

Kwan-Terry, A. and Kwan-Terry, J. (1993) 'Literacy and the dynamics of language planning: the case of Singapore'. In P. Freebody and A.R. Welch (eds) *Knowledge, Culture and Power: International Perspectives on Literacy as Policy and Practice*. London: Falmer Press.

Labov, W. (1972a) *Sociolinguistic Patterns*. Oxford: Blackwell.

Labov, W. (1972b) 'Some principles of linguistic methodology'. *Language in Society*, 1: 97–120.

Labov, W. (1975a) 'Empirical foundations of linguistic theory'. In Austerlitz (ed.) *The Scope of American Linguistics*. Lisse: Peter de Ridde.

Labov, W. (1975b) *What is a Linguistic Fact?* The Hague: Reidel.

Ladd, D.R. (1978) *The Structure of Intonational Meaning*. Bloomington: Indiana University Press.

Lakoff, G. and Thompson, H. (1975) 'Introducing Cognitive Grammar', *Proceedings of the Berkeley Linguistics Society*, 1: 2295–313.

Lee, D. (1992) *Competing Discourses: Perspectives and Ideology in Language*. London: Longman.

Leech, G. and Svartvik, J. (1975) *A Communicative Grammar of English*. London: Longman.

Levinson, S. (1983) *Pragmatics*. Cambridge: Cambridge University Press.

Liberman, M.Y. and Prince, A. (1977) 'On stress and linguistic rhythm', *Linguistic Inquiry*, 8: 249–336.

Lieberman, P. (1986) 'The acquisition of intonation by infants: physiology and neural control'. In C. Johns-Lewis (ed.) *Intonation in Discourse*. London: Croom Helm.

Longman, J. and Mercer, N. (1993) 'Forms for talk and talk for forms: oral and literate dimensions of language use in Employment Training Interviews', *Text*, 13: 91–116.

Lyons, H. (1990) 'What Katy knows about language'. In R. Carter (ed.) *Knowledge about Language and the Curriculum: The LINC Reader*. London: Hodder & Stoughton.

Lyons, J. (1968) *Introduction to Theoretical Linguistics*. Cambridge: Cambridge University Press.

Lyons, J. (ed.) (1970) *New Horizons in Linguistics*. Harmondsworth: Penguin.

Lyons, J. (1977) *Semantics I and II*. Cambridge: Cambridge University Press.

McCloskey, J. (1988) 'Syntactic theory'. In F.J. Newmeyer (ed.) *Linguistic Theory: Foundations*. Cambridge: Cambridge University Press.

McEwan, C. (1990) *The Innocent*. London: Jonathan Cape.

Mackey, W.C. (1976) 'Parameters of the smile as a social signal', *Journal of Genetic Psychology*, 129: 125–30.

McNally, J. and Murray, W. (1962) *Key Words to Literacy*. London: Schoolmaster Publishing Company.

MacWhinney, B. and Snow, C. (1985) 'The child language data exchange system', *Journal of Child Language*, 12: 271–96.

Malinowski, B. (1923) 'The problem of meaning in primitive languages'. In C.K. Ogden and I.A. Richards (eds) *The Meaning of Meaning*. London: Kegan Paul, Trench & Trubner.

Malinowski, B. (1935) *The Language and Magic of Gardening*. London: George Allen & Unwin.

Mandler, J.M. and Johnson, N.S. (1977) 'Remembrance of things parsed: story structure and recall', *Cognitive Psychology*, 9: 111–51.

Mehrabian, A. (1969) 'Significance of posture and position in the communication of attitude and status relationship', *Psychological Bulletin*, 71: 359–72.

Miller, G.A. (1990) 'Linguists, psychologists and the cognitive sciences', *Language*, 66: 317–22.

Milroy, J. and Milroy, L. (1985) *Authority in Language: Investigating Language Prescription and Standardisation*. London: Routledge & Kegan Paul.

Minsky, M. (1975) 'A framework for representing knowledge'. In P. Winston (ed.) *The Psychology of Computer Vision*. New York: McGraw-Hill.

Montgomery, M. (1986) *An Introduction to Language and Society*. London: Methuen.

Moorhouse, A.C.M. (1946) *Writing and the Alphabet*. London: Cobbett Press.

Morris, D., Collett, P., Marsh, P. and O'Shaughnessy, M. (1979) *Gestures*. London: Jonathan Cape.

Murphy, R. and Altman, R. (1989) *Grammar in Use*. Cambridge: Cambridge University Press.

National Association for the Teaching of English (NATE) Language and Gender Committee (1988) *Gender Issues in English Coursework*. Sheffield: NATE.

Nguyen, T., Heslin, R. and Nguyen, M.L. (1975) 'Meanings of touch: sex differences', *Journal of Communication*, Summer: 92–103.

Nihalani, P., Tongue, R.K. and Hosali, P. (1979) *Indian and British English: A Handbook of Usage and Pronunciation*. Delhi: Oxford University Press.

O'Connor, J.D. (1973) *Phonetics*. Harmondsworth: Penguin.

O'Connor, J.D. and Arnold, G.F. (1961) *Intonation of Colloquial English*. London: Longman.

O'Grady, W. and Dobrovolsky, M. (eds) (1992) *Contemporary Linguistic Analysis: An Introduction*. Toronto: Copp Clark Pitman.

Ochs, E. (1979) 'Transcription as theory'. In E. Ochs and B.B. Schieffelin (eds) *Developmental Pragmatics*. New York: Academic Press.

Open University (ed.) (1991) *Talk and Learning 5–16: An In-service Pack on Oracy for Teachers*. Milton Keynes: Open University.

Palmer, F. (1971) *Grammar*. Harmondsworth: Penguin.

Palmer, F. (1981) *Semantics* (2nd edn). Cambridge: Cambridge University Press.

Palmer, F. (1984) *Grammar* (2nd edn). Harmondsworth: Penguin.

Perlmutter, D. and Postal, P. (1983) 'Towards a universal characterization of passivization'. In D. Perlmutter (ed.) *Studies in Relational Grammar*. Chicago: University of Chicago Press.

Propp, V.I. (1958) *Morphology of the Folktale*. Austin: University of Texas Press.

Quine, W. (1953) 'Two dogmas of empiricism'. In W. Quine (ed.) *From a Logical Point of View*. New York: Harper Torchbooks.

Quine, W. (1960) *Word and Object*. Cambridge: Cambridge University Press.

Quirk, R., Greenbaum, S., Leech, G. and Svartvik, J. (1972) *A Grammar of Contemporary English*. London: Longman.

Quirk, R., Greenbaum, S., Leech, G. and Svartvik, J. (1985) *A Comprehensive Grammar of English*. London: Longman.

Reisman, K. (1974) 'Contrapuntal conversation in an Antiguan village'. In R. Bauman and J. Scherzer (eds) *Explorations in the Ethnography of Speaking*. Cambridge: Cambridge University Press.

Romaine, S. (1982) 'What is a speech community?' In S. Romaine (ed.) *Sociolinguistic Variation in Speech Communities*. London: Edward Arnold.

Rutter, D.R. and Stephenson, G.M. (1977) 'The role of visual communication in synchronizing conversation', *European Journal of Social Psychology*, 7: 29–37.

Sacks, H., Schegloff, E.A. and Jefferson, G. (1974) 'A simplest systematics for the organization of turn-taking for conversation', *Language*, 50: 696–735.

Santarita, P. and Martin-Jones, M. (1991) 'The Portuguese speech community'. In S. Alladina and V. Edwards (eds) *Multilingualism in the British Isles 1: The Older Mother Tongues and Europe*. London: Longman.

Sapir, E. (1949) *Culture Language and Personality: Selected Essays* (selected by David G. Mandelbaum). Berkeley: University of California Press.

Saussure, F. de (1974) *Course in General Linguistics*. London: Fontana-Collins.

Schank, R.C. and Abelson, R.P. (1977) 'Scripts, plans, and knowledge'. In P.N. Johnson-Laird and P.C. Wason (eds) *Thinking: Readings in Cognitive Science*. Cambridge: Cambridge University Press.

Scheflen, A.E. (1964) 'The significance of posture in communication systems', *Psychiatry*, 27: 316–31.

Schegloff, E.A. (1984) 'On some gestures' relation to talk'. In J.M. Atkinson and J. Heritage (eds) *Structures of Social Interaction*. Cambridge: Cambridge University Press.

Schegloff, E.A. and Sacks, H. (1973) 'Opening up closings', *Semiotica*, 8: 289–327.

Seidel, G. (1985) 'Political discourse analysis'. In T.A. Van Dijk (ed.) *Handbook of Discourse Analysis Vol. 4: Discourse Analysis in Society*. London: Academic Press.

Shannon, C.E. (1948) 'A mathematical theory of communication', *Bell System Technical Journal*, 27: 379–423.

Sinclair, J.M. and Coulthard, R.M. (1975) *Towards an Analysis of Discourse*. London: Oxford University Press.

Smith, P.T. and Baker, R.G. (1976) 'The influence of English spelling patterns of pronunciation', *Journal of Verbal Learning and Verbal Behaviour*, 15: 267–85.

Sommer, R. (1962) 'The distance for comfortable conversation', *Sociometry*, 25: 111–16.

Spencer, N.J. (1973) 'Differences between linguists and non-linguists in intuitions of grammaticality-acceptability', *Journal of Experimental Psycholinguistics*, 2: 83–98.

Sperber, D. and Wilson, D. (1986) Relevance: communication and cognition. Oxford: Blackwell.

Stier, D.S. and Hall, J.A. (1984) 'Gender differences in touch: an empirical and theoretical review', *Journal of Personality and Social Psychology*, 47: 440–59.

Stokes, A. (1978) 'The reliability of readability formulae', *Journal of Research in Reading*, 1: 21–34.

Stokes, G. (1974) 'The story of P: a computer unmasks the man behind the transcripts', *Harpers Magazine*, 249: 6–12.

Stork, E.C. and Widdowson, J.D. (1974) *Learning about Linguistics*. London: Hutchinson.

Stubbs, M. (1980) *Language and Literacy: The Sociolinguistics of Reading and Writing*. London: Routledge & Kegan Paul.

Sunday Times Magazine (1993) Why the World is Still Painted Pink. London: Wordpower Part 3, The global language.

Swann, J. and Graddol, D. (1988) 'Gender inequalities in classroom talk', *English in Education*, 22: 48–65.

Thompson, J.J. (1973) *Beyond Words: Non-verbal Communication in the Classroom*. New York: Citation Press.

Thompson, S.A. (1991) 'Functional grammar'. In W. Bright (ed.) *Oxford International Encyclopaedia of Language Volume 4*. Oxford: Oxford University Press.

Thorndike, R.L. (1932) 'Reading as reasoning', *Reading Research Quarterly*, 9: 135–47.

Todasco, R. (ed.) (1973) 'An intelligent woman's guide to dirty words: English words and phrases reflecting sexist attitudes towards women in patriarchal society, arranged according to usage and idea', Vol. 1 of *The Feminist English Dictionary*. Chicago: Feminist Writers' Workshop, Loop Center YWCA.

Trew, A.A. (1979) 'Theory and ideology at work'. In R. Fowler, R. Hodge, G. Kress and A.A. Trew (eds), *Language and Control*. London: Routledge & Kegan Paul.

Trudgill, P. (1983) *Sociolinguistics: An Introduction to Language and Society* (rev. edn). Harmondsworth: Penguin.

Umeda, N. (1982) 'Fødeclination is situation dependent', *Journal of Phonetics*, 10: 279–90.

van Dijk, T.A. and Kintsch, W. (1978) 'Cognitive psychology and discourse: recalling and summarising stories'. In W.V. Dressler (ed.) *Current Trends in Textlinguistics*. Berlin: W. de Gruyter.

Venezky, R.L. (1970) *The Structure of English Orthography*. The Hague: Mouton.

Voegelin, C.F. and Voegelin, F.M. (1977) *Classification and Index of the World's Languages*. New York: Elsevier.

Wainwright, G.R. (1985) *Teach Yourself Body Language*. London: Hodder & Stoughton.

Wells, G. (1985) *Language Development in the Preschool Years*. Cambridge: Cambridge University Press.

West, M. (1927) *The Construction of Reading Material for Reading a Foreign Language*. London: Oxford University Press.

Whalley, P. (1980) 'A partial index of text complexity involving the lexical analysis of rhetorical connectives', *A.L.L.C. Journal*.

White, L. (1985) 'The acquisition of parameterized grammar: subjacency in second language acquisition', *Second Language Research*, 1: 1–17.

White, L. (1986) 'Implications of parametric variation for adult second language acquisition: an investigation of the pro-drop parameter'. In V. Cook (ed.) *Experimental Approaches to Second Language Acquisition*. Oxford: Pergamon.

Winograd, T. (1972) *Understanding Natural Language*. Edinburgh: Edinburgh University Press.

Winograd, T. (1983) *Language as a Cognitive Process Vol. 1: Syntax* Reading, MA: Addison-Wesley.

Wong, L.Y. (1991) 'The Hong Kong Chinese speech community'. In S. Alladina and V. Edwards (eds) *Multilingualism in the British Isles 2: Africa, The Middle East and Asia*. London: Longman.

Zimmerman, D.H. and West, C. (1975) 'Sex roles, interruptions and silences in conversation'. In B. Thorne and N. Henley (eds) *Language and Sex: Difference and Dominance*. Rowley, MA: Newbury House.

Index